Principles of Church
GROWTH

Principles of Church
GROWTH

by Dr. Jack Schaap
Pastor, First Baptist Church
of Hammond, Indiana

Hyles Publications
Hammond, Indiana

CREDITS:

PROJECT MANAGER: Dr. Bob Marshall
ASSISTANTS: Rochelle Chalifoux, Kristi Wertz
PAGE DESIGN AND LAYOUT: Linda Stubblefield
The church pictured within the pages of this book is the Grange Hall Baptist Church, Brother Jack Hyles' first full-time pastorate.
PROOFREADING: Mrs. Debbie Borsh, Mrs. Rena Fish, Mrs. Martha Gilbert, and Mr. Jack Mitchell
COVER DESIGN: Linda Stubblefield
COVER PHOTO: Groundbreaking for the new auditorium at First Baptist Church of Hammond, Indiana Groundbreaking Sunday, November 3, 2002

To order additional books by Dr. Jack Schaap, please contact:
HYLES PUBLICATIONS
523 Sibley Street
Hammond, Indiana 46320
Website: www.hylespublications.com
E-mail: info@hylespublications.com

Dedication

O N MARCH 7, 2001, I was voted in as pastor of the First Baptist Church of Hammond, Indiana. For more than 40 years, this church had enjoyed one pastor, a man who under God's leadership had taken them to indescribable heights: "World's Largest Sunday School," "World's Largest Bus Ministry," and "World's Largest Independent Baptist Bible College."

Three years later, this church has shown that she has not lost her vision but rather has taken that vision to a new level. Her zeal has increased, and her members have challenged God's promises.

First Baptist Church is committed to New Testament, Book of Acts growth. History is not always kind to large ministries that lose the aggressive pastor, but First Baptist Church members have dedicated themselves to rewrite history in this case. To those members whose zeal I admire, whose love I appreciate, whose work is tireless, and to those members who have risen to a great challenge, I affectionately dedicate this book on *Principles of Church Growth*.

I love you, First Baptist Church. Thank you for the privilege of serving our Lord Jesus Christ with you.

– Jack Schaap
March 2004

Table of Contents

CHAPTER ONE

Rich, Fat, Salty, Lazy, and Dead

"That the waters which came down from above stood and rose up upon an heap very far from the city Adam, that is beside Zaretan: and those that came down toward the sea of the plain, even the salt sea, failed, and were cut off...." (Joshua 3:16)

AN INTERESTING PLACE is this Dead Sea, also known as the Salt Sea. It is located in southwestern Asia and is bounded on the west by Israel and the West Bank, and on the east by Jordan. The Dead Sea forms part of the Israeli-Jordanian border. The surface of the Dead Sea is 1,340 feet below sea level, which is the lowest water surface on earth. It is 50 miles long and 11 miles wide at its widest point. It occupies the north portion of the Great Rich Valley. It varies in depth from 20 feet in the south to a depth of 1,300-plus feet in the northern part. The Dead Sea is fed mainly by the Jordan River. It has no outlet. The heavy flow of fresh water is carried off solely by evaporation. Due to large-scale projects by Israel and Jordan to divert water from the Jordan River for irrigation and other water needs, the surface of the Dead Sea has been dropping for at least the past 50 years. It is nearly seven times as salty as the ocean. In fact, at a depth of 1,000 feet, the Dead Sea contains some 27% solid substances. It contains no life of any kind. Fish put into its waters soon die. The Dead Sea is economically important as a source of potash, bromine, gypsum salt, and other chemical products which are extracted inexpensively.

Two major seas are referred to again and again in the Scriptures: the Dead Sea and the Sea of Tiberius, which is also known as the Sea of Galilee or the Sea of Chinnereth. Located in the northern part of Israel and fed by many, many streams that flow from the mountains when the snow melts, the Sea of Tiberius is a well-stocked, well-fed sea. It supplied the fish that fed the multitudes, and it supplied fish for the disciples. This sea was the site of many miracles. It was a place of life and health for many folks during Bible times and still provides fish for the sustenance of many who live in that region. The Jordan River flows from that Sea of Tiberius southward into what is called the Salt Sea or the Dead Sea. Chiefly fed by the Jordan River, the Dead Sea is a receiver. It has no outlet. There is no life in it of any kind. As I already mentioned, any life put into the Dead Sea soon dies because of the sea's excessive salt content. Quite bluntly, the Dead Sea is rich, fat, salty, lazy, and dead.

The congregation of the First Baptist Church of Hammond has been and continues to be very well-fed. I do not apologize for that statement. I am not ashamed to admit that I am a student of the Bible, I study it diligently, and have been studying and preaching it for nearly 30 years. When I first began teaching at Hyles-Anderson College, my wife can testify to this, there was rarely a night that I went to bed before 1:30 in the morning because I was studying and laboring. With my books all around me, I had no idea that I was gathering into the storage files of my mind the tools necessary to bring to the First Baptist Church congregation the truths that I teach and preach week after week.

I was also a student of Brother Hyles and other good men. I love good books. I have been a reader of good books and a student of good men for these nearly 30 years that I have been in the ministry. Even before that, when I was a young teenager, for some reason God put in my heart and mind to be a student. I studied and worked hard for my grades. I say all of that to say this: First Baptist Church was well fed by Brother Hyles. First Baptist Church continues to be well fed from the pulpit—that is important to me. I work hard at it. I want the First Baptist Church congregation to be well fed, and they will continue to be well fed.

My Bible says, "...*For unto whomsoever much is given, of him shall be much required: and to whom men have committed much, of him they will ask the more.*" (Luke 12:48) Those who have been well fed are required to do something with what they have been given. The parallel between well-fed Christians and the Dead Sea is very important as we continue in this chapter.

The Dead Sea is well fed by the Jordan River which is well fed by the Sea of Galilee which is well fed by the many tributaries that bring nourishing waters to its fresh-water area. Our Christians at First Baptist Church are well fed; however, it is so important to understand that there is more to the Christian life than just receiving. To whom much is given, much shall be required.

I think of all the soul-winning teaching of Brother Hyles through the years. How many times he pounded his fist on the pulpit, thundering out to the First Baptist Church members to be soul winners. Two of Brother Hyles' greatest messages, "If You Can't Be a Soul Winner, Be a Soul Warner" and "The Four Calls to Soul Winning" were filled with powerful, powerful truths.

Again and again Brother Hyles thundered out the truths about soul winning, the King James Bible, separation, the body of Christ, and the blood of Jesus Christ. His studies of the Proverbs and the Song of Solomon gave us teachings that helped us with our marriages, our child rearing, and our families. These truths make us more accountable because we have received much.

The First Baptist Church people continue to be very richly nourished from Brother Hyles' many tributaries: his books, his Bible studies, his preaching, and his counseling. Many tributaries flowed into our lives. First Baptist Church and Christians across the world are recipients of a rich, flavorful menu as we have our libraries stocked with Brother Hyles' materials; our minds and our memories are filled with his voice and his teachings. We have been well fed.

Let me admonish those of us who have been well fed with the following five truths:

1. Use it or lose it. As I conducted the graduation services for our Hammond Baptist Schools, City Baptist Schools, and Hyles-Anderson College, I thought of all that the students took in during their four or five years of college training. Some of the graduates were in Hammond Baptist Schools for 14 years, coming in as junior kindergartners and then graduating from Hyles-Anderson College. I thought of the incredible amount each student has been given. They will either use it or lose it.

Does a Christian high school graduate have a right to sit for three months of summer and molt before he gets involved in a ministry? He has been given years of soul-winning training at Teenage Soul Winning. Shouldn't he be there the Saturday after he graduates? For several years, the teenager has been involved in teenage soul winning or some other ministry of his church. Now that he has graduated, for the next three months until he gets into the ministry at Hyles-Anderson College or some other Bible college, is he going to just sit around and get rich, fat, salty, lazy, and dead?

Graduates, don't sit around your church for three months and become like the Dead Sea, taking in and taking in! Get busy right away! Get a pack of tracts. Young preacher boys who are called to preach, do not wait until September to start preaching. Do not wait until September to join a bus route. Get on a bus route now, pass out tracts, knock on doors, and win souls!

This attitude of, "I have three more months to be lazy" is unscriptural. Lazy is not found in the Bible. Nobody has ever been used by God who is a lazy person. I have said it again and again, and I will say it until I die of old age or until Jesus comes back: God has used adulterers, fornicators, liars, cheaters, thieves, and rabble-rousers, but He has never used a lazy person—never one time.

This business of going to school nine months and then being off for three months is an idiotic idea. I wish we had 12-month schools. I know teachers need a break. However, what am I supposed to do as a pastor?

I have heard more teachers say to me, "I'll tell you what. I am so glad school is over. Nine months—I could not take one more week."

When does the pastor take off his three months? When does the choir get their three months off? When do the Sunday school teachers get their three months off? When do the plumbers get their three months off? When does John Rice, our contractor, who is working with me on our new building get to say, "I want three months off. I'm tired of pounding nails. I'm tired of driving in drywall screws. I'm tired of troweling concrete."

Bless God! The real world works 12 months out of the year. This business of three months off work breeds a rich, fat, salty, lazy, and dead Christianity. Bus routes suffer for three months. Soul winning goes down for three months because there are no activity reports to complete. For three months, teenagers do not have to answer to their youth director for soul-winning reports. For three months, teachers do not have to turn in reports to their principals. For three months, those teachers can get rich, fat, salty, lazy, and dead.

During the three months of summer, high school graduates hang in the balance. Their pastors, youth directors, Sunday school teachers, and parents fret and worry and get anxious about them. These leaders are concerned about the decisions their teenagers made at their school revival, reaffirmed at Pastors' School, reaffirmed again at youth revival, and recommitted to even on graduation night when they hugged their friends and said, "Let's stay together. Let's do right. Let's make a difference." They fear those decisions could all be trashed during the summer because these graduates get rich, fat, salty, lazy, and dead.

Graduates have taken in and taken in and taken in—fed by the greatest youth director in the world, fed by the greatest high school principal in the world, fed by the greatest junior high principal in the world, fed by the greatest grade school principal in the world, fed by the greatest bus captains and teachers and best Sunday school teachers and best custodians and best electricians and best preaching from Brother Hyles and other preachers. Graduate, do not throw it away in three months by sitting around and taking it in—dying like the Dead Sea.

Our City Baptist (bus kids' school) graduates have been the recipients of loving bus captains who came here from all across the country to attend college. These college students fell in love with their bus kids. They gave their lunch money and even their tuition money, and some of them forfeited their college education because they gave and they gave and they gave. They sacrificed so their bus kids could attend a Christian school. When these college students attend the City Baptist graduation service and see their bus kids walk across the platform and receive diplomas, they proudly stand and applaud for the graduates. They present balloon bouquets or flower bouquets to them, take their pictures, and make a big deal about their graduates, making them feel like heroes.

Where are those City Baptist graduates in September? Some will get jobs at Navy Pier in Chicago during the summer months and rub shoulders with some creepy old mangy dogs there. They will sell their purity, sell their Christianity and godliness, sell the love, sacrifice, and dedication of others who gave their hearts, souls, minds, and strength to get those bus kids out of the fires of Hell. They are a bunch of Dead Sea Christians—rich and fat and salty and lazy and dead.

Some City Baptist graduates will say, "I have three months to live it up before going to Hyles-Anderson College."

You have no right to live it up before going to Hyles-Anderson College! Get on a bus route! Start passing out tracts! Start knocking on doors! Start right after graduation doing the same thing your bus captain did. Go out and get one of those children who is just like you were several years ago—a gang-banger ragamuffin who was mouthy, bossy, arrogant, cocky, and bratty. Lasso the spiritual rope around that child's soul, drag him on that bus, and say, "Hey, Buster, I know what it is like. Sit down! Shut up! Get saved!"

Christian Graduate, forget the idea of waiting three months before selling out for God. The whole world can go to Hell in three months. Use it or lose it! Graduates who do not put the pedal to the metal and get busy immediately will have less to give in September because their spirituality will evaporate from them. They will go to college in September less spiritual than when they left high school. Do not let your high school days be your most spiritual days. I would hate to think I reached the zenith of my Christianity in my public high school. I would hate to think I reached the zenith anytime in my life!

> I'm pressing on the upward way,
> New heights I'm gaining every day…
> But still I'll pray till heaven I've found,
> "Lord, lead me on to higher ground."

Graduates, I know you have parties to attend, and I am glad for you to take a few days off with mom and dad. That is wonderful. But do not get rich, fat, salty, lazy, and dead during the summer.

Those high school graduates who say, "I am going to Hyles-Anderson College," why don't you start acting like a Hylander right after graduation? It is time for some 17-year-old and 18-year-old boys to square their shoulders and say, "Guess what, Mama? I choose to be a man now." It is time for you boys to realize that you do not become a man in three months. You do not ever become a man; you choose to be a man. Manhood is not something given you by inheritance. Manhood is not a gift from Daddy nor is it bestowed upon you by Great-grandpa. Manhood is not given to you by birth. Boys are male by birth, but men by choice. A boy decides to be a man. He becomes a man by choice. Manhood has nothing to do with age; it has to do with what your soul is and what your passion is.

It is time for high-school graduates to say, "I have graduated. Now, like the Apostle Paul, *'When I was a child, I spake as a child, I understood as a child, I thought as a child: but when I became a man, I put away childish things.'* I now choose to move on to adulthood."

Mama, let your boy move on to adulthood. Daddy, let your daughter move on to adulthood. Parents, let your children start acting like adults. When your child comes to you and says, "I think I am going to join a bus route," you say, "Praise God! Amen! I will join it with you." Make the summertime a time of great evangelism, great fervor, and great aggressive, passionate soul winning. Reap a great harvest of souls.

Use it or lose it! Those who do not get that fervor right out of the chute when they are fresh out of high school will only cool and cool and cool and will start college a backslidden old carcass whose dead soul will have to be revived. Kick up the heat a few notches so that September, October, and November are not spent trying to re-warm a cold coal. Graduate, keep the same emotional fervor that you felt on graduation day when your heart was stirred and your mind was aflame saying, "Boy, it is good to be part of this ministry." I want the graduates feeling that same way in September.

In September, do not have to say, "Well, I've had a few beers, and I've had a few women, and I've had a little marijuana. I hope the college doesn't find out because I wouldn't be admitted."

Graduate, don't you dare let that happen during the summer! Jump in a ministry. Get in the Phoster Club or the Fishermen's Club or the Bus Ministry. Start knocking on doors. Soul winning is the best way to keep the fire from burning out.

Christians, we have been well fed and fattened up by Brother Hyles' teaching and preaching and the preaching of other great men of God. We have no right to sit in our pews for the three months of summer and molt or rot or get rich, fat, salty, and lazy, and then die. I do not want that for First Baptist Church. I am not interested in First Baptist Church ever becoming like many other churches which have a big surge in the spring and then deflate in the summertime. My Bible says, "...and so much the more."

How can Christians watch the China Mission Team all band together and bind their souls in a covenant with God to go open up the door in China, and watch a Congo team go off and preach the Gospel there, and watch missionary deputation folk prepare to get to the foreign field, and sit back and say, "Well, it's summertime; I guess I had better go to the cabin and go fishing." We need to do our fishing on Sundays—bus-route fishing and lost-soul fishing!

Some Christians have the idea that summertime is a big, collective sigh. Take a sigh for about 48 hours, then take a deep breath and go again.

Families should take a vacation together. However, remember Brother Hyles' admonition? "Leave on Monday and come back on Saturday." Christians should not miss church. I know members have to miss church occasionally, but they should still go to a good church while they are out of town on vacation. Better still, just be in your home church every weekend. With many members, every Sunday they miss, their church loses their tithe. Every Sunday a Sunday school teacher misses, his Sunday school boys and girls miss a teacher. Every Sunday a bus captain misses, his bus route falters and stumbles a little more.

I am not against anyone missing once in a while for a vacation, but the rest of the time Christians should put the pedal to the metal and keep that axe to the grindstone; keep it sharp and hot and busy. Don't you get rich, fat, salty, lazy, and dead during the summer. Use it, or you lose it.

Every pastor across America dreads summertime. People's clothing comes off, and their morals go down. Christianity gets lost, and everybody becomes rich, fat, salty, lazy, and dead. Go ahead and get some sun, play with your family, play some golf, go bowling, have some picnics, and have some barbecues, but while you are having fun, keep the fires of Hell in your mind as you realize that the Devil is working overtime to get people into Hell. Use it or lose it.

2. Do not evaporate! Irrigate. Winning the lost is not a passive evangelism; it is an aggressive evangelism. I am not interested in lifestyle evangelism. A Christian should live a good lifestyle but should not just evaporate and hope that people somehow catch the moisture of the Gospel from his evaporation. Open the spigot and flood the unsaved! Pour it out! The Bible says, *"For I will pour water upon him that is thirsty…,"* and *"He that believeth on me, as the scripture hath said, out of his belly shall flow rivers of living water."*

I am not interested in sprinkling; I am not a Catholic. I want to dunk the unsaved! I do not want to get around people, and then after 25 or 30 years have them look at me and say, "Oh, you are a Christian." I want those people to know it after 30 seconds. I am not trying to offend people. I am trying to get the lost baptized in the Spirit of God and filled with the truth of God's Word. The water of the Dead Sea just evaporates, turns to clouds, and moves over and sprinkles on somebody else.

Not me, bless God! I want to irrigate. I want to dig ditches. I want to dig bus routes. I want to dig ditches to the houses and knock on doors and say, "Hey, watch the spigot open up and flood you with the Holy Spirit of God!" I am tired of this evaporation kind of Christianity! This kind of Christianity that says, "If I smile right, look pleasant, and wear perfume, the world will know I am a born-again, saved, fundamental, independent Baptist."

No, they will not! A Christian should smile and smell good and get dressed up and be appropriate, but the bottom line is that on top of the smiling, on top of the perfume, on top of the proper demeanor and decorum, a Christian must open his mouth and say, "Can I tell you the good news about Jesus Christ? Are you saved? Are you born again? Are you a Christian? Let me ask you something; if you died today, would you go to Heaven?"

I do not care if folks laugh at you, mock you, or snicker at you; open the spigot and let it flood out. Irrigate this old world! Irrigate your hometown and local area! Irrigate it! Grab a pack of tracts this summer and pass them out in the grocery store. Pass them out in the gas station. Pass them out in the convenience stores. Pass them out everywhere! The world is not afraid to advertise! Why are Christians?

While driving down Highway 394 and the Bishop-Ford Freeway, I see all the billboards, and it makes me angry every time. The world does not mind advertising their rock 'n' roll. They do not mind advertising their rhythm and blues. They do not mind advertising their punk rock. They do not mind advertising their liquor. They do not mind advertising their cigarettes. Hollywood does not mind advertising their sewer movies with filth and incest and lust and sodomy. Why should Christians be ashamed to advertise Christ? Because we are rich, fat, salty, lazy, and dead—that is why!

3. It is more blessed to give than to receive. The Sea of Tiberius knows that. If the Dead Sea and the Sea of Tiberius could talk, the happiest one would be the Sea of Tiberius. Its fish abound. I wonder what the Sea of Tiberius felt when a little handful of fish from its waters was taken and used to feed the 5,000. It puffed out its chest and pulled up its waves and built up a crest and said, "Those fish came from my sea." No fish ever came from the Dead Sea. Nobody has ever been fed a meal from the Dead Sea. Only death and destruction and saltiness are out there. I want to be like the Sea of Tiberius. I want to be fresh. I want to give out.

The happiest Christians are the ones who are giving; and yet, a happy Christian often becomes a troubled Christian. Something happens to him. In his soul-winning zeal and fervor and his passion to get the lost saved, something happens. There is a little marriage struggle. There is a little trouble with the college rules or a little demerit trouble. When a Christian gets in some trouble, sometimes he dams up that flow and becomes like the Dead Sea. There are a whole lot of married couples whose marriages have soured their giving. A couple becomes so focused on their marriage trouble that they have built a dam across the Jordan River of their life, and nothing goes out. They keep taking in and taking in.

The unhappy Christian comes to hear me every Sunday morning and says, "Boy, I hope Brother Schaap can get me through another week." That unhappy Christian needs to get filled with the Holy

Ghost Who will get him through seven days a week, 24 hours a day. How does the pastor get through a bad day? The same Holy Ghost living inside of the pastor is living inside of the layman. The same Bible I have is the same Bible my members have. The same promises of God that I have are the same promises for every Christian. The same Spirit of the living God lives inside all believers. Every promise of the Book is mine—and yours, too. What happens is, a so-called happy Christian stumbles, skins his spiritual knee, and gets depressed and saddened and stricken in his heart. He has built a dam and said, "That is it! If that is what giving out means, I am going to dam it all up."

Too many Christians are wrestling with the struggle; struggling with the struggle instead of struggling for the goal. A happy Christian becomes a troubled Christian because he stops giving. Then he becomes a rich, fat, salty, lazy, Dead-Sea kind of Christian. Go ahead and let your troubles stop you, Christian. Tumble down with your problems and say, "Oh, I've fallen, and I can't get up."

The sourest Christians are those who stop giving out. The happiest Christians are those who are getting out the Gospel. The happiest Christians are those workers in our Nursing Home Ministry; they are tired, but happy. One Sunday, the workers brought 408 nursing-home residents to church and saw 55 saved and 27 baptized. That is a happy crowd.

On one Sunday, the First Baptist Church Bus Ministry baptized 1,100! That was a happy crowd. The happy crowd is that Bible-Club crowd that had over 150 baptized on one Sunday. The happy crowd is that bus captain and those bus workers who ran the same number on a summer Sunday that they ran during the Spring Program. Why are these folks the happy crowd? They are happy because they are giving out and giving out and giving out.

Some Christians become sour because they decide to stop giving. Everyone has reasons to stop giving: life is hard, people are mean, people are unkind, people do not treat you fairly. An unhappy Christian says, "Brother Schaap, you really do not know what I am going through." Yes, I do! I counsel an average of nearly 150 people each week, many of whom are unhappy Christians. The truth of the matter is these people are so focused on fixing themselves that they have stopped giving to anybody else. Even for those who do go on a bus route, it has become purely a perfunctory, mechanical action.

Bus captains, how many new visits do you make each week? Some bus captains will say, "Well, it's not Spring Program." Oh, so nobody goes to Hell except during Fall and Spring Programs?!

Let me speak to the Devil for a moment. "Hey, Devil, what days and weeks and months of the year do people go to Hell? Just Spring and Fall program, right? That is what I thought. All the other weeks everybody goes to Heaven."

Most Christians live as though the Devil only sends people to Hell during the Spring and Fall Programs; that is why Christians work extra hard during those times. I am not asking bus workers to make every week a Spring Program, but I think they ought to make new visits every week on their bus route.

First Baptist Church has over 600 Sunday school teachers. If each teacher brought just one visitor to church each week, think what the results would be in one year's time. If each teacher made a commitment this year to bring one visitor a week to Sunday school and averaged one visitor per week, with 600 teachers that would be 600 visitors per week—over 30,000 visitors per year!

When lazy people read the book of Acts, somehow they feel that the time of the early church was a different dispensation. I think that is heresy out of Hell! I think it is the Devil telling Christians that souls only went to Hell in the book of Acts, and souls do not go to Hell today. Yes, they do go to Hell! And Hell is hot and nasty, and the Devil is going to torture lost souls for eternity!

Church members, you do not have 50 visitors like you did during the Spring Program, but how about one visitor?

Some say, "But it is summertime, Brother Schaap."

Oh, that's right. I forgot. It's not hot in Hell during the summertime.

It is time that Christians realize and understand that the Jack Hyles they loved and adored and whose signature they wanted and whose hand they wanted to shake, and the other great men Christians love and adore, are men who were trying to get truths across to those who were listening. They were trying to transmit truths like "if you do not use it, you are going to lose it," and "it is more blessed to give than to receive." If these truths are not for the First Baptist Church, then let's just shut the doors right now before it becomes a social club. Let's just call our church the Jack Hyles Memorial Social Club. The members will all get golfing memberships. We will all ride in luxury vehicles and have stretch limos take us to church. The First Baptist Church will just get smaller and smaller and smaller and smaller and smaller until eventually we can meet in the chapel. After the chapel, we can meet in my office. After the office, the last one out can close the door, shut off the lights, and let the world go to Hell.

It bothers me—in fact, it aggravates me when I find in the book of Acts that the church in Jerusalem grew to a membership of 100,000 people in two years. Multitudes were added! Multitudes multiplied! I told my father-in-law, Dr. Jack Hyles, and I told God that there is no way I am taking the pulpit of the First Baptist Church of Hammond and just kind of riding it out. I will not ride on that horse and just bide my time and baby-sit the saints. I am not trying to baby-sit my church members until I bury every single one of them in coffins! I am trying to win the world to Christ!

First Baptist Church of Hammond has been given the biggest opportunity. To whom much is given, much shall be required. I want every single boy and girl and adult in my congregation to stand before Christ and say, "God, I gave it everything I had; You know I did." That is why First Baptist Church is raising the money to refurbish our sailor home.

I want the sailors from Great Lakes Naval Base to go back to that naval base and get excited about First Baptist Church. There is a world of sailors going to Hell. Those sailors who got saved and now attend First Baptist Church do not come to our church just to get a free meal from us. They do not come to First Baptist Church just to get preached at. Sailors come to First Baptist Church to have their lives changed. First Baptist Church is not in the sailor babysitting business. We are not in the truck driver babysitting business. Truck drivers who come to First Baptist Church and get born again and get baptized, need to get out on those roads and get on that CB and say, "Hey, Good Buddy, let me tell you about the Son of the living God." Sailors and truck drivers can pass out tracts and round up people telling them about Jesus. It is time all Christians realize that we are in the soul-saving business.

A happy Christian gets hit by an emotional dart. A fiery dart from the Devil flung off his bow smites the Christian's spirit, and he stumbles and falters. The old bitterness creeps in and the Christian starts pulling in. The Christian keeps receiving and says "Help me, Pastor. Feed me." The pastor nurtures him and helps him through his tough time. The unhappy Christian gets comfortable getting fed. He thinks, "This is nice. Feed me some more, Pastor." My whole idea is to feed the weak Christian until he gets strong enough to get up and say, "Back to giving out. Back to giving."

Some Christians have lost the joy of their salvation, not because they got stung by the Devil or because people have it in for them; it is because they have stopped giving. They need to get back on that bus route and start giving, and get back in that Sunday school class and start giving. Grab that pack of tracts and start giving them out. Grab that New Testament, blow off the dust, and start giving out the Romans Road—the precious wonderful Gospel of Jesus Christ, the Son of the living God Who came and was born of a virgin, buried, and, hallelujah, rose again from the dead! That is good news! It is time that the unhappy Christian understands that he stopped giving out. He has become rich, fat, salty, lazy, and dead. It is more blessed to give than to receive.

4. Too low to flow. The Dead Sea is so low that it cannot flow out. There is no place in the world lower than the Dead Sea. Some Christians are living down there in the low life. They cannot make it flow uphill. All the sludge and the sewer of the world are flowing into them. They pour all that filth of the world into their lives. They live a low life; and low life people have nothing to give out. The Dead Sea is dead because it is so low that it cannot flow.

Christian, get up on higher ground. Kick it up a notch. Stop hiding behind the excuse, "Well, I've just got an addiction." No, you are just a sorry Christian who thinks he is the only one who is tempted. Get that spiritual thumb out of your spiritual mouth. Stand up, square your shoulders, and say, "I am a man." Are you telling me that you are addicted to three inches of paper with tobacco inside? Kick that stupid habit. Do not come to my office and say, "I am having a hard time, but I was too busy to go to Reformers Unanimous on Friday night." Do not come see me. First Baptist Church has pumped $100,000 into the Reformers Unanimous addiction program, to buy materials, to hire workers, and to provide a meeting place. Addict, get your carcass to the meetings, and we will help you get off that addiction. The Reformers Unanimous program will get the addict in the Word of God and on higher ground.

When the addict gets to higher ground, he can start flowing out to somebody else. By the way, Reformers Unanimous is not a crutch for addicts to say, "I am making it." No! Reformers Unanimous is to teach the addict that the answer is found in Jesus Christ and the Word of God.

Some may say, "Brother Schaap, you have never been a drunk. It is easy for you little Sunday school boys."

They are right! I have never tasted alcohol. I know I could become a drunk, but greater is He that is in me than he that is in the world. An army of people had the same addictions, but one day they realized something is more important in life than living down in the cellar. Addicts have to get out of the cellar and out of the septic tank! They need to kick off that lid, swim out of that sludge, and shake themselves off like a dog and say, "I am coming up." Too many are kicking the lid off and diving in head first. Addict, get out of that low life; you are too low to flow.

The reason why many Christians do not win souls and pass out tracts is because they are living lives that are not in tune with the pastor's preaching. Go ahead, teenagers with earrings, tell me how many tracts you passed out this week. Teenagers who have on the headphones, pumping all the garbage into your mind, how many souls did you win this week? Compromising church member, how many converts do you have sitting beside you in church on Sundays? How many nursing home residents do you love on, and give the Gospel to, and help with their palsied step to get over to the baptistery? Show me your converts by your compromising lifestyle, and I will show you my converts by my Bible Christianity.

Compromising Christian, if your kind of living is so good, how big is your bus route? If your kind of living is so good, then where are the changed lives that have been influenced by you? If your kind of compromise is so good and your kind of worldliness is so good and if that kind of low-life living is so good, then how many people can look at you and say, "You made a difference in my life"? No! You are just rich, fat, salty, lazy, and dead.

5. One source, one failure. The trouble with the Dead Sea is that it has only one source of refreshment, the Jordan River. The Sea of Tiberius has dozens and dozens of sources. Some Christians hang all of their Christianity upon one person. If that person hurts their feelings, then Christianity is no longer any good.

These same Christians will say, "You do not know what my mama did to me." Well, how about your dad? How about your pastor? How about your Sunday school teacher? How about your friends? How about your school teacher? How about your principal? How about your Saviour?

Some say, "You do not know how hard it was living with my family." However, their family members tell me how hard it was to live with them. Everybody has a crutch to lean on. Everybody has a sad, sorrowful story to hide behind. Everybody has somebody that has offended them. If a Christian's whole source of inspiration is dependent upon one person, he has a very big failure coming. A handful of First Baptist Church members, and even some Christians across America, put all their confidence in one man who graced the First Baptist Church pulpit. Unfortunately for them, Brother Hyles is now with our Saviour. But the rest of us listened as Brother Hyles told us to put our confidence in his God. A whole lot of us said while Brother Hyles was alive, "I think God is Brother Hyles' source. I think his source is the Holy Spirit. I think his source is the King James Bible. I think his source is the fellowship of believers in the local church. I think his source is prayer with his Heavenly Father. I think his source is giving out and giving out. I think his source is all the good things he did for other people. I think his source is his prayer life. I think his source is his wife. I think his source is his family and loved ones he had." Brother Hyles had multitudes of sources and a whole lot of us caught onto that truth so that when Brother Hyles was gone, we sorrowed and we wept; but we still got fed. The Bible did not die on February 6, 2001. God did not die in Heaven on February 6, 2001.

Please do not misunderstand. First Baptist Church of Hammond is an empathetic place and a sympathizing place, but Christians cannot put all their confidence in just one source. Believers need many sources coming in. I know people whose only source is the Bible, and when they run into a tough verse or some problem text that is hard to understand, they get all hung up on that. I know Christians whose only source is prayer. They do not read much Bible or go soul winning much; and woe be to God if He does not answer their prayers. The first time these Christians ask for a big answer and God does not answer in the manner in which they want Him to, they lose their confidence in God. Enough of this one-source Christianity! I have multiple streams coming to me.

I spent time with my Heavenly Father today. I asked Him to fill me with His Holy Spirit today. I spent time on my face praying to God. I spent time reading my Bible. I spent time with my wife today and time with my family today. I ate a good meal today. I came to the house of God today and got fed. I have brothers and sisters in Christ. I enjoy good Christian music. I have multiple sources coming in. I could lose five of my sources and still be a happy, refreshed Christian. I do not want to lose anything, but life tells me that I will. Life tells me that I will lose some of the sources I lean on for joy and gladness. Too many have leaned too heavily on just one source—the Jordan River of their lives—and when that Jordan River is pinched off, those Christians die. I do not want just one source; I want it all.

These five truths will keep the happy, productive Christian from becoming a Dead Sea Christian: (1) Use it or lose it; (2) Do not evaporate, irrigate; (3) It is more blessed to give than to receive; (4) Don't be too low to flow; and (5) One source, one failure. I do not want anyone to be a Dead Sea Christian. I want the entire Chicago area to know there is a fresh source of life at First Baptist Church. Let's not become rich, fat, salty, lazy, and dead.

CHAPTER TWO

In One Accord

"And in those days Peter stood up in the midst of the disciples, and said, (the number of names together were about an hundred and twenty)." (Acts 1:15)

NOTICE THE PARENTHESIS in this verse. According to the first chapter of the Book of Acts, the church in Jerusalem had grown to 120 members.

Acts 2:41, *"Then they that gladly received his word were baptized: and the same day there were added unto them about three thousand souls."* This was the marvelous day of Pentecost. Notice the words *"added unto them."* Added unto whom? Unto the 120. Some people say Pentecost was the start of the church; however, the church in Jerusalem had 120 members before Pentecost because Acts 2:41 says, *"added unto them."* So the 3,000 saved at Pentecost plus 120 is 3,120. At that time, there were 3,120 members in this church.

Acts 2:47 says, *"Praising God, and having favour with all the people. And the Lord added to the church daily such as should be saved."* If you add daily, what is the smallest number you can add? One. It might have been that God added 10 or 3,000 daily. Anything 3,000 or less would be Scriptural. I am going to use the lowest possible numbers. I will add one. The course of time we are discussing here is two years. Let's say that God added for only one year. The Jewish calendar has only 360 days, so I will add 360 people (one daily for 360 days of one year). Now 120 plus 3,000 plus 360 more converts is exactly 3,480 people. The church was now one year old with at least 3,480 members.

Acts 4:1-4 adds, "*And as they spake unto the people, the priests, and the captain of the temple, and the Sadducees, came upon them. Being grieved that they taught the people, and preached through Jesus the resurrection from the dead. And they laid hands on them, and put them in hold unto the next day: for it was now eventide. Howbeit many of them which heard the word believed; and the number of the men was about five thousand.*" This is an amazing story. It was common in the Bible to count mainly just the men; occasionally they would mention the number of women. These verses do not say how many women believed or how many children believed. Since the Bible only gives me the number 5,000, I will add that number. Nearly an entire chapter is devoted to the adding of 3,000 members to that early congregation, and then in the fourth chapter only one verse casually mentions this huge addition, as if Paul were saying, "By the way, on another day we added about 5,000. That's just the men; I couldn't even count the women and children." We now count a total of 8,480 disciples in that church.

Acts 5:12-14, "*And by the hands of the apostles were many signs and wonders wrought among the people; (and they were all with one accord in Solomon's porch. And of the rest durst no man join himself to them: but the people magnified them. And believers were the more added to the Lord, multitudes both of men and women.)*" When I studied this passage, I decided to let the Bible interpret its own words. The word *multitude* is defined on two occasions in the Bible. One time the Bible describes a multitude as being 4,000 people. If I choose the Bible to define the Bible and do not give my definition of a multitude or the dictionary definition, I will use the smaller number of the multitude which is 4,000. The Bible does say that it was multitudes—plural. I believe as Brother Hyles did that the King James Bible is preserved. I believe it is preserved not only in word but also in the plurality of words. When the Bible says *seed* of Abraham, it uses the singular form of the word. God said, "I am smart enough to put an 's' on the word if it means plural." God is the best English teacher you will ever find in the world. God says in these verses that *multitudes* were added—more than one multitude. So if the Bible defines itself, then a multitude could be a minimum of 4,000. If I have multitudes, then the smallest would be at least two multitudes. It also says, "multitudes both of men and women." If I wanted to be very generous, I could say that phrase means "two multitudes of men and two multitudes of women" which would be 16,000 people; however, I want to show you the smallest possible measurement that the Bible is defining of what a church did in two years. So, if I say there are at least two multitudes and the smallest multitude in the Bible is 4,000. We will disregard the men and the women multitudes and just choose one of them. Then as of Acts 5:12 there would have been 16,480 Christians.

In Acts 6, things really began happening. Acts 6:1 says, "*And in those days, when the number of the disciples was multiplied....*" In chapter one, God was smart enough to know what a number was. He said the number of the disciples was about 120. Here the same Holy Ghost using the same language says, "Now the number is multiplied." What is the smallest number by which you can multiply? If I multiply by the smallest number, which would be two, I would now be at 32,960 people in my count of the membership of the church in Jerusalem.

But wait, according to Acts 6:7, we're not yet finished, "*And the word of God increased; and the number of the disciples multiplied in Jerusalem greatly; and a great company of the priests were obedient to the faith.*" I do not think it is a mistake in Acts 6:1 when it says, "*The number of the disciples multiplied,*" and in verse 7, "*the number multiplied greatly.*" If I choose the number three by which to multiply, because the Holy Spirit uses the adverb *greatly* in this verse, then the minimum size of that church in Jerusalem was 98,880 people. This was two years after Jesus went to Heaven. No wonder people have a hard time believing Paul in Acts 19 when he said that in two years everyone in Asia heard the Gospel.

There is a Christianity in the book of Acts that most Christians, apart from a handful of people in a few little pockets around the world, cannot comprehend. Oh, what could be done if God's people ever said, "Yes, not only is John 3:16 inspired, but Acts chapters 1, 2, 3, 4, 5, 6, 7, and 8 are also inspired and just as available to us as they were to the early Christians."

I dare anyone to take their King James Bible and prove me

wrong. The smallest that church in Jerusalem could have been was just under 100,000 people. Many Bible scholars state in their commentaries that in true, honest estimation, the church was probably in the neighborhood of 250,000 members in two years. These Christians had no building and no auditorium. They took over the temple and got kicked out of there. This huge congregation of 100,000 to 250,000 met in the streets and in houses.

Keep in mind this was not Hammond, Indiana; or Seoul, Korea; or Mexico City, Mexico. The hardest city in the world to reach would have been Jerusalem, where two years before, the Son of God had been hung on a cross and tried for blasphemy and treason. God said, "I want to show everyone, whoever picks up My Book, that I am going to start a church in the hardest city in the world. In two years, I am going to put 100,000 people in that church which will say to all of Christendom for every century thereafter, 'If I built a church of 100,000 in two years in the hardest city, what are you doing in your city?' "

Every time I read the book of Acts, I get so convicted that I close the Bible, set it aside, and say, "God, I find myself as wicked in my heart as the people who want to take your Book and say, 'Well, that is not really what it means.' " What does it mean then? What do you think God is telling Christians in the book of Acts? Some say, "The day of Pentecost was a day that we cannot have now."

Suppose we throw out the 3,000 people saved on Pentecost. Refiguring the numbers, we still arrive at 80,880 members. Wow! That's still a profound number for any church anywhere for any length of time. The power of God was mightily working in the book of Acts. That power is still available for Christians today. In fact, never in my life have I felt it as available for anybody as I have felt it is available for the First Baptist Church of Hammond.

First Baptist Church of Hammond is located in the midst of approximately six million people in the Chicago area. When I look at the number of people in Jerusalem relative to the number of people who were in that church, it is phenomenal what could be done at First Baptist if all our members would heed this simple Bible study of the ingredients that so quickly built the early church.

I was reading a biography of what is considered to be the largest Baptist church in the world in Seoul, Korea. That church began in

1969 with seven members; today, it has about 60,000 members. Every Sunday the church has about eight to ten services, running about 5,000 people each service, totaling 40,000 to 50,000 people every Sunday in attendance. I told God, "You know what, Lord? It bothers me that such enormous church growth is being done someplace else; it needs to be done right here." It needs to be done right here in the United States of America by God's people who once built their fundamental churches to the largest in the world.

Again and again, I feel that First Baptist Church of Hammond has come to another very important station of life. The first year and a half of my being the pastor, the First Baptist Church members were nurturing each other and trying to help each other through our great loss. We were holding up each other's weary arms and heavy hearts and wiping our tear-stained eyes as we wept together because of the loss of Brother Hyles. We kind of looked at each other and said, "We have to go on. We have to face the future. We have to step up."

Then as we realized that life was going to go on, we began adding new ministries and almost accidentally, without setting any numerical goals (really just wondering if we would still be a church in two years), we have grown by 1,800 in the last two years. I am amazed when I realize what First Baptist Church has done without really trying. We have only had one big day, our Great Commission day when we were just trying to get out the Gospel. That one day 48,000 were saved through the work of the First Baptist members—a phenomenal day. However, I began to see that God was hungry and willing to work with First Baptist Church of Hammond again. I ran to the book of Acts and said, "God, I want to see that old recipe again."

What is that recipe that God used to build the church in Jerusalem from 120 to 100,000 in two years? I haven't read anyone's books on this subject. I haven't gone to any resource material. I haven't studied anyone else's Sunday school literature. I have just studied one book—the book of Acts.

Let's continue the study with the following verses: Acts 1:14 says, "*These all continued with **one accord** in prayer and supplication, with the women, and Mary the mother of Jesus, and with his brethren.*" Acts 2:1 continues, "*And when the day of Pentecost was fully come, they were all with **one accord** in one place.*"

Acts 4:24 adds, "*And when they heard that, they lifted up their voice* to God with **one accord**, and said, Lord, thou art God, which hast made heaven, and earth, and the sea, and all that in them is."

Acts 5:12 says, "And by the hands of the apostles were many signs and wonders wrought among the people; (and they were all with **one accord** in Solomon's porch."

The phrase that is common in these verses is "*one accord*." One great reason that the church in Jerusalem grew is because of "*one accord*." Most Christians think that "*one accord*" means that the Christians all got along with each other. However, that is not what this phrase means. Let me prove it. One chapter smack-dab in the middle of all this growth tells about a man and woman who were killed because they did not get along with the local church. Ananias and Sapphira lied to the Holy Ghost and stole the tithe and offering. They had promised some building fund money and used it for a vacation instead, and God killed them.

Also in Acts 6:1 it says, "And in those days, when the number of the disciples was multiplied, there arose a murmuring of the Grecians against the Hebrews, because their widows were neglected in the daily ministration." Christians were murmuring and felt neglected. People were upset. Widows were angry with the preachers, and there was a little strife going on. So I know that "*one accord*" does not mean that the church members all got along.

If "*one accord*" means that all Christians must get along with each other to have church growth, then fundamental Baptist churches have no chance of growth. I will be honest with you, I spend a majority of my time in my office trying to help people get along with each other. If I have to wait for every husband and wife to love each other and all the kids to love their parents in order to have church growth, then let's close the doors today. There are a bunch of touchy, "feely," deeper-life people that want to stand around and hold hands and sing, "Kum Bah Yah," and have this warm fuzzy feeling where everybody loves everybody else.

If we have to wait to build a great work of God until we all have that warm, fuzzy feeling in our hearts and every church member loves every other church member, then First Baptist Church will never grow. I do not believe the notion that we all have to get along and that there cannot be any strife or discontentment before God can bless the church.

In the church in Jerusalem, the widows were irritated with the pastor because they were being neglected. Then Ananias and Sapphira were conspiring against the church and holding back money they promised. That *"one accord"* does not have anything to do with their all getting along with each other. There has never been a local church where everybody got along with each other all the time. A church like ours is a hospital, and at any given moment there are 25 to 40 marriages that are hanging on the very edge. In a church like ours, at any given minute there are probably 30 to 50 teenagers that are giving their moms and dads fits and cursing mom and dad and listening to their rock 'n' roll music. The truth of the matter is, last fall when we started our school year, I would have said that 85% to 90% of our Hammond Baptist kids were listening to the wrong kind of music. Right now I would say it is about 75%. Critics will say, "Wow! How can God bless First Baptist Church?"

If our churches have to wait until we get out all the sin, and get out all the strife, and until all the married couples are getting along, and all the teenagers love mom and dad before God will use our churches, then we are never going to be used of God! First Baptist Church is filled with people with heartaches, marriages on the fritz, teenagers upset with mom, and mom and dad upset with each other. That is part of life!

The Bible says that the church in Jerusalem had strife in it and still grew to 100,000 people in two years. They had widows upset with the pastor, and the church still grew to 100,000 people in two years. They had people killed in the church because they were stealing money from God, and still the church grew to 100,000 people in two years. How in the world did God ever use that church?

Mark 16:14 says, *"Afterward he appeared unto the eleven as they sat at meat, and upbraided them with their unbelief and hardness of heart, because they believed not them which had seen him after he was risen."* The word *upbraided* means "chided or scolded harshly." We would say today, "He ripped off their faces!" The word means, "To take them to task, to step on their toes, to stick a bony finger in their chest and accuse them of a great fault." What was the fault of these disciples?

After Jesus rose from the dead, Mary Magdalene saw Him and came back to the disciples. I can imagine the conversation. She excitedly said, "You will not believe Who I saw. I saw Jesus!"

The disciples said, "We do not believe you. You are that fallen woman that had seven devils in you." They would not believe her. Peter and John ran to the tomb, went inside, saw the empty grave clothes, rushed back, and said, "You will have a hard time believing it, but the tomb is empty."

Jesus said that the disciples had all this proof that He was alive. "I met you; I talked to you. I walked with two of you on the road to Emmaus. When I broke the bread, you saw the holes in My hands. You knew it was I, but when you told the rest of the disciples, they did not believe you. I spent three and a half years with you, and I told you that I was the Son of the living God. Peter, I asked you saying, *'Whom do men say that I the Son of man am?'* You answered, *'Thou art the Christ, the Son of the living God.'* You hard-headed and hard-hearted unbelievers! Whom do you think I was? What do you think I came to do? I told you I came to seek and to save that which was lost. I told you I came to die. I told you I would be buried. I told you I would rise again. I am so angry with you!"

Mark 16:15 records the very next words out of Jesus' mouth, "*And he said unto them, Go ye into all the world, and preach the gospel to every creature.*" The greatest commission was given to a bunch of backslidden disciples who did not believe who Jesus was. Jesus was angry at the disciples and frustrated with them. He ripped off their faces. He said, "I spent three years with you men, and you still do not know Who I am. You know what I am going to do about it? Get out of here and go win the world to Christ!"

That is why in Acts 1 (which describes this same event), all the disciples are standing around with their mouths open as Jesus went to Heaven. The angel said, "You heard Him, didn't you? Why are you standing around? Get out of here and go preach!" Somewhere in there, the disciples got the message, because two years later, there are 100,000 of them—not just members, but they were called disciples—people who were physically, actively involved in the church.

I have "*one accord*" with my associate pastor, Johnny Colsten, not because he is courteous and kind and has a warm personality and a warm handshake. I have "*one accord*" with Brother Eddie Lapina, the business manager and youth director of First Baptist Church, not because we do not have any harsh words or because we laugh together and enjoy the same kinds of humor and love for life and love for our families. I have *"one accord"* with my assistant pastors and staff, but not because we have warm feelings or warm handshakes or are buddy-buddy or socialize together.

In *"one accord"* means people are in agreement about a certain matter. I am in agreement about some things with Brother Tom Vogel, the academic vice president of Hyles-Anderson College. If Brother Vogel and I laid out all our beliefs, we would probably find some areas in which we disagree or see things a little differently. But I know one thing: we have one accord because we agree on one thing. There had better be one thing on which we are in agreement. There had better be one thing we agree on with the bus ministry and Dr. John Francis. There better be one thing we agree on with the Fishermen's Club and the "A" Bus Ministry and Dr. Roy Moffitt. There better be one thing we agree on with the Spanish Ministry and Brother Freddy De Anda. If First Baptist Church does not have that one agreement, then we are not in *"one accord."*

Literally *one accord* means "one passion." Did you know that passionate people often have strife? If you put a passionate husband and a passionate wife together, you are probably going to have more likelihood of strife than two boring "oatmeal and cardboard" spouses. Miss Oatmeal marries Mr. Cardboard. They have their 2.3 kids and their 1,200-square foot house and their 1.7-stall garage. They have all the statistical averages, and they are normal. They probably do not have any strife. However, if you have two passionate people together, you are going to have some strife. If you have passionate deacons and a passionate pastor, there might be a little rub once in a while. If you have passionate leaders of ministries and a passionate pastor and passionate followers in the ministries, you will probably have some friction once in a while because passionate people sometimes have troubles.

An angry, passionate mob murdered Stephen in Acts chapter seven. At the end of Stephen's sermon, he makes a statement that infuriates the crowd. Notice their reaction in verses 57 and 58: *"Then they cried out with a loud voice, and stopped their ears, and ran upon him with one accord, And cast him out of the city, and stoned him...."* Did you notice that this crowd was in one accord? Yes, they were in one passion with each other. The only thing they had on their minds was killing Stephen, and they did so. They weren't concerned with their differences or their daily duties, or even what the consequences would be of their actions. They were driven by one consuming passion. Oh, that God's people would be united in their passion for winning the lost as was that crowd for destroying Stephen.

Moses was a passionate man. One result of his passion was that he got in trouble and killed a man. I know Moses was a passionate man because he argued with God. You have to be pretty passionate to argue with God.

He said, "You are not going to do something stupid like destroy Sodom and Gomorrah, are You? That is not fair. You are fair, aren't You, God?"

Every time I read those passages, I jump a few pages because I am afraid God is going to burn me for reading it. Some of those people in the Bible were downright "in God's face." They almost upbraided God. It was a passionate Saviour Who "ripped off the face" of His passionate disciples who were willing to forsake all and follow Him.

Sometimes the people who forsake all and follow you turn tail and run from you. It is just a matter of passionate people. God knew if He could round up a passionate man like Moses and harness that passion, He could do a great work with him and part the Red Sea. It took the passion of man to stand up there in front of all the Egyptians and say, "...Fear ye not, stand still, and see the salvation of the LORD, which he will shew to you to day...." (Exodus 14:13)

It took a passionate boy like David when he was 17 years old to say, "I will go out and kill Goliath and lift off his head from him."

Saul said, "You cannot do that. You are just a youth."

David said, "I may be a youth, but I killed a lion and bear that were after my sheep." That same passionate man could have an immoral relationship with Bathsheba.

You see, "one accord" does not mean that they all got along. People who get along are sometimes just plain old lazy. How many splits do you read about in the United Methodist churches? When was the last time you heard about an American Baptist Convention church splitting? They don't split; they just dribble out. They just die off, die off, and die off until the last guy turns off the lights when he leaves. The people who do not do anything at all get along.

I get along great with my neighbors. We don't do anything together. Our neighbors from across the street came over to our house last week. The most we do with them is wave and say, "Hey!" Maybe once a week we will say, "How are you doing?" That's it. We get along beautifully.

This phrase *"one accord"* is so vital to understanding why the early church grew from 120 to 100,000. Churches across the world are saying, "We're going to grow if we all get together. There's too much strife going on. How can fundamentalists grow? They're all bickering and fussing with each other."

If we have to wait to grow until we are done bickering and fussing with each other, turn out the lights, the party's over! If *one accord* means "getting along together," there's not a Baptist church that stands a ghost of a chance. First Baptist Church of Jerusalem didn't grow because they had a "Kum-Bah-Yah" love fest, nor did they have a bunch of rock 'n' rollers come and produce a warm feeling between them all. The early church had problems and strife.

The phrase *one accord* means of "one passion." The church was being persecuted. People were getting fired because they were Christians. People were losing money because they were Christians. People were losing friends because they were Christians. That church was growing so fast that the city was scared. The leaders were put in jail and beaten and scolded and threatened. In Chapter 8, along comes a man named Saul.

Acts 8:1-4, *"And Saul was consenting unto his [Stephen's] death. And at that time there was a great persecution against the church which was at Jerusalem; and they were all scattered abroad throughout the regions of Judæa and Samaria, except the apostles. And devout men carried Stephen to his burial, and made great lamentation over him. As for Saul, he made havock of the church, entering into every house, and haling men and women committed them to prison. Therefore they that were scattered abroad went every where preaching the word."*

This church was in turmoil. It was being attacked. One of their finest had just been murdered by a mob. They had endured internal problems and external persecution; still, they were in one accord. The members went everywhere preaching the Word. One of the church members might not have gotten along with the fellow who was sitting on the deacon bench with him or with his wife sitting on the pew next to him. The kids might not have gotten along with mom and dad. Their mom and dad might not have gotten along with the preacher. The preacher might not have gotten along with the deacons. The deacons might not have gotten along with the widows. The widows might not have gotten along with the pastor. The pastor might not have gotten along with the school teachers. That is not the point! The point is when it came to this church in Jerusalem, they had one mind about one thing. It was the passion of their life. They breathed it, they ate it, they slept it, they dreamed it, they lived it—they wanted to spread the Word of God! Their passion was to get the lost saved. The disciples "got their faces ripped off" by Jesus. While they were still red with embarrassment, they walked up to someone and asked, "Can I tell you the wonderful news about salvation?"

Church members might not agree on many issues. The choir might have a disagreement sometime with Brother Cuozzo, the choir director. Brother Cuozzo might have a disagreement sometime with the choir. Baptist Boys Battalion might have a disagreement with the parents or the parents with the Baptist Boys Battalion. Blue Denim and Lace might have a disagreement with the parents and the parents with the leader or the leaders with the girls. The pastor might have a disagreement with the deacons, the deacons with the staff, or the staff with the pastor. We have disagreements. Bus captains are ticked off with the bus driver or workers. I do not care with whom you are ticked. You must be consumed with one passion: do you have the same mind, the same agreement, the same passion that lost souls go to Hell and that it is the job of Christians to get them out of Hell.

If we have to wait until we are all in peace and harmony, it is never going to happen. In the heart of man is lust and greed and revelry and rivalry and contention and strife and every evil speaking. Galatians 5:19-21 tells us, *"Now the works of the flesh are manifest, which are these; Adultery, fornication, uncleanness, lasciviousness, Idolatry, witchcraft, hatred, variance, emulations, wrath, strife, seditions, heresies, Envyings, murders, drunkenness, revellings, and such like...."* We are full of sin! I have all kinds of hell inside my heart like you do. However, there is one great consuming passion that burns like an inferno in my heart and that is, *I want the world to know the One Who loves them so. Like a flame it's burning deep inside. To be used of God is my desire.*

Christian, do not wait around until Junior becomes a

respectable, fine teenage boy. He might grow up to be a prodigal. While you are struggling with his being a prodigal son, why not go get some other prodigal saved? Your marriage may never be what it ought to be. I have no magic wand to wave over you.

Some of you say, "I went to Brother Hyles for 20 years, and he didn't help us either."

Then why are you coming to me? I checked that office. There is no magic wand! I use Brother Hyles' oil to anoint sick people; some get healed, but others do not. The truth of the matter is I may never be able to heal a couple's marriage like it ought to be. I may never be able to help Junior to become the young man he should be. Some may live in financial discord the rest of their days. Others might be in misery and contempt with other people all of their lives. However, members of First Baptist church had better have one consuming passion: Many of the six to eight million people in the Chicago area are going to Hell, and it is the responsibility of the First Baptist Church to get these lost people saved.

First Baptist Church will not grow because the members get along with each other. First Baptist Church will grow because the members are consumed with one passion. The co-president has to have a passion not just to take care of the college, but also to build First Baptist Church.

Jesus said, *"On this rock I will build my church."*

Brother Johnny Colsten and I never disagree; however, our never disagreeing is not why First Baptist Church will grow. Churches do not grow because they have kind, good, sweet-natured, gentle Christians. Churches grow because Christians have a single passion to win the lost to Christ.

I do not know of anybody I enjoy working with more than Brother Eddie Lapina, our business manager. Nearly every financial dealing in this whole ministry (college, schools, and church) is done between Brother Eddie and me. Just this past year, we have worked together on the remodeling of 57,000 square feet of property. In addition, we are trying to add 20,000 square feet more by refurbishing old buildings behind us which would house another 100 Sunday school classes. Brother Eddie and I work together well. We get along well. However, we are not going to build a church because the business manager and the pastor see eyeball-to-eyeball on money. We are not going to double the size of First Baptist Church and get 100,000 members, like they did in the book of Acts, because we get along or because I enjoy working with my staff. No! First Baptist Church will grow because we have one consuming passion: lost souls are going to Hell, and we had better get busy winning them to Christ.

I could not have asked for a greater gift from God for our Spanish Ministry than Brother Freddy De Anda. I talked to one of Brother De Anda's men recently and asked, "How is Brother De Anda doing?"

He said, "Brother Schaap, I think you would be very pleased. Brother De Anda even preaches your sermons. Every decision is 'We will check with Brother Schaap about that and do what the pastor tells us to do.' "

Brother De Anda's loyalty to the pastor may be one reason that the Spanish department has improved, but First Baptist Church will not grow because Brother De Anda preaches my sermons or because he likes me or because he shakes my hand or because we have a warm, fuzzy feeling together. A church is built because the Spanish pastor is consumed with one passionate mind set—to get the lost out of Hell. That goes for all the ministries of the First Baptist Church.

I would like to have a nice meal with all the men who work for me or take them on a hunting trip to Montana some time or go four-wheeling in Alaska or out shooting pistols or a round of golf or whatever they want to do. Fellowshipping with my staff men is not going to make this church grow. I will tell you what is going to make First Baptist Church grow: when all the staff men have one brilliant, consuming, white-hot passion; and when they are in one passion with the pastor, in one passion with Christ, and in one passion with the Book—the passion that lost people are going to Hell, and it is the job of all Christians to get them saved.

Even a backslidden teenage boy who has a hard time with mom and dad can have one passion and be in agreement in one area— winning lost souls to Christ. School teachers and administrators, I am glad you have a passion to prepare lesson plans and to teach your students; however, from the principals of the schools to the bus drivers, teachers, and custodians, the passion of your life better be to get those young people to become soul winners to get lost souls out of Hell. If the Christian school does not teach that one passion, it has failed at the most important passion of life. I care not at what you excel unless you excel at soul winning. That is the passion that Brother Hyles had.

Bus kids, instead of just feeding off the goodness and kindness and love of your bus captain, thinking somehow that the whole reason you exist is to be that bus kid who gets the captain to swallow the goldfish, you had better realize that your job is to become a bus kid like Brother Robert Wilson who is going to Mexico as a missionary. He has the same mind and agreement and passion as the bus ministry that saved him from South Chicago—that the world is going to Hell, and it is Brother Wilson's job to get them saved. First Baptist Church supports missionaries to win souls to Heaven, not to tend flower gardens or to have a nice town home or condominium and wait several years before they start winning souls. Missionaries should win souls their first day on the field!

A man came to me and told me that he was going to a certain country in Africa as a missionary. "I am proud of you," I said.

He asked, "How long after I get to Africa should I start a church?"

"I cannot tell you because I did not train you," I answered. "I do not want to contradict anyone who may have already advised you."

"I am asking you, Brother Schaap," he countered. "How long would you wait to start a church?"

"One week," I said. "I would have a Bible study in my house the first Sunday I was there."

"What if nobody came?"

I said, "I would have a Bible study with my wife then. I would go get somebody. If I had to pay somebody to come to my house, I would pay an interpreter to come, and I would win him to Christ. I am not going to take God's money from God's people and God's churches and sit for two and three and four and five years doing nothing but learning their language."

The first words you learn in their language are John 3:16. I would write it out and read it to the people and show it to them on a piece of paper. I would draw a diagram if I had to. I understand there are places where you have to go where it takes a while to teach them even basic truths; but missionaries who go to those places that have the Gospel and speak English should immediately start winning those people to Christ. The Mexican people are hungry for the

Gospel. Win them! The Filipinos are hungry for the Gospel. Win them! *"One accord"* means my heart beats one thing: win the lost, win the lost, win the lost!

A young college boy meets me in the church alley every Sunday night. Recently, he said, "Brother Schaap, I had 11 people saved yesterday."

Glory to God! That is what Christianity is all about—getting lost souls saved!

A young teenage girl told me recently she had won her first soul to Christ. I was thrilled. The next week she saw me and said, "Preacher, I won 13 souls to Christ yesterday."

I was overjoyed. She was in *one accord* with me and this church and our Saviour.

First Baptist Church has summer camps and school camps for our children. Our kids may come home from camp and say, "We all had warm, fuzzy feelings. We all went to bed feeling so cozy. We had a wonderful bonfire, and we all made some very precious decisions. We decided to write our moms and dads love letters."

That is wonderful! I want our kids to go to camp and make all those wonderful decisions. However, if our camps do not bring them back as better soul winners, we have failed our kids. The truth of the matter is if the First Baptist Church Sunday night crowd of 4,000 to 5,000 people all got on the same page, in one accord, with one passion, and each said, "I know one thing I agree upon: I agree it is my responsibility to win lost people to Christ," the Chicago area would be turned upside down for God and for good. Enough of saying, "That church in Jerusalem had it." Let's add, "and I want it, too!"

Brother Wayne Cowling went to our college years ago. He built a church and pastored and now is working for Reformers Unanimous helping churches get RU programs started. When Brother Cowling was an unsaved serviceman with orders to ship out to Vietnam, his mama came to Brother Hyles and said, "My son is going to Vietnam. If he gets killed, he is going to Hell. What do I do?"

Brother Hyles said, "Go soul winning. Every time you win a boy to Christ about your son's age, you say, 'God, I got that boy saved. Now You send someone to get my boy saved.' " That lady was winning as many as 100 people a week to Christ. For several years, she won 200-300 people yearly to Christ. She was an amazing soul winner. Eventually, her boy did get saved and became a Baptist preacher.

Some mamas labor and worry about their boys. They are so fixated on their boys' problems that they are unfocused on the great passion of getting lost souls saved. The best hope a wayward boy has of getting the power of God to change his heart is a praying mama who knocks on doors and says, "May I tell you some wonderful news? Jesus saves." Husband, you may have trouble with your wife, but get in the Fishermen's Club or join the bus ministry. Get active and involved in knocking on doors.

I want the First Baptist Church of Hammond to be in one accord, one passion, and one mind. We must be in agreement on one thing: a white-hot, consuming passion that the six million people from North Chicago to Joliet to Michigan City and each one of the 485,448 people in Lake County, Indiana, need some church to say, "You're in my sights, buddy. I may have trouble with my spouse or my children or my money or another brother in Christ, but I am focused on one thing: without Christ, people go to Hell, and I have the wonderful words of life. Jesus saves!"

We may disagree on many issues, but we had better be in agreement on one issue: The souls of mankind are lost and going to Hell, and we have the Gospel message that can bring them salvation.

A precious couple came to see me in my counseling line. Their tears flowed abundantly. They said, "Brother Schaap, we have tried and tried and tried to have a child."

I have anointed them three times now and prayed for them. They have a passion together. They are two people who are focused. They want so badly to have a child. When the couple left my office, I got on my knees and said, "God, may my passion for lost souls be as great as their passion to have a child."

The lost world needs Christians to win them to Christ. It is our job. That is why we are here. Let's make sure we keep that one passion. Let's be sure we are *IN ONE ACCORD!*

CHAPTER THREE

How to Develop a Passion for Souls

"And being let go, they went to their own company, and reported all that the chief priests and elders had said unto them. And when they heard that, they lifted up their voice to God with one accord, and said, Lord, thou art God, which hast made heaven, and earth, and the sea, and all that in them is: Who by the mouth of thy servant David hast said, Why did the heathen rage, and the people imagine vain things? The kings of the earth stood up, and the rulers were gathered together against the Lord, and against his Christ. For of a truth against thy holy child Jesus, whom thou hast anointed, both Herod, and Pontius Pilate, with the Gentiles, and the people of Israel, were gathered together, For to do whatsoever thy hand and thy counsel determined before to be done. And now, Lord, behold their threatenings: and grant unto thy servants, that with all boldness they may speak thy word, By stretching forth thine hand to heal; and that signs and wonders may be done by the name of thy holy child Jesus. And when they had prayed, the place was shaken where they were assembled together; and they were all filled with the Holy Ghost, and they spake the word of God with boldness." (Acts 4:23-31)

THESE EARLY CHRISTIANS had a consuming passion. It's the same passion I have: I want to get people saved. I want to win the lost. That passion has to be there. I will build on that thought as we look at one area in which we are supposed to be in one passion. Acts 1:14 says, *"These all continued with* **one accord** *in prayer and supplication, with the women, and Mary the mother of Jesus, and with his brethren."*

Acts 2:1 says, *"And when the day of Pentecost was fully come, they were all with* **one accord** *in one place."*

Acts 2:42 says, *"And they continued stedfastly in the apostles' doctrine and fellowship, and in breaking of bread, and in prayers."*

Acts 2:46 continues, *"And they, continuing daily with* **one accord** *in the temple, and breaking bread from house to house, did eat their meat with gladness and singleness of heart."*

Acts 4:24 says, *"And when they heard that, they lifted up their voice to God with* **one accord,** *and said, Lord, thou art God, which hast made heaven, and earth, and the sea, and all that in them is."*

Acts 4:31 says, *"And when they had prayed, the place was shaken where they were assembled together; and they were all filled with the Holy Ghost, and they spake the word of God with boldness."*

I know I am supposed to have one mind about winning the lost, one passion about getting souls saved. Ministry leaders are supposed to have one passion—not for ministries, but for getting people saved. The men on the church softball league are supposed to have one passion—not for softball, but for soul winning. Youth baseball league players are supposed to have one passion—not baseball, but soul winning. Should a bus driver's one passion be driving a bus? No! It should be winning souls to Christ! Should a Sunday school teacher's one passion be building his class? No! It should be winning souls to Christ! Should the choir members' one passion be to sing the best song they can sing? No! It should be winning souls to Christ! Should the one passion of the organist and the pianist be to play those instruments the best they can? No! It should be winning souls to Christ! Should helping with the church business be the one passion of a deacon? No—winning the lost! Should the preacher's messages be his one passion? No! The preacher's one passion must be to win lost souls to Christ. We must all win the lost at all cost.

This one-passion mentality comes by concentrated focus. We are all supposed to focus in one direction. When I was a kid, I would take a magnifying glass and go outside to burn ants! All guys did that. My friends and I would go outside on a hot day when the sun was right overhead, and we would focus that sunbeam into that magnifying glass and would watch those ants as they started slowing down, then stopping, rolling over, curling up, and smoking. That magnifying glass focused that little beam of light going through it.

When energy is focused on one spot, one finds the power of concentrated effort. It is one beam of light—one passion of light, so to speak. That is what First Baptist Church is supposed to be. That is what every local church is supposed to be—one concentrated force or one passion.

Why are Christians at church? To win souls. Why was First Baptist Church organized 116 years ago? To win souls. Why do our congregations meet together Sunday morning, Sunday night, and Wednesday nights? To learn how to be better soul winners. Why does the choir sing? To stir our hearts to get ready to hear the preaching so we can get ourselves equipped to be better soul winners. The passion of the local church is getting lost souls out of Hell.

How do we get that passion? What is the magnifying glass that can pull the energy together? I am in favor of all the activities our church has. Our Best Years Club goes on outings and picnics and has fun. We have junior camp. We have high school camp. We have college summer school. We have reading programs and child-care programs and youth baseball leagues and men's softball league and golf outings. I am for all these wonderful things 1,000%.

However, with the bigness of a church like First Baptist Church with all its different ministries, what can happen is that that powerful beam of light starts going in different directions until eventually that little ant can walk in the hot sunlight and not get burned because the heat is not focused on one spot. First Baptist Church can pass sinners by the thousands on their way to a camp and not win one of them. First Baptist Church members can pass lost souls at the grocery market and never give one tract to anybody. You may be at the grocery market to pick up food for the junior camp or some other ministry. However, the whole purpose of the Christian life is not to buy and sell, but to concentrate that light of the Gospel and say, "Let's get lost souls out of Hell."

If a church has a small group of 25 people and the pastor says,

"Let's have a big day. Let's all invite somebody," it does not take much to grow from 25 to 50. But it takes a whole lot to grow from 5,000 to 10,000. In a church of 5,000 members, there are hundreds of activities and Youth Conferences and Educators' Conventions and Christian Womanhood Spectaculars and Pastors' Schools and camps. All of these are wonderful ministries serving the people. But a church of 5,000 can become so busy serving the people that nobody is out there trying to get lost souls saved.

How does the pastor and congregation of a big church keep their minds focused? How do they all look through the same magnifying glass and focus all together so as not to lose that one
passion, that one zealous focused ray of energy that says, "When I go to the grocery store, I am going to pass out a tract. When I am walking through the neighborhood, I am going to see if I can win my neighbors to Christ."

How can a Christian have that *"one-accord"* passion to get people saved? Through passionate prayer. I do not mean the little prayer time, the little ditty ritual most Christians go through for about three to five minutes in the morning before going to work or the little five to six minutes before going to bed at night. It is not the mumbled prayer said before eating lunch or the perfunctory, necessary prayer before breakfast, lunch, and supper. I am talking about how to gather your minds together and focus and get that energy where you have one accord, one passion in a church.

In Acts 1:14, the Bible says, *"...prayer and supplication...."* The Bible says that I must continue in one accord, one passion in prayer and supplication.

What is supplication? The word *supplication* comes from the root word "supple, bendable, flexible, and conformable." The word *supplication* literally means "to want to conform, to want to mold, to want to bend." If I supplicate, I am actually praying that I could be conformed or molded or bended to another pattern.

Brother Ray Young, the Co-President of Hyles-Anderson College, took a group of contest winners on a seven-day trip to Europe. Suppose I had wanted to go on that trip with him. Supplication is my begging and pleading for him to take me with him where he is already going.

Supplication is finding out where Brother Young is going and saying, "Brother Ray, can I ask a really big favor? I heard you are going to Europe tomorrow. I know you are going to have a lot of fun, aren't you? You're going to be in Normandy. I would love to go to Normandy with you. I don't suppose you have room, do you? Could you squeeze one little skinny guy on board? Could I go with you to Europe?"

That is supplication. Supplication is begging and pleading and petitioning and praying that you could go along where God is going. It is saying, "God, I think You are going somewhere, and I would just really love to go with You."

Let me illustrate. My grandpa used to own a trailer park in Holland, Michigan. Many Friday nights when I was a young boy, I would stay overnight with Grandpa and then spend all day Saturday with him. Grandpa and I would work around the trailer park together. One Saturday morning he got up early and said, "Hey, Jack, let's go to the dump. I need to take all the garbage to the dump." Back before the environmentalists passed all the clean air laws, Grandpa had a little incinerator where he burned all the garbage from the trailer park. Once in a while the ashes would pile high and the items that would not burn would accumulate, and Grandpa would have to empty the incinerator and take the garbage to the city dump.

I said, "The city dump? Is it fun?"

He said, "No, it's not fun at all. It's a lot of hard work. It stinks there. There are rats and flies. It's a mess. You want to go along?"

I said, "No, I don't want to go." I stayed home and played army with my buddies. About two or three hours later, I saw one of my buddies for whom I had been looking. As he walked toward me, I noticed he was licking the remnants of a butter pecan ice cream cone.

I met him and said, "I missed you. We were playing army."

"I went with your grandpa to the dump," he said. "He was heading out, hollered at me, and asked if I wanted to go along. So I jumped in the pickup truck with him. On the way home, we stopped at Mills Ice Cream Parlor, and I got me an ice cream cone."

I said, "You're eating MY ice cream cone. I was supposed to go with my grandpa, and I should have been eating that ice cream cone." I covenanted with God right there that I would never again miss going to the dump with Grandpa. About a month later, I spent the night at Grandpa's house. Saturday morning I got up bright and early, and I ran to his bedroom. He and Grandma were still asleep in the bed, but I said, "Hey, Grandpa, Grandpa, Grandpa! Isn't it time to go to the dump?"

He said, "Son, it's six o'clock in the morning. It's not time to go anywhere right now."

I said, "Grandpa, are we going to the dump today?"

He said, "Yes, I'm going to the dump today, but I didn't think you would want to go."

I said, "Oh, I'd love to go to the dump. Grandpa, can I please go to the dump with you?"

He said, "Boy, what is the matter with you? We're going to go later on. Why do you want to go anyway?"

I said, "I love going to the dump."

He said, "Last month I asked you to go, and you didn't want to go."

I said, "Grandpa, that was a whole month ago. I'm a big boy now. I've grown up a whole lot!"

Why was I excited about going to the dump? I did have an ulterior motive—I wanted that ice cream cone! And that Saturday I got that ice cream cone!

In the months that followed, I went to the dump dozens of times with Grandpa and got several ice cream cones and hamburgers and all kinds of good things. I supplicated. I was trying to convince Grandpa that I wanted to go to the dump with him. I wanted to be supple, bendable, moldable, and flexible. I wanted to conform with Grandpa where he was headed.

One day I was going to Schilling Brothers Lumber, and I said to my four-year-old daughter, "Jaclynn, Daddy's going to the hardware store. Do you want to go along?"

She asked, "What are you going to get there?"

I said, "I have to buy some nails and screws and a hammer and screwdriver. Do you want to go with me?"

"I don't think so," she answered.

"You're going to be sorry," I warned.

She said, "No, I don't think so."

I got in the car and went to the hardware store and bought a hammer and screwdriver and nails and screws. On the way home, I noticed the Dairy Queen sign said, "Special! Peanut Buster Parfaits 99 cents." The will of God convicted me, and the Holy Ghost of God led me, and I felt compelled to stop at Dairy Queen. I bought a Peanut Buster Parfait. By the time I pulled in the driveway, I had caramel all over my knuckles from scraping the spoon way down in the bottom of the container. I walked inside the house with the empty container, and my daughter asked, "What's that?"

"That **was** a Peanut Buster Parfait," I answered.

"You got that at the hardware store?"

"No, sweetheart," I answered. "I got that at Dairy Queen."

"But Daddy," she declared. "You didn't tell me you were going to Dairy Queen."

"I wasn't planning to go to Dairy Queen," I replied.

She said, "You told me you were going to the hardware store."

"I went to the hardware store," I agreed, "but I saw the Dairy Queen sign, and I stopped."

"Dad, if I had known you were going to Dairy Queen," she said, "I would have gone to the hardware store with you."

"If you loved me, it wouldn't have mattered where I was going," I said.

Don't miss that truth. That is what supplication is. Supplication is the next time Jaclynn saying, "Daddy, Daddy, Daddy, are you going to the hardware store? May I go? In fact, Daddy, are you going anywhere? May I go? I don't care where you go. May I go with you?" That is supplication.

Supplication is convincing God that you do not care where He is going; you just want to go along. Until you are willing and convincing to God, God is not much interested in focusing your passion.

God magnifies a church's passion. God puts that focus on a community. It is God Who begins to work and use a local church. Listen, God is not obligated to use First Baptist Church, folks. Do you think God up in Heaven says, "Oh, my, I am pretty impressed. A big church down there in Hammond, Indiana, has My arm behind My back. I have to use them."

God does not have to use First Baptist Church. Many churches have closed their doors because nothing is happening. God is not using a whole lot of people who once were being mightily used of God. Do you think God has a special affection for Hammond,

Indiana? If He does, He's the only One Who does. I love what Jack DeCoster said while he was here for Pastors' School looking at our building projects.

He said, "Do you know what I call this place, Brother Schaap? I call this Mount Zion."

I asked, "Why is that?"

He said, "Because that is God's favorite place. I think First Baptist Church is God's favorite place."

I think God does love First Baptist Church, but God does not owe our church any favors. My Bible says that God is able to do exceeding and abundantly above all that we ask or think. But it does not say that God is always willing to do that. Sometimes we think because God is able that He automatically wants to. My opinion is that God looks for us to provide the "want-to" so His ability is turned loose and unharnessed. My willingness determines how much of God's ability I get to see work in Hammond, Indiana. God is able to save every soul in Hammond because the blood of Jesus Christ was shed for every soul in Hammond, Indiana. Then why isn't everyone in Hammond, Indiana, saved?

Some will say, "Well, not everybody is going to get saved."

One time in Samaria, everyone got saved. Why did every child, every teenager, every mom, every dad, every adult, every senior citizen in Nineveh get saved that one time when Jonah preached? They were all saved because God is able; but, He is waiting for some church to want it badly enough.

God is saying, "I am able, but I have confined My ability to your willingness. I will only work with a willing vessel." My Bible says that there must first be a willing mind. II Corinthians 8:12 says, *"For if there be first a willing mind, it is accepted according to that a man hath, and not according to that he hath not."* God is not looking at your ability; He is looking at your willingness.

The one thing I can provide for God that determines whether we get the job done is the willingness. I heat up the passion; God does the work. I provide the magnifying glass; God provides the sun. People will say, "I have been soul winning, but my bus route is in a very hard area."

You don't think Samaria was a hard area! Samaria was where Jews were hated. Jesus even had a tough time in Samaria. However,

Philip went to Samaria, and Philip got wound up! Philip got that passion. Philip got magnifying-glass power, and God used Philip, and that whole city, with one accord, turned to the Lord.

When we talk about hard areas, there is not any area harder than Jerusalem. That is where the people murdered God. They put God on a tree and said, "If You are the Son of God, come down and show us." Less than two months later, the church began growing, and within the space of two years, it grew from 120 to a membership of 100,000 people—nearly the entire city. That is more people than there are residents of the city of Hammond.

You see, Hammond may be a hard place, and where your bus route is may be a hard place, and your city may be a hard place, but nothing is too hard for God! The ability of God is not in question. It is the willingness of God's people to be magnified or focused with the power of God.

A big church gets distracted by so many things: softball games, youth baseball league games, t-ball games, Billy Sunday league games, Best Years Club activities. Don't get me wrong, I love all our programs, but because there are so many things that dissipate our interest, before we know it, we get more impassioned about a game than we do about the lost. Some men get more bent out of shape about baseball and softball than about their neighbor going to Hell. If everybody in First Baptist Church brought one visitor next week, we would have no place to put the crowd. We are building an auditorium that is 60 percent larger than our present congregation.

People have asked, "Are you going to be able to fill that new auditorium?"

We can fill it in less than one Sunday. Filling that new auditorium is only a problem of our willingness and has nothing to do with God's ability. God could fill that auditorium until we must have five services every Sunday. Would to God that we had to do so!

I told God the other day, "God, we will build the new auditorium, and God, You are going to have to help us fill it; but I don't mind if we have three, four, five, or ten services a week with 70,000 people attending every Sunday. What I am interested in is seeing how big a God I have."

God said, "I am big enough; are you willing enough?" God says the willingness comes when you have a singular passion in prayer and supplication that says, "Oh, God, I want that. I want to go where You are going. I want my neighbors to be saved. God, I want my friends to be saved. God, I want it."

God says, "You must spend the time in prayer to get that passion equal to my ability." Far too many people have written off God's ability as being inadequate and too weak to handle a situation.

Dr. Lee Roberson said to me a couple of years ago that he personally had read where over 7,000 Southern Baptist churches had not baptized one convert in that year. At First Baptist Church, we baptize thousands of converts every year, and I am glad we do. The bottom line is First Baptist Church is in a hard area like anyone is in a hard area. The difference is that there are some willing people in the church. What would happen if everyone in First Baptist Church decided to get focused on one thing?

Missionaries say to me all the time, "Brother Schaap, you have no idea how hard the mission field is."

Yes, I do know. I am not going to sit in judgment of you. All I know is you serve the same God as I do.

I was talking to a missionary who said, "Brother Schaap, I am going to a pastors' convention in such-and-such a country."

I said, "That country?"

"Yes."

I said, "A convention? How many are you expecting?"

When he said, "Three thousand," I was shocked!

"Three thousand?" I exclaimed. "I do not even know of a missionary that is running more than ten in that whole country."

He said, "Brother Schaap, our boys have bought into the lie that such-and-such is a hard country. There are pastors that preach the Gospel just like we do. They use the same Bible we do, but nobody has told them yet that their God is not able to do it. They will have 3,000 people at that convention—3,000 pastors and preachers."

"You are lying to me," I responded. "Nobody goes to that country and does it."

He said, "Nobody who believes that way does. Do you believe God can do it in Hammond?"

"Well, He has been," I answered.

He asked, "Do you believe God is still doing it?"

"Sure I do," I replied.

"That is what you believe," he declared. "Your belief is probably why your church grew 1,800 last year."

Any place where a man wants to go and believe that God's ability is only limited by man's willingness, that place is where God can work. The number-one reason why Christians do not get their prayers answered is because 99.9 percent do not pray. I don't call those little ditties before each meal praying. Praying is asking God to do something. Praying is focused energy saying, "God, I want You to do something specifically."

I am all for praying for our food, but I am talking about the kind of praying that says, "God, move my heart from the extremity, from the fringe to where it is hot, right under the magnifying glass of Your power so I am with You, God. I am going to the spiritual dump with You where my heart is hot in passion to win the lost for whom You came to die."

That is where I want to live. I don't want to visit there on Saturdays; I want to live there 168 hours a week.

So often, my wife will say to me when I come home from work, "You have that look in your eye. You're thinking again, aren't you?"

I say, "It's hard to get it off my heart. I have taken hold of the reins of something the likes of which could change the world. If we don't do it, I don't want to meet Jesus and have Him say, 'I gave you the most powerful, independent, fundamental Baptist church in the world. I gave you the horsepower of the bus ministry the likes of which no other church in the world has. I gave you the world's largest Sunday school. I gave you deacons who have a heart to serve Me. I gave you 600 Sunday school teachers. I gave you a college with over 1,000 young men and women who are set on fire for God. And what did you do with it, Schaap?"

I do not want to meet Jesus without saying, "God, I took it all the way under the magnifying glass. We set this world on fire for You, God." That is what I want to say when I meet Him!

Independent Baptists ought to have 10,000 missionaries on the foreign field. First Baptist church alone ought to have 1,000 missionaries out of our congregation in the next ten years. A thousand First Baptist young people should say, "I am so hungry to get out the Gospel, let me go somewhere and tell the lost about Christ."

When high school students come for their senior appointments,

I ask them, "What do you want to do?"

Some will answer, "Oh, I don't know."

I can tell them what to do! The world is going to Hell! Go any place and get out the Gospel!

That passion did not start in me two years ago when I became the pastor of this great church. That passion started when I was a little boy. That passion started when I was five years old and God lit a fire inside of me which burns hotter every day. That fire has waned from time to time, but has never gone out. That fire just gets hotter and hotter. Sometimes I feel there is a fire burning deep inside me that is indescribable. That's passion!

I'll tell you how I got that passion. I got that passion by spending time alone with God—long times of regular, frequent prayer. I poured out my heart to God.

We sing, "Sweet hour of prayer, sweet hour of prayer! That calls me from a world of care." The truth of the matter is, I doubt if 50 percent of Christians know what it is to pray for an hour—an hour on your face until tears stain your cheeks. Pray for an hour on your face arguing with God. Pray for an hour on your face begging and pleading—not for a boyfriend, not for a girlfriend, not for a nicer car, not for a better job, not for a pay raise—but for the mighty baptism of the Spirit of the living God to fill you so that you can win the world to Christ.

Supplication is not just for preachers; it is for plumbers and truck drivers as well. Supplication is not just for staff members; it is also for laymen. Supplication is for junior-age boys and girls and teenagers. Supplication is for every Christian! Thousands of Christians should have a hunger and passion to get under that magnifying glass and say, "God, may I please go with You? May I please do something to win the lost?" Yes, pass out a tract. Yes, preach the Gospel. Yes, go to teenage soul winning. Yes, run a bus route. "I want that passion like You have beating inside of You. That is what I want, God!" That passion comes from spending a lot of time with God.

Christian, spend all the time you want with Hollywood; it will not give you a passion for souls. Spend hours in your music; it will not give you a passion for souls. You will not get a passion for souls by watching your television. Is Hollywood a friend of God? No! It is a vile, filthy enemy of the very passion which I am addressing. It robs you of the fire. It comes like a cloud between you and God and takes away the fire.

However, I know what heats up the fire. Take an hour a week, fall down prostrate on your face, and say, "God, I will pay any price. I do not care what it takes, God. Set me ablaze for You. God, help me get that passion for the lost that You have, God."

I love the story Dr. Tom Williams tells about a lady who came to him one night after he preached an evangelistic sermon. He had preached about getting your lost loved ones saved. This very well-attired and distinguished-looking woman came to him and said, "Dr. Williams, my husband is unsaved. Would you pray for my husband to get saved?"

"I would be happy to," he said. He got down on his knees but noticed that she remained standing. "Do you want to pray?" he asked.

She said, "I would love for you to pray."

He said, "Why don't you join me here at the altar?"

"I suppose I could," she answered. She got on her knees next to Dr. Williams.

"Oh, God, this dear woman loves You," he began to pray. "Her husband is lost and going to Hell. God, I am asking You to put him in an accident or put him flat on his back where the only place he can look is to Heaven. Break a bone, crack a rib, bring a heart attack, produce a stroke...."

The lady tapped Dr. Williams on the shoulder and asked, "What are you talking about?"

He said, "Do you want your husband saved?"

"Well, I want my husband saved," she said, "but I don't want him in an accident."

He asked, "How badly do you want your husband saved?"

She answered, "Not that badly."

Dr. Williams began praying again, "Well, God, go ahead and send ·her husband to Hell." Brother Williams got up off his knees and turned to the next person.

The lady stopped him and said, "Just a minute! I don't want my husband to go to Hell."

Dr. Williams replied, "Until you want your husband saved as badly as God wants him saved, he will not get saved."

Like that dear lady, we want a convenient Christianity that says, "God, win Hammond and the world to Christ, but God can You do it in about 30 minutes? I have a ball game to get to. I have to watch the Cubs or the Sox play. I have a heavy date, and I have to spend hours with my girlfriend watching television. We have to spend hours in lovers' lane. I have books to read. I have shows to watch. I have fun things to do. Hey, God, can You kind of squeeze it in a little bit to help me be a soul winner?"

God says, "I am not going to squeeze it in! I want you to get a white-hot passion like I have all the time."

Until God sees a group of people with that kind of passion, His power sits off to the side and says, "I am not going to do it."

God has limited His winning the lost to His people's willingness. God does not save people without human agency. God does not save anyone unless some soul winner gets excited about it and knocks on the sinner's door and cares about him. Look how casually teenagers go to teenage soul winning and how many souls they just kind of stumble over and win. God is so hungry to win the lost that a teenager can go soul winning with a bad attitude, ticked-off at mom and dad, and angry at his girlfriend. When he passes out a tract and asks another teenager, "Do you want to get saved?" the teen says, "Yes, I do."

It is amazing to me that some of our First Baptist Church kids come back from soul winning and tell me, "Brother Schaap, I won 11 people to Christ this week." I sometimes wonder, "God, if those kids ever got impassioned about soul winning, what would happen? If they ever have that white-hot passion about it like You have, God, what would happen?" Chicago would get saved! We would see a Samarian incident where the whole city turned to Christ. We would see a Nineveh where one backslidden, angry, unhappy preacher went to the city of Nineveh, and the whole city got saved. God is so hungry to win the lost that He is willing to use anybody.

When Jesus looked at the disciples and upbraided them for their unbelief, He also told them to go preach the Gospel, and that is the group who turned the world upside down. Let me share some practical help on getting a white-hot passion.

1. Learn how to win a soul. I guarantee you there are hundreds of people in my congregation who really do not know how to win a soul to Christ. I am asking my staff men who have soul-winning ministries to have quarterly training sessions in our church to teach soul winning. Even though many Christians have learned how to be soul winners, the truth of the matter is I dare say there are hundreds of others that really do not know how to win a soul to Christ.

2. **Covenant to pray one hour per week.** I wish an army of my members would say, "I am going to set aside one solid 60-minute hour where I do nothing but beg God to make me a soul winner and to set our church ablaze." This is not a time to pray for the sick in the hospital or anything else except for one pure purpose only—that God would set our church ablaze with a white-hot passion to win the lost. I promise you, if everybody in the First Baptist Church spent that time in prayer, Hammond had better watch out!

I was remembering a story about a church that was once the largest Baptist church in Europe—the Second Baptist Church of Oradia, Romania, our missionary George Pordea's boyhood church. Brother Pordea told me that when his mother and father attended that church, the church ran as many as 8,000 on big days. He said that at 5:00 every morning, several hundred of the church members would meet, and once a week as many as 5,000 people would meet to pray for an hour! At times, I don't care about anything at 5:00 in the morning!

"George," I asked, "what did those people pray for?"

George said, "They prayed for one thing. They prayed that the Christians in America would wake up to the opportunity they have in America."

Every time I think about George's statement, my heart breaks to think that people who were living in Europe on about $15 a month in squalid, cheap, filthy government housing owned and operated by the Communists were praying for American Christians. At one time when the church building was filled with 8,000 people, the prime minister gave the order for bulldozers to tear down the building.

The dozer operators refused saying, "No, those are relatives of ours. Those are people we live with. We will not tear down that building."

The prime minister said, "Tear down the church building, or I will put you in prison."

The workers did not tear down the building because 8,000 people were inside. I get convicted when people under those conditions were praying for me. They were not praying that I would be blessed or have a good day or be healed, but that I would wake up to the opportunity I have in America.

Within the first eight chapters of the book of Acts, three times God persecuted the church in Jerusalem and said, "You are not doing enough." This was a church that in two years went from 120 to a minimum of 100,000 members! In two years, they had three persecutions: three vicious attacks against their leadership until eventually in Acts 8, the Bible says there arose a great persecution against the church in Jerusalem, and the members were scattered everywhere. The soldiers went house to house and put Christian believers in jail. The Bible says, *"Therefore they that were scattered abroad went every where preaching the word."* (Acts 8:4)

You and I are saved because of that persecution in Acts chapter 8. God said, "I am so eager and so hungry to have a church that is on fire just a little bit, that I grabbed them and said, 'Come on! Do not stop now! Put on the fire. Get in the center under the magnifying glass. Get white-hot for Me!' " That is what He is talking about.

Three times God grabbed the pastors of the churches and shook them and put them in jail. Three times He put stripes on the backs of those men who went away saying, "Glory! Hallelujah! We are counted worthy to suffer shame for the name of Jesus Christ." God said, "That is not good enough. You are catching it, but your church is not catching it!"

Sometimes I wonder if it would help the First Baptist Church members if I got put in jail or if my assistant pastors got persecuted and arrested and beaten in the town square? The truth of the matter is, if you study prophecy at all, you will find that during the Tribulation, 144,000 Jews get saved. Those Jewish converts are called the firstfruits of the Tribulation, being the first Jews to get saved. These Jews immediately trust Christ, and they are so happy that they all get together in Jerusalem. God sends the Antichrist three and one-half years later to persecute those believers with the greatest persecution in the history of the world. Why? God persecutes these Jewish believers to spread them around the globe to preach the Gospel.

Persecution has always been God's tool because people do not want to wake up and do right out of their own motivation. I have told God thousands of times that He never has to persecute me to get me motivated. Every day and every week I spend a long time on my face saying, "God, I will persecute myself so that You do not have to persecute me. I want to see what You can do at First Baptist Church of Hammond."

To most Christians, "sweet hour of prayer" is about 30 seconds of mumbo-jumbo nonsense. Their whole prayer life consists of statements like, "God, change my life so it is more comfortable for me." Ninety-nine point nine percent of every Christian's prayer life consists of, "God, would You make my lifestyle more comfortable?" They do not necessarily mean more money; they just want people to treat them nicely. They want their boss to change or their spouse to change and treat them nicer. They may want a pay raise. The truth of the matter is if Christians changed their selfish prayers and said, "In .1 % of my prayer life, I am going to pray for me, but 99.9% of my prayer life is going to be set aside for God to set me ablaze, to set me afire and my church afire. God, let's see what the mighty, omnipotent power of God can do."

I believe there would be no limit to what God could do. First Baptist Church would outgrow our new auditorium in 30 minutes. Around the globe, there are churches that believe like us. They believe the Bible is the Word of God. They believe salvation is by grace through faith. They believe Jesus Christ is the Son of God. They believe in the same doctrines we do; and those churches are five to ten times larger than First Baptist Church. First Baptist Church can try to hide behind, "We are the world's largest Sunday school." That title does not mean diddley!

God is not looking down from Heaven and saying, "Wow! First Baptist Church is the world's largest Sunday school." No, God is saying, "Tell you what I think about that. Show Me what you can do. Hey, World's Largest, show Me what you can do if you are the world's largest."

While First Baptist Church quietly hides behind our nomenclature, God is not impressed when He sees our stationery. When I show God my business card which reads, "Jack Schaap, Senior Pastor of First Baptist Church of Hammond, home of the World's Largest Sunday School," God does not say, "Ooh, Jack, back down."

God is not impressed. Rather, God says to me, "Then see what you can do. World's Largest Sunday School, do you have the most missionaries on the field? Do you have the world's largest number of preacher boys? Do you have the world's largest number of souls being saved each year? Do you have the largest number of baptisms each year? Do you have the world's largest congregation in that church? Hey, Schaap, are those people distracted with all the fun and delightful programs, or are they burning white-hot with a passion to see the lost saved?"

Hey, senior citizens, on your activity, get somebody saved! Hey, little leaguers, win the lost to Christ. Hey, all you teenagers, on your way down to camp, witness to every gas station attendant you see. When you stop at a fast-food restaurant, witness to every worker. Let this world know that there is a church that is set ablaze for God. Covenant to pray for one hour a week. That gives you 167 hours a week to do what you want. Take that hour a week to pray, "God, set my church ablaze."

I am asking for one hour per week on your face before God saying, "God, set my soul afire. Lord, set our church afire. Lord, set our preacher afire. God, set our deacons afire. God, set our teens afire. God, set our Sunday school teachers afire. God, set our Christian schools afire. God, set our youth ministry afire. God, set our church afire. Oh, God, set me afire!"

3. Covenant to fast one to three days a month. If you are healthy, set aside one day a month to fast and say, "God, I am not going to eat a thing. I want You to know that I am going to persecute myself so You do not have to persecute my church to remind me how important it is to get the lost saved."

Do not fast for your husband to treat you nice or your teenage boy to behave himself in school or your teenage daughter not to like the wrong boy. I am not asking for 40 days like the Saviour did or 80 days like Moses did at Mount Sinai. I am not talking about the great people who really made a difference. I am only asking for one to three days a month where you take that time and say, "God, I am not going to eat. I am not going to tell anybody. I want You to know, God, that I want to be set ablaze. I want my church to be set ablaze. God, I want my local area to know there is a church that is set on fire of God." I am asking you to get God all over you. I am asking you to get the power of the Holy Ghost on you.

Five times last Sunday morning in the privacy of my office, I put a drop of oil on my finger and touched someone's forehead and said, "God, those early Christians said, 'God, as I stretch out my hand, grant that you would heal.' Are you a respecter of persons?"

No, God is not a respecter of persons. Call me anything you want. I am an old-fashioned, sin-hating, independent, fundamental Baptist who believes in the Holy Ghost and the power of the Spirit of the living God. Bless God! I know that God will pour water on him who is thirsty, and I am a thirsty preacher! I am a hungry preacher! I am thirsty for the fire of the Holy Ghost to win the world to Christ! That is what I want.

I do not want some line of people throwing away their crutches and my putting on my white patent-leather shoes and white tuxedo with my mansions all over and my Rolls-Royce. That is a sham and a farce in the sight of God! However, I am interested in seeing people's lives transformed by the Gospel of Jesus Christ. My Bible says, *"Open thy mouth wide, and I will fill it."* I cannot get my mouth any bigger! Sometimes I go to God with my mouth open as wide as possible and I say, "God, I want it badly!"

Teenage boys, when is the last time you ever got together with two or three of your friends and said, "Why don't you come to my house, and let's pray for the teenagers of our church." I am serious about that. I did.

I remember when a dear friend of mine and I were 18 years old. I called him, and he said, "Brother Jack, can you do me a favor?"

I said, "What is it?"

He said, "I don't mean to be goofy or super-spiritual, but could you and I meet once a week and just pray?"

"Brother," I said, "that is right up my alley; that's my language."

Every week for three hours we got on our faces and just poured out our hearts until we cried. God did not do anything that moment, but I sometimes wonder if those hours of prayer are why I am standing in the First Baptist Church pulpit. I sometimes wonder if the blessings I have seen in my preaching are because of all those hours of praying.

Recently, I took my family to play a round of golf at Balmoral Golf Course in Crete, Illinois. I could hardly keep my mind on the game because when that course was being developed, I used to walk and pray in that very area. I would leave my dormitory and walk around that course for hours begging for the power of God. Every hole my family shot, I would think, "That is where I used to walk and pray." What wonderful memories!

I go to Baptist City where our schools are located, and I remember how I used to walk those streets sometimes until 1:00 in the morning praying, "Oh God, do something for me. Give me the mighty baptism of the Holy Ghost. I am not a charismatic, God. I am just a young Baptist preacher who wants the power of God. That is what I want! I want to see the book of Acts come alive today; that is what I want!"

That power is what I still want in 2004. That is what I want for the next 25 years if God grants us the time and tarries His coming. I want First Baptist Church of Hammond to burn white-hot. Some of you teenage boys need to get together and take 30 minutes or so to pray for your church's teenagers and pray for your youth director that he would have the power of God on him.

We hear the story about the women who prayed for D. L. Moody to have the power of God. Do any of you women ever get together for prayer? Most pastors are scared to death to let their women or men get together and pray. Let me add that I am not for mixed praying at all, but I am talking about some ladies inviting their friends to their house and saying, "We are not going to pray for anything except that our church will have the mighty power of the Holy Ghost."

House to house every day those in the book of Acts met to pray—one accord in prayer, passionate praying. Where I grew up, our Wednesday night service was called Wednesday night prayer meeting. We would have a little Bible study, and then we would all break up in groups, and we would pray. I remember some of those dear saints praying. As a young boy, I was scared because I thought God would move in, and I could almost hear the fluttering of angel's wings as some of those dear old saints would pray many times for us teenagers.

The man who became the youth director at my home church (running around 100) left a church running over 2,000. I asked him, "Why would you leave a church as a youth director of a church running 2,000 and become the youth pastor of my little old home church running less than 100?"

He said, "In all the years that church of 2,000 has been in existence, they have turned out only three full-time Christian workers—
all women. Your little church of less than 100 has turned out over 40
full-time Christian servants of God."

I sometimes wonder if that large percentage was because of all
those prayer meetings we had, where saints would just humble themselves and get on their knees and say, "God, I am just going to pray
for the power of God."

I wondered for many years why I had to go to Pillsbury Baptist
Bible College, a college with a little different philosophy than Hyles-
Anderson College. My favorite Bible teacher was a hyper-Calvinist
who believed the *New American Standard Version* was better than the
King James Bible. His teaching spun my head. I was confused by him
because I loved him so much.

Now I know why I had to attend college at Pillsbury. Every morning at 4 o'clock I got up. By 4:30 I was on the basement floors of the
classrooms until 7:30 praying for the power of God. God knew if He
put me hundreds of miles away from everybody I knew, I would have
no place to turn but to Him. I prayed for three hours on my face
every morning. My buddy Bob would come downstairs and nudge my
shoulder and say, "Jack, the class members are waiting to come in to
start class. You're down here in your bathrobe. You have to go
upstairs and change clothes."

I said, "Bob, I don't want to leave. I feel like God has met with
me. If I leave, I feel like I am leaving the presence of God Himself."

Bob would lead me upstairs to my room. I wept my way through
every day saying, "God, I read those biographies, and I read Your
Book. God, there is a Christianity that I am not familiar with—the
Christianity of the baptism of the Holy Ghost. It is a Christianity
where even the hard cases get saved. It is a Christianity where the
whole world is evangelized. God, someday, somewhere, sometime let
me be a part of a place that is busy about the right kind of business."

It is no accident or mistake that God brought me to First Baptist
Church of Hammond. God's placing me at Pillsbury Baptist Bible
College was a divine intervention itself. I know as sure as I am saved
that I am supposed to be the pastor of First Baptist Church—a
church where it has been happening and where it ought to continue
to happen.

4. Join some soul-winning ministry. Christians need to be with other people who are like-minded. Get on a bus route. Become a Sunday school teacher. Join one of our 90-minute soul-winning sessions. Get with others who are banding together saying, "Let's go win the world to Christ. Let's go do something big."

Christian, you need to be part of an army. I do not want these one-man soldiers trying to win the world by themselves. I want an army. We need a group of men and women who are trained to win the lost. Join a soul-winning ministry and be faithful to it.

5. Ask God for divine appointments. Get on your face and say, "God, I am going to go soul winning and become part of a group, but Lord I am going to ask You to bring people across my path where it is unmistakably clear that You want me to be the messenger with some specific role to play where You get all the glory and all the credit. It was not just my knocking on doors; it was You stepping in and saying, 'Jack, I want you right now, right here.' "

I was driving toward our church one day on Highway 41. My heart was very burdened. I was on my way to meet Brother Hyles for an appointment, and I said, "God, I am just consumed with this idea of winning people to Christ." I had left about an hour early giving me plenty of time to get to the church. I was driving slowly, and I said, "God, I really want to win a soul."

When those words were out of my mouth, I saw a man hitchhiking on the side of the road. A vehicle stopped by him, then took off and left. I said, "God, I want to witness to that guy right there." After I drove over the bridge, I turned around. As I drove back over the bridge, I saw a van stop, and the man got inside the van.

I said, "So much for that leading of the Spirit of God! There he goes in that van." Still, I just knew I was supposed to stop and witness to that man. I drove on and found a place to turn around to head back toward the church. When I came back, I saw that same man standing on the side of the road again. I thought, "This is weird. I just saw the guy get in the van." I quickly made a u-turn, pulled over, rolled down the window, and called, "Before you get in the car, let me ask you a question. Didn't you just get in a van?"

He said, "Yeah, how did you know?"

I said, "I want to know why you got out of the van."

"I can't explain it, man," he answered. "I got in that van, and it was like an audible voice said, 'Get out of this van now.' Can you feature that? What do you make of that?"

I said, "Get in the car, and I will tell you what it means. I want to ask you a question: 'If you died today, would you go to Heaven?' "

He said, "You know how to go to Heaven? I just got off of a third-shift job. I have asked everybody at work how to go to Heaven. Nobody knows. I am so scared of dying. Would you tell me how to go to Heaven?" Divine appointments!

My wife and I became burdened about our neighbors. They started talking about moving, and we started praying, "Oh, God, please save our neighbors." About 2:30 in the morning, I heard an explosion like a big firework going off. I jumped out of bed, and I saw my neighbor's garage in a wall of flames. I pulled on a pair of blue jeans, shoes, and a sweatshirt. I grabbed the fire extinguisher and told my wife, "Call 911! Then call their house and tell them to get out of the house!"

I ran outside, banged on their door, and my neighbors came running out. Then I grabbed a hose and put out the fire. My neighbors thanked me and thanked me and thanked me. The next day my wife went next door and won them both to Christ.

"God, burn down any house You want if it keeps people out of Hell!" Ask God to give you the opportunity to have those divine appointments.

Jesus said, "I must needs go through Samaria."

Why did He want to go through Samaria? Jesus had a divine appointment with a woman at a well who needed to trust Him, and that meeting was going to be written forever in the Book. When the disciples returned, the Samaritan woman was getting saved. Was she a soul winner when she got saved!

Another time, Jesus told His disciples, "Go to the other side of the sea."

Jesus had a divine appointment with a demoniac of Gadara over there. When the man got saved, the whole city got saved because of him. Jesus was not welcome in the city, but the demoniac won the whole city. Why? Because of one divine appointment.

6. Get your neighbors saved. Some ladies are socially outgoing, and they like people. They know how to sell Amway or Tupperware or Mary Kay. Why don't those ladies get all their representatives together and tell them the greatest news that ever was heard? Why not invite your acquaintances over for lunch and say, "Ladies, I go to the greatest church in the entire world. Can I tell you about the greatest news of Jesus Christ?"

Why not get your friends and neighbors together and get them saved. Let's get our lost neighbors saved. I know it is a whole lot easier to go to some neighborhood where you do not know anybody. If those people say, "No," it does not matter so much. I am asking you to covenant with God to claim your neighborhood for Christ. First Baptist Church, we ought to be setting the pace in the world. It is time for us to set the standard in this country.

Get yourself under that magnifying glass and say, "God, get me white-hot! Get me passionate! Get me in one accord with my pastor; in one accord with the deacons; in one accord with You, Christ; and in one accord with the Holy Ghost of God!"

Learn to win a soul. Covenant to pray one hour a week. Covenant to fast one to three days a month. Join a soul-winning ministry. Ask God for divine appointments. Let's win our neighbors to Christ. Let's set this world ablaze by the power of God!

CHAPTER FOUR

Why Do Large Churches Stop Growing Larger?

"Nevertheless I have somewhat against thee...." (Revelation 2:4)

T HERE IS LITTLE doubt in my mind that the church of Ephesus in the book of Revelation was the largest church of the first-generation churches. It was an amazing church with pastors who read like a hall of fame: the Apostle Paul, who founded the church; the Apostle John; and Timothy—to name but a few. Most Bible students and researchers believe that the church of Ephesus was no doubt the largest church of its kind in the world.

Through the inspiration of the Holy Ghost and through the human agency of the Apostle John, the Lord Jesus Christ wrote a letter to this church at Ephesus. It was a letter of a mere seven verses long in which He complimented them, scolded them, threatened them, and encouraged them, especially concerning one problem in the church.

I was doing research on some large churches built during the last 100 years in America's history. In 1949, the largest church in the world was a Baptist church which averaged 5,200 people in attendance with about 12,500 members. Between 1949 and the mid-1960's, two other churches sprang up and became the largest churches in the world. All three of these churches were Baptist churches averaging between 5,000 and 6,500 people in Sunday school at their peak. This was back before the bus ministry caught on; and yet, these were huge churches. Twenty years later, the largest of those three Baptist churches now averages 500 people, and one church no longer exists.

I have been consumed with this business of church growth. What is it that makes churches grow and then just stop growing? When Brother Hyles talked to me time and time again about the future of the First Baptist Church and about my pastoring the church, I would stand my ground saying, "I just need you to tell me that First Baptist Church of Hammond will grow."

Brother Hyles said, "I can't. But I believe that the same God Who has built our church is the same God Who will see you through it. Maybe part of the problem is that you are focusing on history and not on prophecy and the Bible. Maybe you ought to stop studying what history tells you cannot be done, and maybe you should study what God can do." Those were very pointed words to me. I remember wincing many times in places as we fussed about this matter.

I have studied and continue to study the large churches through the ages, through the last century, and even the large churches in the present. What makes a church grow? What has caused great churches to cease growing? I'll be honest with you, I'm going to fight and give it all I have—heart and soul and mind and strength and blood, sweat, and tears to keep First Baptist Church from going the way of history and becoming what all of the great mega-churches of the past eventually became. If First Baptist Church is to die, it is not going to die while I am on watch. First Baptist Church will live, or I will die making it live. The First Baptist Church members and I will stand shoulder to shoulder and build this together. One man will not make a church live. However, it is my duty as pastor to stand in the pulpit and speak vicariously on behalf of all of my church members what many of them feel; that is, we have an opportunity that has been handed to us—a great, effectual door has been opened.

God said to the church at Ephesus, "You have made a mistake. You left your first love." Notice, God didn't say, "Therefore, go back and rekindle your love." God said, "*Remember therefore from whence thou art fallen, and repent, and do the first works....*"

In the previous verse, God did not say, "I have somewhat against you because you left your first works." He said, "*...thou hast left thy first love.*" This church in Ephesus had a work problem which affected their love, and their love affected their work. Eventually God said, "If you don't fix the work problem, it won't matter how much you love Me."

Many churches across America are very much in love with God. They have praise services where they all hold hands and sing "Kum Bah Yah." The people lift up their hands toward Heaven. They are loving, affectionate, sweet, and kind churches. Jesus is saying to them, "You've forgotten that the love has to produce work." Jesus said, "*If ye love me, keep my commandments.*" (John 14:15) He didn't say, "If you love me, have a warm fuzzy feeling all over." A mistaken Christianity equates a deep growth with warm fuzzy feelings.

I am in favor of altar calls. First Baptist Church is going to have revivals and old-fashioned preaching. We are going to try to get sinners converted and souls saved and Christians right with God. However, warm fuzzy feelings are not going to build a church.

There are specific reasons that churches stop growing. I don't think that God just decides to stop blessing a church. If First Baptist Church does not grow, I don't think it is because God said, "You know what. I'm tired of First Baptist Church being the big one." God doesn't feel about First Baptist Church like the average sports fan feels about the New York Yankees. Seemingly, everyone loves a hero. However, as soon as the hero is on top, we want that hero taken down. Something is very carnal about man's thinking. Mankind wants a Superman, but then he wants somebody to beat Superman. He wants kryptonite to weaken Superman.

Something in mankind wants greatness to rise to the occasion, and then there is something wicked in our hearts that wants greatness to stumble and fall. We want David to be king, and at the same time, our sinful nature wants to kind of pull for him with Bathsheba. We want to watch him stumble and fall with her. Then after he falls, we say, "You poor sap!"

God is not that way. God does not look at First Baptist Church and say, "First Baptist Church, you have been big enough long enough. Why don't we let someone else be the big guy now?"

That attitude is not scriptural at all. There is not one shred of evidence that God believes that. So, one of the reasons churches stop growing is not God's randomly saying that He does not want a big church to grow larger. There are things that big churches do or fail to do that bring those big churches to a halt and make them slide backward until they go from 6,500 to 500 to 0 to closing the doors to bulldozing the buildings to selling the corporation to dissolving the assets and the church.

Allow me to share several reasons why large churches stop growing larger.

1. Large churches stop growing larger because they stop believing in growth. I do not believe in mediocrity. I do not believe in stagnation. I do not believe in standing still. I believe in growth. In my own life, I want to keep growing mentally and spiritually.

For instance, I do not want my marriage to stop growing. My wife and I are still growing in our marriage. We are more advanced in growth in our marriage now after 24 years than we were 24 years ago. We were very much in love when we stood on the church platform 24 years ago, but the bottom line is we are much more in love and more affectionate and more advanced in our marriage. I want to keep growing.

One must keep believing that the purpose of the church is to keep on growing. A church cannot get to the point where the members' attitude becomes, "We've got all we need." When First Baptist Church has won the last sinner in Lake County, Indiana, then we will go to the three million people in Chicago and get them saved! As long as there is one lost sinner on this globe, First Baptist Church needs to keep growing.

I wonder how many more lost people are wondering how to keep from going to Hell. How many unsaved people are wondering as they put their head on their pillow at night after a binge weekend of drugs, "I wish someone could tell me that if I didn't wake up, I would wake up in Heaven."

A survey was made of 2,500 pastors and 98% of them said, "I have enough." Pastor, if you have enough, then get out of the ministry and go get a decent job! College preacher boys and missionaries, First Baptist Church is not sending you out from Hyles-Anderson

College so you can "get enough." There should never be "enough" in your church! Souls are going to Hell, and the job of the church is to go after every one of them! I don't mean to just go across the street I mean go around the globe.

First Baptist Church of Hammond was given the Great Commission—not just the eleven disciples who were left at Christ's ascension. For that reason, First Baptist Church sent a team of our own staff members to China. That is also the reason we have missions training conferences to train missionaries, fire them up, and get their souls stirred up to go out and build something big for God. We still believe in growing here at First Baptist Church. The day we stop believing in that, we begin dying.

2. Large churches stop growing larger because they become evangelistic and revivalistic instead of soul winning. Instead of winning souls, the church becomes evangelistic. What is the difference? Soul winning is Christians going out and telling people how to be saved. After getting the lost person saved, the soul winner brings his converts to church. "Evangelistic" is Christians going out and inviting people to ride their bus, bringing them to Sunday school. Then the Sunday school teacher wins the visitors to Christ, or the preacher preaches them down the aisle.

What is wrong with that? The pastor and the Sunday school teachers are not supposed to be the only soul winners in the church. Evangelistic churches say that the Sunday school teacher or the pastor or the superintendent or the division leader or the junior church preacher are the soul winners in the church. No! Every Christian is supposed to be a soul winner in the church. Everybody who breathes air in the First Baptist Church is supposed to be a soul winner!

When my assistant pastors stand before the Judgment Seat of Christ, I am not going to give an account to God for the souls my assistant pastors did not win. I will give an account of the souls I did not win. God expects me to be a soul winner, not because I am the pastor of a New Testament church, but because I am a born-again child of God. As a child of the living God, it is my responsibility. Woe unto me if I preach not the Gospel of Jesus Christ! That statement is not a pastor speaking. That is a Christian speaking. A title that I prize higher than "pastor" is "Christian." It is time that God's people understand that their churches are not to be evangelistic churches. I don't want the members of my church just bringing in lost souls. Don't get me wrong. If a member brings an unsaved person to church and cannot get him saved, I will do everything I can to get him saved. However, bringing lost people to church and the pastor preaching them down the aisle is not the primary purpose of the church. The church is for Christians to bring in their converts.

Psalm 126:6 says, "*He that goeth forth and weepeth, bearing precious seed, shall doubtless come again with rejoicing, bringing his sheaves with him.*" A sheave is a bundle of grain that has already been harvested. Christians are to go out into the field (the world) and harvest the grain (win souls) and bundle that grain into a sheaf and bring the sheaves (converts) to the church already saved.

Soul winning is going out as a Christian, winning a soul to Christ, and bringing the convert to church. The convert walks the aisle with the soul winner who helps the new convert get baptized. That is a soul-winning church. An evangelistic church is where the members go out and invite people to come to church, bring them to church, and trust the pastor to preach them down the aisle.

A revivalistic church is a church that brings in a "hired gun" twice a year. The church members invite all their lost friends and relatives to the services and let that "hired gun" bring the lost down the aisle with his high-powered stories and preaching. First Baptist Church of Hammond is light years from being revivalistic. I pray to God that that never happens to First Baptist Church.

Where I attended college in Minnesota, some people used to say, "The problem with Jack Hyles is that he doesn't bring in any evangelists to preach and get people saved."

My roommate had visited First Baptist Church and said, "I can't speak on behalf of Jack Hyles, but I tell you this, I visited First Baptist Church of Hammond for two Sundays and heard him preach. He doesn't need an evangelist! He preached on women wearing britches and men with long hair, and the aisles were flooded with converts. I don't know how that happened."

I know how that happened. A whole bunch of soul winners had been out soul winning the week before and had won folks to Christ! Brother Hyles didn't preach sinners down the aisle. He invited saved folks to come and rejoice with their converts!

Bus captains, do you visit just your regular riders each week? I am for visiting your regular riders, but that is not soul winning. When bus captains have that type of thinking about soul winning, it will kill a big church. That is not soul winning! When a bus captain visits a regular rider, he should get that rider's mama and daddy saved and his brother saved and his sister saved. He should get everyone saved in that house.

When I was a bus captain here in First Baptist Church, I built the second largest bus route in the church. If I hadn't given up my route to become pastor, I believe I would have had the largest bus route by now. How did I do it? By winning souls! I recruited an army of people to knock on doors and told them to win souls and keep on winning souls because the way you build a bus route is to be a soul winner. God blesses soul winning, not just knocking on doors and inviting people to have a Happy Meal with you on Sunday. When bus captains stop winning souls and just visit their regular riders, their routes will die and the church will die.

Sunday school teachers, how many converts were in your class Sunday? My Bible says that the first thing you are to teach your pupils is "the things that I have commanded you." Matthew 28:19, 20 says, *"Go ye therefore, and teach all nations, baptizing them in the name of the Father, and of the Son, and of the Holy Ghost: Teaching them to observe* **all things whatsoever I have commanded you.** *...."* Teachers are supposed to win souls to Christ, and then the first thing they are supposed to teach their converts is how to go and get people saved.

At the time of this writing, our Sunday school lessons are about the miracles of Christ. The most important lesson about the miracles of Jesus Christ is to get people to Jesus Christ, and He will change their lives. The greatest miracle is not that Jesus walked on water or turned water to wine. It is the miracle that God can take a poor lost sinner, lift him from the miry clay, and set him free! Hallelujah, what a Saviour! The other miracles are very minor miracles compared to the miracle that when you bring an individual to Jesus, He will save his soul, change his life, convert him from darkness to light, and write his name in the Lamb's Book of Life. Jesus will put the light of the glory of the Gospel of Jesus Christ shining abroad in his soul—the greatest miracle of all! Large churches stop growing larger because Sunday school teachers think it is their duty to teach, not to win souls.

First Baptist Church of Hammond will die the moment Sunday school teachers think their only job is to teach. No! It is the job of a Sunday school teacher to be a soul winner. Sunday school teachers who do not win souls are killing their church. Superintendents who do not win souls are killing their church. Division leaders who do not win souls are killing their church. Bus captains who do not win souls are killing their church. Bus workers who do not win souls are killing their church. I don't care how many visitors a member brings to church. I'm interested in how many souls he won to Christ.

When a bus captain pulls up in his bus on Sunday morning and gets out, he should be able to say, "I've got my regulars and three brand-new converts." That is the life blood of a church—the transfusion that every sin-hating, Devil-fighting Baptist church needs.

The revivalistic church brings in their "hired guns" twice a year so that the other fifty weeks out of the year the members can be lazy, backslidden, and worthless children of God. God does not want our churches to be revivalistic or evangelistic. God wants our churches to be soul-winning churches.

3. **Large churches stop growing larger because they become compartmentalized because of growth and thus unionized in their thinking.** As a church grows, different people must take charge of different departments. Therefore, First Baptist Church has a deaf department and a blind department and a Pathfinder department and a Sunbeam department and a rescue mission and a nursing home department and the department of ushers and the choir department and the bus drivers department and custodial department and the PA department and many more. What often happens in big churches like First Baptist Church is that members become union workers. What is a union worker? It is someone who says, "That's not my job; I don't do that. I don't change light bulbs; I'm a carpenter." Good night! Your job is not your assigned task! Your job is to get out the Gospel. We are not union workers at First Baptist Church. As pastor, I'm not too important to pick up the garbage in the street. That is not just the custodian's job; it is my job.

At a Pastors' School, I walked into one of the bathrooms, and it was not cleaned to my standard of cleanliness. In my suit, I got down on my hands and knees and cleaned those toilets and those urinals. If the pastor can do it, the members can, too! Everything in the church is the members' business. The business of the church is getting people out of Hell. We are all in that business. The church has custodians to change light bulbs to allow others to work in the rescue mission or in the nursing home ministry or the PA booth or sing in the choir or be a staff member. However, there is one job that church members better never think is not their job—getting people out of Hell!

This union mentality of, "All I do is drive the bus" will kill a church. Bus drivers better start passing out tracts and preaching the Gospel. Their job is not to drive the bus. Their job is to win souls.

Some say, "Well, I'm a bus worker who writes the number on the riders' hands."

He had better put the bus number on the hands of brand-new converts he got saved that week! A custodian, a PA man, an usher, a staff member, a choir member—a church member's position doesn't matter. The big duty in the church is to win souls.

Each church member will determine if his church grows or not. The pastor doesn't decide church growth; the members do, bus captains do, staff members do, choir members do, PA men do, ushers do, custodians do, maintenance men do, bus drivers do, rescue mission workers do, pathfinders do, blind department workers do, deaf department workers do, and church members decide if their church grows or not!

4. Large churches stop growing larger because they grow beyond their ability to grow. Brother Marshall, one of my assistant pastors, began a new adult Sunday school class. Recently, he had 81 on Sunday morning. He is now in a dilemma—he cannot have 81 people come to his house for an activity.

What happens is a church gets excited and grows and grows until the inevitable happens. Let me use my former bus route as an illustration. I took a bus route of seven kids and in two and one-half months built the route to 86 riders.

My workers came to me and said, "What do we do?"

I said, "Just keep growing."

We put 117 bus kids on a 52-passenger bus. (Don't ever do that!) One of my workers, Truitt Suhl, came to me and said, "I hate big days!"

We had bodies everywhere. I sat down with my bus workers and said, "Folks, we have to make the difficult choice. We have to have two buses. That means half of you workers will stay with me and half of you will work on the other bus."

My workers didn't want to leave me. We did split the route and eventually had seven buses. When Brother Dan Mock took my place as captain he told me, "Brother Schaap, the day will come when we will have ten buses on that route!"

A church comes to a point where it cannot grow anymore; so it stagnates, and then the law of attrition sets in and the church starts losing and losing and losing. The United Methodist churches are a good example. These churches used to take in 400,000 new members every year. Now they take in 230,000 people every year. The denomination is losing more than they are bringing in, so they are dying off. This illustrates my point. If a bus captain builds a large bus route, he must split his route to continue the growth. If a Sunday school teacher builds his Sunday school class big enough, he has to split his class. That is an unpopular view because churches have their little group of people, and they get rich, fat, salty, lazy, and dead!

A church member begins thinking, "Hey, I'm happy in my class just the way it is." Do you want to grow your church, or do you stop believing in growth?

In Brother Marshall's Sunday school class, his 81 members will soon become 100. Brother Marshall will run out of space. He will not be able to visit the absentees. He will not be able to help everyone in his class that needs help, so some class members will be neglected. Then his class will start settling and settling.

In First Baptist Church, some uncomfortable changes must happen in the future in order that the church can grow. Someone asked me, "Are you sure you want to build the new auditorium?"

I answered, "Well, First Baptist Church can either build a new auditorium, or we can have two or three services in our present auditorium." At some point, division is necessary for growth. If Brother Marshall wants to build his Sunday school class to 1,000, he will probably have to divide his present class and continue to grow and divide until he has ten different classes within his department. Growth means division, and division can be a painful experience as well as an insecure experience.

It was not comfortable for the church in Jerusalem to be persecuted, but that persecution divided that church into many smaller groups that went everywhere preaching the word and building many larger works.

5. Large churches stop growing larger because they are afraid to take a risk. When my dad started his business, my family risked it all. My dad went to the bank and told the banker, "I'm worth $30,000, but I want to borrow $60,000."

That banker probably said, "You're not worth that much."

My dad said, "I want you to risk it on me." The banker did stick out his neck and gave my dad more than he deserved to have. My dad risked it all.

I well remember those days when the business wasn't doing much, and Dad was living on about two hours of sleep a night. As a young boy, I wondered, "What if Dad's business doesn't fly? What are we going to do?"

My dad's attitude was basically, "Don't talk that way. The business has to fly, because we won't have a bed to sleep in if it doesn't fly."

When an organization gets big, the popular word becomes *secure*. Big businesses say they cannot take risks because they cannot hurt their shareholders. The only shareholder of the First Baptist Church is Jesus Christ! He's the One Who bought this church!

A church may say, "How much does Jesus want us to risk?"

As Jesus hangs on the cross, ask Him what He was willing to risk for the church! Jesus said, "I'm not going to put a little dime in the pot; I'm going to put in My own body. I'm going to lay Myself down and die for the church. I'm risking it all." Jesus did risk it all. He gave everything.

When a Hyles-Anderson graduate starts a church, he risks it all. A young preacher and his wife rent a storefront and invest all the money they have. The graduates call me and say, "Brother Schaap, I've invested all my life savings. I've borrowed money from my parents. I've stuck my neck way out. If it gets cut off, I'm going to lose everything I have." Ten years later, many of those graduates who risked it all are recognized with doctoral degrees from Hyles-Anderson College because their store-front church has grown to 2,000 in Sunday school.

A young, small church is not afraid to risk; they don't have a lot to lose. However, when the small church grows and becomes a larger church, the members are tempted to say, "We can't take the risk. We've got too much to lose."

Too much what to lose? To go soul winning three or four hours weekly? Too much what to lose? To sacrifice occasionally financially and dig deeper than you care to dig and give to missions or the bus ministry or to the building program? What will the church lose? The church will lose face at the Judgment Seat of Christ when its members stand before the Son of the living God and say, "I did not want to take the risk to be a bus captain. I did not want to take the risk to go out soul winning. I did not want to take the risk of embarrassing myself by putting a Gospel tract in the waitress's hand. I did not want to risk shame or embarrassment."

Then you will hear Jesus say, "I risked Hell for you!"

Big churches get fat and lazy because its members want to be secure. They want to protect their assets. I don't want to protect anything but the name of Jesus Christ and the souls who are lost and going to Hell. That is for Whom I am risking all.

6. Large churches stop growing larger because they begin focusing on serving the saints rather than winning the lost. I love all of our service groups at First Baptist Church. I love our Blue Beret. I love our Red Beret. I love our Baptist Boys Battalion. I love our Blue Denim and Lace. I love our Cornerstones. I love our Far Above Rubies. I love the cheerleaders' organization. I love the basketball and the wrestling and the soccer and the baseball teams. However, do any of our service groups win any souls? Young churches do not have all these service groups. Their one purpose is to knock on a lot of doors and get a lot of people saved. As long as winning souls is a church's focus, the church will grow. Then as the larger church has more saved people, it starts groups and activities to serve their members.

Brother Hyles used the illustration of a car dealership. A car dealership must have a sales department and a service department. When a car dealership sells cars and sells cars and sells cars, eventually some of those cars come back with problems that need to be fixed. The dealership then opens a service department to repair those cars and to help keep them on the road. However, if the dealership becomes service-oriented and stops selling cars, eventually they will lose the whole dealership. The dealership must have both, and a church must have both. A church can't say, "A few of our members will serve, and others will win souls." No. Everybody must "sell the cars."

When I worked at Hyles-Anderson College, the college performed several studies on why students came to Hyles-Anderson College. Of course, Brother Hyles was the number-one person who influenced students to attend Hyles-Anderson College. I was the number-two person. I believed with all of my heart that if I was going to draw a paycheck from that school, I had better be bringing money into that college. I believed that if I was going to work at the college, I should be bringing in students. An average of 35 students per year came to Hyles-Anderson College because of my influence. I believed I had a moral obligation to keep the doors of that college open.

If I am a member of the First Baptist Church, I believe I have a moral obligation to make sure that in a year's time I am bringing fresh blood into the church. As a born-again child of God, I believe it is a moral obligation to say to the One Who paid for me to go to Heaven, "I brought someone with me to make your payment more efficient." I am interested in making God understand that if I am part of an organization, I will also build that organization. Those who draw a paycheck from the First Baptist Church organizations must do their part to keep those organizations open.

Recently, someone called one of our schools interested in enrolling their child in the school. It was obvious that the folks were not ready for their kids to go to our school. The family was very different from First Baptist in many respects, and perhaps they were not even saved. The person who answered the call said, "I don't think our school would be appropriate for your child."

I told that staff member, "You missed a great soul-winning opportunity. If somebody is ineligible for our schools, guess how they become eligible? They get saved, get to our church, make a public profession, get baptized, and then get growing in the Lord, and then they put their child in our Christian school!"

Hammond Baptist Schools are built on soul winning. The most important subject in our schools is how to get people out of Hell. Every part of the First Baptist ministry has to be on the lookout for how they can get somebody saved, how they can convert a situation into a soul-winning opportunity. The school staff and faculty have to think, "How can I use a school to put people into the First Baptist Church of Hammond?" If I were a school teacher in one of our schools and I was not regularly bringing people down the aisle who became families in this church, who took money out of their pockets to pay to put their kids in the school where I teach, I would feel like I was taking advantage of a good situation.

If I had to pay my church staff a salary based upon the number of converts that our Christian school teachers brought in during all the years they have taught in our schools, I wonder if I could pay the salaries of my church staff. Does a teacher have a right to teach children in a Christian school how to be Christians if he doesn't have anyone in the church who is helping pay his salary? If I, as the pastor of First Baptist Church, had to feed my family on the converts' tithes and offerings that staff members and all the others who draw paychecks from this ministry brought into this church, would I be able to feed my family? Could the church keep even one bus rolling if the bus ministry was to be financed by the tithes and offerings of your converts?

When a church gets big, fewer and fewer people bring in anyone who pay tithes and offerings, and the church starts getting top heavy with many people supported by a very small number of soul winners. As the number of soul winners gets smaller and some of the soul winners die off or leave the church, the church collapses.

Deacon, are you like the deacon, Philip, who preached in Samaria and saw one of the two greatest revivals in world history? The entire city of Samaria got saved because of the preaching of a deacon!

The duty of a deacon is not attending deacons' meetings or approving budgets or watch dogging the pastor and staff or trying to get new paint in a hallway. No, sir! The duty of a deacon is to win souls out of Hell. Deacon, can you point to families in your church whom you have won to Christ, who are faithful members, and who pay tithes and offerings that help pay the bills? Have your converts brought enough tithe money to help pay for running the bus ministry in your church? Where do churches get the money to support its ministries? If everyone in the First Baptist Church said, "Within the next 12 months, there will be a bona fide family in our church who is saved because of my Gospel witness, who is baptized because of my influence, who is sitting in these pews because of my interest and my energy, and who is tithing because of my teaching," then praise be to God! First Baptist Church could run an unlimited number of buses. This whole matter of building and growing is evidenced when everybody gets on the same page and says, "We're with you, Pastor. We're united. We're in one accord."

7. Large churches stop growing larger because they stop bathing their work in prayer and begin to rely upon organizational skill and experience. Those who plan our Youth Conference or our Christian Womanhood Spectacular or Pastors' School or the Christian Educators' Convention or the opening days of the fall semester at Hyles-Anderson College must not rely upon the wisdom they have gained from years of experience. They must fall on their faces and say, "I need Thee, God. I cannot do this by myself. I must have the blessing of God. Without You, I can do nothing!"

If leaders don't bathe their work in prayer and instead rely upon their own skill and experience and wisdom, then we may as well get jobs at GE or IBM because that is what their employees do. Leaders must not lean on the arm of the flesh instead of the arm of God. Everything must be done by falling on our faces and praying. Bus captains and bus workers should have their prayer meetings, and Sunday school teachers and superintendents should pray when they meet together. They should beg the Holy God to bring down power from on high. "All is vain unless the Spirit of the Holy One comes down."

Large churches stop growing larger because they stop bathing their work in prayer. Most have heard the statement, "I must pray like everything depends upon God and work like everything depends upon me."

I believe in prayer. However, I also believe in work. Of course, one must pray a whole lot for a big day, but one will only have a big day if he works as hard as he prays. That is the formula for big days.

8. Large churches stop growing larger because they become defensive in their position. Critics will rise up and accuse and criticize. I will not respond to my critics because that takes me away from the focus of the ministry. I know the issues out there. I know what the critics say about First Baptist Church and about me. I see what is going on, and I choose to shut up. Some say, "Brother Schaap, don't you think you ought to address your critics?" I am. First Baptist Church is building and growing!

Monday through Friday, I am picked up at my house and driven to the church by one of our security guards, Brother Dave Sisson. At Pastors' School in 2003, I gave all the pastors small trash cans for their negative mail. Brother Dave keeps one of those Pastors' School trash cans between the seats. As I finish reading my mail, I throw the trash in that trash can.

One day I opened a letter, read a few lines, and shoved it in the trash can. I said, "Thank God for that trash can!"

My driver said, "You feel better now?"

"Yes I do," I responded. "I just want to get rid of the stuff that keeps me from being focused on what the ministry is all about."

Imagine being taken to the hospital emergency room; and while the doctor is working on you, suddenly somebody criticizes your doctor. If the doctor said, "Just a minute, patient, I have to go answer this critic," you would say, "Doc, I don't care what he is saying about you. Fix me! Let him criticize you! Just get over here, Doc, and keep me alive!"

Six million people in the Chicago area are dying and going to Hell. Let me say to all the critics, "I'm sorry. I don't care what name you call me. I don't care what finger you point at me. I have souls in the spiritual emergency room who will die if I don't pay attention to them." The larger church starts saying, "Well, we better answer that question and respond to our critics."

I like what Cicero said, "I criticize by building bigger."

9. **Large churches stop growing larger because the church does not want to pay the price.** Its members come to a point where they say, "I paid my dues." Would someone please tell me the chapter and verse for that statement?

Long-time members may say, "I put in my time in the bus ministry" or "I put in my 20 years." Show me in the Bible where those verses are! Older members will say, "I'm 55 years of age, and I taught Sunday school for 30 years. I'm tired."

Show me in what book of the Bible that is found! There is a point when the church people say, "I just don't want to pay the price. I'm going to let a younger generation do it." No, Sir! I want to pay the price all the way until my body lies in state or the Lord calls me up in the Rapture. I will have 1,000 years to rest. I will have 1,000 years in which to sleep. I will have 1,000 years to have a beach-front condominium. I will have 1,000 years to do nothing but be lazy. I want to give it all I have while I have something to give.

> "Work, for the night is coming,
> When man works no more."

Christians should have some fun. Everyone should take a family vacation every summer. We need to take some time with our families and loved ones. We should enjoy our lives. However, if the members are going to build First Baptist Church, there is a price to be paid. Maybe that means some should take the money they spend on cable television and give it to faith promise missions instead.

The truth of the matter is, it will cost everyone something to get our new building built and fill it—a whole lot of hard work and a whole lot of walking with God. As for me and my house, we're going to pay that price. We are going to roll up our sleeves and go to work and bathe our work in prayer. When I go to Heaven, I want to walk up to Brother Hyles and say, "I beat history."

I want Brother Hyles to say, "Well done, Jack." I want First Baptist Church members to meet their former pastor, Brother Hyles, in Heaven and have him say, "You did it!"

I want to walk up to my Saviour, and I want to fall on my knees and cry, "Glory!" I want to look in His face and say, "Jesus, I did it for You."

God has given much to First Baptist Church; and to whom much is given, much is required. I want this "much" that God has given us to become multiplied many times over.

Christians, get out your old, dusty New Testament and put it on the whetstone and put a sharp edge on that Sword. Dust off your dog-eared tracts and start passing them out. Start asking people, "Are you saved? Are you born again? Do you go to church anywhere? Can I give you some good news? If you died today, would you go to Heaven?" It's time for the First Baptist Church of Hammond to rise up as a mighty army and say, "Hey, Chicagoland. Hey, America. Hey, world! We are a sleeping giant, and we just woke up. Watch out. You happen to be standing where the Gospel gun is about to shoot!"

First Baptist Church is a large, large church that doesn't want to stop getting larger. Growth is why we are in business. Twenty years from now, I don't want some pastor saying, "There was a big church in Hammond, Indiana, at one time. They were the world's largest Sunday school. Now, all the people fit in just two center sections." There is no way that is going to happen—not without a fight! I pledge my life to be sure it never happens.

CHAPTER FIVE

Hindrances to Church Growth

"Then he that had received the five talents went and traded with the same, and made them other five talents." (Matthew 25:16)

A CHURCH IS MADE up of families and individuals. Thus, if a church is to grow, the families and the individuals must grow. That is just good common sense. If a Christian is not growing, then his church cannot grow. If an individual is not doing his part, then his part is not getting done. We fundamentalists are local church in our belief, yet tend to be universal church in our practice. We believe that this body of blood-washed believers called the First Baptist Church of Hammond is a physical and spiritual entity. The building at 523 Sibley Street is not the First Baptist Church of Hammond. First Baptist Church could meet any place—the gymnasium at the Hammond Baptist Schools or in the Hammond Civic Auditorium or even in a large tent in the parking lot. Where the local church meets does not make it a church. The church is not a building; the church merely assembles in a building for convenience.

However, when it comes to growing a church, Christians somehow think that some spooky, ethereal, universal, mystical something or other makes churches grow. Christians make churches grow. Pastors make churches grow. Church members make a church grow. In other words, what the members of the First Baptist Church do and what they are have a direct bearing upon the health and growth of the First Baptist Church of Hammond. What I do not do and what I refuse to be is a direct hindrance upon the growth of the First Baptist Church and what it could become.

Christian, you are not a non-important entity. You may sit in the reaches of the balcony or the mezzanine or in the shadows underneath the mezzanine or even right down front. Your heart is cold, your spirit is calloused, and your walk with God is nonexistent. You are backslidden and barely attend church except that your mom or dad make you go, or you may be in church out of obligation because you play on the church softball league. For whatever the reason you attend church, the last thing on your mind is church growth. You are a debilitating factor in your church's growth. You are a cancer that is causing the body of Christ to be ill and not able to function. Just like when your body is affected with a cold or influenza, you do not feel like going gung-ho for anything. The healthy parts of the body are affected by the not-so-healthy parts of the body. When a person is afflicted with cancer, even though it might be just one small tumor the size of a quarter in your brain, somehow it has a magical way of slowing down the feet and the hands and every other part and function of the body.

Therefore, if a Christian is a part of a local church, as he functions with the church and gets on board with the church, he becomes a part of the growth of the church depending on what he does. If a church member just sits back and says, "I am just putting in my time. I know I am a member of the church, but...," then he becomes a debilitating cancer to the church. Instead of leaving the church, he should change and jump on board. Each believer is in his church for a reason, which is not just to take up 18 inches to 40 inches of pew depending on his posterior size. First Baptist Church members are here to make a significant contribution to this body, your family, the First Baptist Church of Hammond.

So, if the local church is to grow, its individual members must grow. If the church does not grow, it is because Christians in the church do not grow. There are hindrances in the growth of a church. If a family does not grow spiritually, the church does not grow spiritually. If individuals do not grow spiritually, the family does not grow spiritually. If individuals grow spiritually, then families grow spiritually, and the church grows spiritually. When a church grows, it can have a profound influence on its local community. I want the whole Chicago area to feel the effect of the First Baptist Church of Hammond. The whole world needs to feel the effect of the First Baptist Church.

Let's just assume for a few moments that we actually believe the Bible is true. I know we say we do, but let's pretend that we really do believe it. When Jesus said, *"Go ye into all the world, and preach the gospel to every creature,"* to whom do you think He was talking? There are three choices.

1. He was talking to 11 men called His disciples or apostles. If this be true, then we have wasted much time and money and effort since the early church in Jerusalem. If only those 11 men were to obey that command, then why should we even open our doors, unless it's to serve as a social club under the name of a church. And if Christ was addressing only 11 people, then what 11 is He addressing in our church? Let's find those 11, and the rest of us can go home and watch a ball game.

2. He was talking to a particular church—namely the church in Jerusalem. In that case, Jesus was talking to 120 people because Acts chapter one says that there were about 120 members in that church. And if He was talking to only that church, then likewise, all the other churches since that day have foolishly wasted their efforts.

3. He was talking to all believers everywhere who would ever read those words. Whether it is to 11 or 120 or to all believers including you and me, what are you doing to get the Gospel to the entire world? Any way that you want to interpret that passage, we have a really significant problem because if God really meant what He said, then what are we doing to get the Gospel to the entire world? What is the church doing as a body of believers to get the Gospel to the world?

The interpretation gets deeper than that. If Jesus commanded each believer to get the Gospel to the world, I do not believe He idly gives commands. If there are 116 countries that do not have a Gospel witness, I wonder whose fault that is!

Some say, "Brother Schaap, those are closed countries."

Are you saying that God is not big enough? The simple, honest truth is, I believe those countries are closed because God says, "It would not matter if I opened up those countries; you would not do anything about it anyway." I think God looks at First Baptist Church and other churches of like faith around the world and says, "If I opened up every country and threw the doors wide open, what difference would it make in how you live and how you give?" The truth of the matter is, if God opened up those countries, it probably would not make any difference. It would just be a statistical change, and all those billions of people would still go to Hell.

Independent Baptist churches must look at themselves. If we are autonomous, self-governing, independent Baptist churches, meaning there is no denominational leader telling us what to do or where to send our church's money or what missionaries to send, then independent Baptists get to decide how big we each want to grow. We get to decide how much influence we want to have. We get to decide how many missionaries we want to send. We get to decide to what degree we want to obey the commands of God. What a wonderful privilege! I believe fundamentalists can reach the world! If we do not, it is our fault and not God's fault.

I believe there are eight hindrances to church growth.

1. Christians do not pass on their faith to their children. If we believers do not pass on our faith to our children, we are failing in the most basic, elemental part of church growth. In the very foundation of church growth, it is incumbent upon believers to say, "If I receive Christ, my children will. If I believe in Christ, my family will. If I serve Christ, so will my family."

I am very aware that many families who have finished their child rearing have some family members who have sorely disappointed them. I am not picking on those people. I am addressing those parents who have the ability to make the change and make the difference right now. Are your children in church tonight? Are your children saved? Are all the members of your family born again and serving the Lord?

I was reading some very interesting statistics recently. A very famous evangelical association conducted a survey of many thousands of people in America. The following question was posed: "Do you consider yourself to have a personal relationship with Jesus Christ?" The results were posted by generation. In the pre-World War II generation, 65% said "yes"; 35% of the baby boomers (those born between 1947 and 1960) said "yes"; 15% of those born between 1960 and 1985 said "yes"; and only 5% of those born 1986 to the present said they have a personal relationship with Jesus Christ. Imagine, from 1947 to the present, we have gone from nearly 2 out of every 3 people confessing to having a personal relationship with Christ to only 1 in 20 people. Christians are failing miserably in getting the Gospel to the world and especially here at home in America and especially in their own homes.

The same article said that statistics show us that as many as 70% of young people reared in Christian homes and attending church regularly have not embraced the faith as their own by the time they graduate from high school and will ultimately leave the faith. One large denomination said if their constituents would only pass on their faith within their church walls, their denomination would more than double its current size within one generation. If all we did as Christians was to make sure those who call us Mom and Dad are as active and involved and as passionate as we are in this business of Christianity, our churches would double in size in one generation.

I am not sitting in judgment on anybody whose children have turned out to be different than what they had hoped, but I am addressing those who have children still under their control and influence. Something has radically gone wrong in fundamental Christian churches that are declining and declining and declining. Evangelical churches that believe the Gospel of salvation by grace through faith have declined 9.5% in the last ten years. The population has increased 11%. We are losing ground! There are a few big success stories, but the bottom line is that in spite of the few doing a great job, thousands more are needed just to keep pace! We are losing ground faster all the time.

One reason that churches do not grow is that they do not pass on their faith to their own children. That beacon of light has to shine brightest in your own home. Fundamentalists have presented a Christianity to our children that is purely a set of values, a code of conduct, and a list of rules. Too often they have inconsistently lived those values, codes, ethics, and rules before their children, and they have not transferred a faith in a real person named Jesus Christ.

I think the biggest reason Christians do not pass down their faith to their children is that their children never realize adults actually pray to a real God. The children rarely ever see their parents on their knees. The children hardly ever see their parents win a soul to Christ or transfer their faith to another individual. The children never see Dad win the neighbor to Christ and never see anybody born again in the home. Their family goes to Sunday school, which is about the only real Christianity the children see. However, the kids know some of the church couples are bickering and fussing, and their marriages are splitting up, and so-and-so is committing adultery in the church; so the kids come to the conclusion of, "Why should I buy into this thing called Christianity?"

Mom and Dad listen to their rock-a-billy music, which is just a slowed-down version of the ungodly music of their kids. Children know that their mothers listen to that filthy music that talks about the heartbreak of their marriage and the sad depressing tunes and then wonder why Mama criticizes them for listening to hip-hop, rhythm and blues, rap, Gothic, and rock 'n' roll.

Some neighbor kids once came to my house. One of the boys had long hair and had two girls with him. They said to my son, "I suppose in that Christian school you go to, you can't listen to Marilyn Manson music, can you?"

"No," my son said.

One of the girls said, "I couldn't live without Manson."

I could not live without Christ! *"For to me to live is Christ!"* Christianity is not about my music or my money or my bass boat or my lifestyle. Christianity is a Person named Jesus Christ!

Until believers pass on their love for Christ and their relationship with a Person, we will not transfer our faith to our children. I am not interested in transferring a code of conduct. I am not interested in transferring a value-orientated system of living. The difference is not your value-orientated society or your lack of values. The difference is found in John 3:36, *"He that believeth on the Son hath everlasting life: and he that believeth not the Son shall not see life; but the wrath of God abideth on him."* It is not a matter of values; it is a matter of a Person.

If you do not pass on that Person to your children, they are not going to have a hangdog care about your values.

Remove Christ from Christianity, and nobody will want to buy into those values. My flesh nature being what it is, I wouldn't. Saying we are a moral majority sounds really good; however, we are not! Morals are dependent upon a person named Christ. The Old Testament is filled with examples of people who were given the very finest of values.

In Deuteronomy 4, God tells the Jews that if they would abide by the rules given them, the surrounding nations would look at them and say, "What nation has so great a God as the Jews?" I do not care if the world in Hammond, Indiana, says, "Wow! First Baptist Church sure is a strict church." I am not trying to build a strict church; I am trying to build Christians who love Christ.

A First Baptist Church teenager who goes out teenage soul winning and still listens to the rock 'n' roll or the rhythm and blues or Gothic music or hip-hop or rap and all that nonsense music, may win another kid to Christ. However, when the new convert sees that the First Baptist kid is an inconsistent kid with the same hangups as he has, the soul-winning teenager has offered him nothing at all. Christianity is a Person named Christ Who should make all the difference in a believer's life. If Jesus is not making a radical difference in the way a Christian lives, in the way he thinks, in the music to which he listens, in the books he reads, and in the television shows he watches, then I do not want that Christ. It is a false Christ with a false Gospel and a false Bible and a false religion. I do not want a Christ Who does not change my life. The number-one reason that Christians do not grow, and thus our churches do not grow, is because we do not pass on our faith to our children.

2. Christians are striving for maturity rather than striving for discipleship. There is a gross misunderstanding about Christian growth in the Bible. What does it mean to be a mature saint? The word *mature* is not a bad word, but the problem is we have a whole lot of "mature" saints. Most of these mature saints are professors in seminaries who are killing the faith of our boys and girls. These professors are very mature with years and years and years and years of experience. However, they also have years and years of cold, dead living and no obedience. Young boys come to Hyles-Anderson College who spend three to twelve hours going soul winning every Saturday. We have professors who get in their required one hour of soul winning. Which one is the growing Christian? Does that teacher who is teaching his students how to be mature in Christ want his students to become like him?

The teacher may say, "Well, that college student is single and does not have as many responsibilities as I do."

How did the Apostle Paul continue as he got older and older? Paul, who wrote the book of Hebrews, said, "...and so much the more, as you see the day approaching." (Hebrews 10:25) So much the more! Paul said, "Push it harder as you get older! Put in more hours and more time!"

But the teacher says, "Brother Schaap, you have got to be kidding. I have mortgage payments. I have kids. I do not have time!"

No wonder the world is going to Hell! Some Christians have bought into this idea that as they mature, they do less and less and less until they eventually rule over all the people that are doing everything for you. They become like King Tut sitting on his throne with all those servants serving him while the "mature" one does nothing. A professor puts in his required hour while the kid he is teaching to be a mature saint says, "I am not very mature. I only put in eight hours of soul winning today." I do not want a maturity that pulls me away into less activity for God. Maturity oversees ministries; disciples knock on doors. Maturity teaches others what he no longer does; discipleship is learning to do more of what he has already been doing.

The word *disciple* means "a learner." A disciple is constantly learning. The mature person has stopped studying. The disciple is curious and wants to know more. The mature person is bored; he knows it all already. The disciple is hungry to know, and he has heroes. The mature person is disillusioned and skeptical. Some church members are so mature that they cannot even go to their pastor for advice. That is just for 18-year-old kids! Adults tell the young people, "Have heroes." We bark and holler about the heroes the kids put on their walls. We do not want Marilyn Manson pictures on the wall. We do not want all those Gothic music heroes or the rock-a-billy crowd on their walls. In fact, if one of your children were to put one of those ungodly heroes on the wall, you good, godly parents would walk into your child's room and say, "Get that garbage off the wall before I apply some needed correction."

That is fine! But let me ask you, Mom and Dad, who are your heroes? Mature Christians are people who have gotten skeptical and have become disillusioned and have said, "I do not have any heroes."

Some parents have gotten to the point where they look at their kids and say, "Get your heroes off the wall, but I cannot give you anyone else to look up to either."

A vacuum is thereby created in their children's lives, and their kids look at them and say, "You don't even have anybody that you want to be like."

Dad sits on the couch and watches x-rated videos and has a stack of pornography, and his kids think, "That's Christianity, Dad?"

A boy whose life was all messed up came to me, and I asked him, "What happened to you?"

The boy said, "My dad was a deacon in a Baptist church. He was a soul winner and bus captain. One day my sisters and I were playing hide-and-seek in our house. We were running up the steps and into my parents' bedroom. I dove onto Mom and Dad's bed, and the mattress slid off the box spring. Since Mom and Dad were coming home, we took off all the covers and began remaking the bed. We found over 50 pornographic magazines that our dad had stashed there."

Many parents live that kind of inconsistency where they preach, "Don't you do it!" but they do it. Mom and Dad will say to their children, "Don't let me catch you with those kinds of ungodly heroes!" In the next breath, they will say, "I don't believe the pastor; I think he is a hypocrite. I don't trust that Christian school teacher because I think he's got it in for us. They only like the staff kids any way."

Parents are giving their kids a model to rebel and to run and flee into the world saying, "I don't want anything to do with that kind of God."

I do not want to be a mature Christian if that is maturity. I want to be a young disciple always learning.

All you mature Bible scholars, show me a New Testament soul winner whom God loved to promote who came to the point where he stopped going soul winning and just taught everyone else how to be soul winners. There are none in the Bible. Peter, James, John, Paul, Thomas and all those men were killed—not because they were teaching others how to do it—but because they were doing it. Stephen was not stoned because he was a professor at a college. He was stoned for telling that crowd of listeners, "You had better get saved!" I do not want to be so mature that I assign someone else to do what I have been commanded to do.

Churches stop growing because individuals stop growing, and that makes families stop growing, and that makes the church dead in the water. Christians do not pass their faith on to their children. Believers are striving for maturity rather than discipleship.

3. Christians seek independence rather than dependence. This is the paradox of Christianity. A Christian thinks he wants to keep getting older and older and say to God, "I need you less and less and less. Leave me alone. I want to do my own thing. God, I needed You a whole lot when I was a brand new Christian, but do you know what? I have really grown a lot, God. I am very mature now, and I do not really need You as much now."

Christians have it backward! If a Christian is really growing in the Lord, he knows he needs God more and more and more every day!

After 40 years of salvation, I can testify of this one fact: I need God a whole heap more now than I did 40 years ago. The Christian life is not a decreasing dependence; it is an increasing dependence until every breath I draw, every swallow of my throat, every bite of food I take, whether I eat or drink, I do it all for the glory of God, and I even do it by His help. I used to pray only for salvation; now I pray for hot water, clean clothing, electricity, and all the things I already have, reminding myself that without God I can do nothing. That is why I come to the First Baptist Church auditorium every Saturday night. I walk down those platform steps and practice, then I stop and pray by Brother Colsten's chair, and by my chair, and all the staff men's chairs; I pray for the choir and each section of the auditorium. I get on my face and my knees and beg God for the mighty power of God. After 28 years of preaching, I need God so much more now.

A Christian grows when he realizes he needs God more now, not less. Jesus said in John 15:5, "*I am the vine, ye are the branches: He that abideth in me, and I in him, the same bringeth forth much fruit: for without me ye can do nothing.*"

4. Christians walk by sight not by faith. When is the last time you really needed God to come through for you? I do not mean just for a sermon illustration or a story in Sunday school. When is the last time you got on your knees and said, "God, I cannot believe the bind I am in. God, if You do not come through, it is not going to happen." Many mature saints say, "I used to have stories like that." When is the last time you knew you needed God to come through for you big time?

The truth of the matter is that as Christians grow, we reach a point where we plateau. We start taking care of ourselves, and God is nothing more than a rabbit's foot we keep to remind us that we are probably a little luckier than the unsaved person because we have the Holy Ghost inside us. We no longer say, "God, I need You so much!"

Faith Promise giving is a wonderful way for Christians to make themselves need God. It brings us into the Holy of Holies with God Almighty where God says to us, "Would you like to hear My heartbeat? Would you like to see the breath of My voice? Would you like to hear the sweet words out of My mouth? Would you like to know where I live? Would you like to walk in harmony with Me? Let us together decide to reach the world." It is you and God entering into a zone where God says, "Would you like to partner with Me? Would you like to go into business with Me? Let us reach the world." It is not an obligation, a necessary part, a perfunctory form and ritual of the worship service. It is a high honor that God would consider you to find you worthy to work with Him. Would you hire yourself to reach the world if you were God? Living by faith is partnering with God.

I remember when Brother Hyles started drawing me in as a staff member and started meeting with me every Thursday afternoon from 1:00 to 4:00. He said, "I am going to teach you the inside working of the First Baptist Church. Jack, I am going to show you things nobody knows."

I remember the thrill as I got out my pen and said, "May I take notes?"

He said, "You have to promise me that no living human being other than you will see those."

I thought, "I am being brought into a holy chamber, and I am learning what only one person knows." That is the same kind of relationship I want with my God—God and I entering into partnership together.

5. Christians are satisfied. The truth of the matter is, it is pretty comfortable being a member of the First Baptist Church of Hammond. A member of our church has a young, healthy pastor who will probably be around for a long time. The pastor will do a nice job for funerals of his members and their loved ones. He will even write a poem for the funeral if asked. He will perform their weddings. He preaches to the congregation three times a week, including practical lessons from the Bible on Wednesday nights.

Truthfully, it is very easy for a member of the First Baptist Church to sit back and kind of "plug in" half way. It is fun to watch those buses line up outside the church. It is fun to hear about the Inner-City Chapel Ministry. It is fun to see all our missionaries with Fundamental Baptist Missions International. It is fun to be a spectator attending the elaborate game that is being played on the field of First Baptist Church and sit back and eat our popcorn and say, "You know what, for $2.00 this is the best show in town!"

First Baptist Church has good music and will soon have an orchestra. The choir is going to double in size when we have our new auditorium. The city architect is working with us to make this a big, huge beautiful campus. Everybody that comes into this zone will immediately recognize that they are in the First- Baptist-Church-of-Hammond zone. This part of Hammond will be the prettiest part of the entire city. Our old buildings are going through a face lift internally and externally, and the day will come when folks will look at all our buildings and say, "These are very beautiful buildings." First Baptist Church of Hammond is a great place of which to be a part. However, it would be easy for a member to become so satisfied with what everybody else is doing around our church that he is not doing anything to contribute to the growth of First Baptist Church.

6. Christians are ignorant of what God expects. In the story of the talents in Matthew 25, one man was given five talents, another man two talents, and a third man was given one talent. If God gives some people five talents, some two talents, and others only one talent, would First Baptist Church be a five-talent church, a two-talent church, or a one-talent church? Looking at all the ministries we have such as the bus ministry, the nursing home ministry, the truck stop ministry, the sailor ministry, the Bible clubs ministry, the deaf ministry, the blind ministry, the homeless ministry, the Gospel League Home ministry, I believe First Baptist Church is a five-talent church.

What did God expect from that five-talent man? That man took those five talents and doubled them. He said, "I have five talents, and I am not going to quit until I have five more." That passage mentions four times that the five-talent man doubled his talents.

I believe God looks at First Baptist Church of Hammond and says, "Do you realize what you have there at First Baptist Church? You have all those ministries, all this horsepower, a lot of potential money coming through you, with the world to reach, and a Book full of commands. You are a five-talent church. How am I going to judge you?"

If I am a pastor of a five-talent church, then when I meet Jesus Christ, I do not want to say, "I took the five-talent church you gave me; and here it is, your five-talent church."

I know what God said to the man who gave him back only what he was given. God said, "…*Thou wicked and slothful servant…cast ye the unprofitable servant into outer darkness….*" (Matthew 25:26 and 30) God was saying, "Your life is so worthless to Me. Anyone can take what I gave them and just give that back to Me. I am looking for you to double what I gave you."

When I read this passage of Scripture, I get very convicted. If we are supposed to give God double what He gave us, that means if First Baptist Church is running 5,000 people in this auditorium, when I die and leave this earth, I want the next pastor to be able to stand up and say, "To you 10,000 people in this auditorium, let me tell you something…." If I do not double what God has given me, then I do not want to meet Christ. That story teaches that if I do not give back to Christ double what He gave me, I am a wicked and slothful servant.

Sunday school teacher, how big was your class 20 years ago when you were teaching it? If you inherited a class of five little boys, what should you do with those five boys? If you became a bus captain of ten people, what should you do with those ten people? There are bus routes all over our church running 10, 15, or 20 people. It costs us over $100 to run one bus each week. Bus captains, put 45 kids on that bus! The national average is 40; at least hit the average! First

Baptist Church is an above-average church; I want our members to show it.

I am trying to get my members and me on the same page. I am trying to get that church member out in the pew to get provoked and understand that our attendance is not going to double by his simply sitting back and listening and doing the same things he has always done. I do not want to meet Jesus that way. First Baptist Church has been given a wonderful opportunity, and there ought to be a challenge inside each Christian's heart that rises up and says, "Be quiet, Brother Schaap! Okay, I will double my class! I will double my bus route. I will double this church with you if you will just shut up!"

I am interested in the First Baptist Church doing what it did before there was a Hyles-Anderson College. The First Baptist Church of Hammond was declared the largest Sunday school in the world, and all the work was done by laymen—not one college kid! We are not going to build this church on the work of college students. I want college kids across America to come to First Baptist Church and say, "You have got to see how those laymen build a church. Nobody does it like that!" I do not want the laymen to hide behind those Hyles-Anderson College kids, but instead to show them how to build a church.

God expects Christians to grab what He gives us and double it! If you really want to get scared, go to Matthew 25:14 where God said that He wants us to multiply times ten. In the Bible, there are two sets of growth God gives: double or multiplied ten times. The largest Baptist church in the world, which is located in Seoul, Korea, averages 38,500 in attendance every Sunday. It is somewhat of a different church than ours, but they do preach salvation by grace through faith and believe the Bible is the Word of God. When I read that church's statistics, I threw down the book and exclaimed, "I hate that!"

No, I don't hate that church. I hate that a church like First Baptist Church of Hammond that has the truth and the answers is not the largest church in the world. Our folks have written the books on marriage and child rearing and church growth. It is time First Baptist Church stopped hiding behind its laurels. I do not want to sit back and say, "Hello, world. Do you realize how great First Baptist Church is?"

No! I am going to humble myself and fall on my face and say, "God, would You please help us to double our ministry? Would you help First Baptist to do more than we have ever done before?" That is what I am interested in. I believe with all my heart there is a young generation coming up in fundamentalism that is saying "I would like that same thing. I would like to see what God could do with us."

7. Christians do not set any goals. How many souls did you plan to win last week? You hit it, didn't you? It is not the not reaching of goals that bothers me. It is the not setting of goals that bothers me. It's the not striving for a goal that bothers me. Bus captain, how many did you plan to have on your bus route Sunday? How many do you plan to have during the Fall Program? If you wait until October to set your goals, you will not reach those goals either. Have you prayed about your goals yet? Have you set numbers in your heart? Have you fasted and prayed and begged and said, "God, I want to do something that has never been done before!" Does it grip you that there is a big God Who could do greater things than what He is doing?

I want to be used of God. I would love it if the First Baptist Church, as a single mind, as one body, would rise like an army and say, "God, we are going to take up Your Word. If You want us to reach the world, You are going to have to help us. We will step out on faith. We will find ways to support the missionaries. We will find time to give. God, would you use us like You have never before used us?"

The Chicago area ought to be able to say, "Have you heard what is happening in Hammond?"

In 1972, the highest attendance First Baptist Church ever had was 12,170. The highest number we have ever had in the history of this church as far as regular Sunday services is 18,700. Sometime in the next few years, I want to double that attendance at 37,400. First Baptist Church has had giant days off property and giant unified services at the Civic Auditorium with many more thousands in attendance.

Last year we had Great Commission Sunday and preached the Gospel all over the Chicago area and had 48,000 saved in one day. However, I am talking about regular Sunday school and church. First Baptist Church should set some big goals.

In 1995, Brother Hyles wrote a list of goals for our church. On his list was a new school for our bus kids. First Baptist recently bought the former Spohn School. A new 7,000-seat auditorium was on his list. We are in the process of building that auditorium. Brother Hyles listed several goals, and First Baptist is just about right on track with his list of goals.

I do not want the First Baptist Church to roll over with its feet up in the air and say, "Scratch my belly, God. Make me feel good because I am a member of a huge church that is fat and lazy."

No! I want this church to say, "God, I want to get back up on my hind legs, and I want to run. We are going to get out missionaries. I am going to give to Faith Promise Missions. I am going to get a bus route. I am going to get a Sunday school class. I want to work in partnership with God, and I want to see what God can use me to do."

One of the greatest thrills of my life is to know that God wants to use me. Do not hide behind your problems. Stand unabashedly and say, "God, if you want to use me, here I am."

First Baptist Church has a great opportunity, and I believe we are a five-talent church. I believe we have been blessed singularly unlike any church since Jerusalem. But the Bible says to whom much is given, much shall be required. I want First Baptist Church to be ready and ripe so that when the Lord comes back, we will not have to stand with our heads hanging down and say, "Our great tribute is that we made it through the funeral of Brother Hyles." That is not the best testimony for us.

I want our testimony to be "We had to jam pack extra chairs in the First Baptist Church auditorium. We had to build a new auditorium because the old one wore out, and we outgrew it. I want God to see that First Baptist Church is very tuned in to the Great Commission. Let's grow!

Chapter Six

The Ingredients of a Mega-Church *or*
The Doctrine of Holiness as a Relative Principle of Church Growth

"And great fear came upon all the church, and upon as many as heard these things." (Acts 5:11)

FIRST BAPTIST CHURCH is called a mega-church by nearly everyone in the religious world. Church researchers say that any church that runs more than 2,000 consistently week after week is considered a mega-church. Another category is called super mega-churches, in which First Baptist Church is listed because we run over 10,000. The word *mega* comes from a Greek word which means "great."

Acts 4:33 says, *"And with great power gave the apostles witness of the resurrection of the Lord Jesus: and great grace was upon them all."* Notice the words "great power" and "great grace."

Acts 5:5 states, *"And Ananias hearing these words fell down, and gave up the ghost: and great fear came on all them that heard these things."*

In the chapter entitled "In One Accord," how this super mega-church in the book of Acts went from 120 church members to a minimum of 100,000 church members in the space of no more than two years was addressed. The church in Jerusalem was a super, super, mega-church because they had the right ingredients of great power, great grace, and great fear.

The word *great* in the previous verses is from the Greek word "mega." The early church had mega-power, mega-grace, and mega-fear.

• **The first ingredient of a mega-church is mega-influence.** Acts 1:7 says, *"And he said unto them, It is not for you to know the times or the seasons, which the Father hath put in his own power."* The disciples were worried about the Lord's return and the restoration of the kingdom of Israel. They were concerned with all the fighting between the Palestinians and the Jews, and the time when the Jews would control the Kingdom of David again and the Messiah would rule. Jesus said, "That kind of power is not your business." The disciples were concerned about positional power. The position of pastor of the church is positional power. The position of the father of the home, the position of assistant pastors, and the position of principals are all positional powers. Jesus was saying, "Don't worry about what position you have. That is the Father's business."

In Acts 1:8, Jesus told the disciples, *"But ye shall receive power, after that the Holy Ghost is come upon you: and ye shall be witnesses unto me both in Jerusalem, and in all Judæa, and in Samaria, and unto the uttermost part of the earth."*

The word *power* in this verse is from a different Greek word which means "influence." Jesus said, "Don't worry about the position you have; rather, worry about the influence you have." I would much rather be an influence in my home than have just a position in my home. I would much rather have influence in the church than just to simply have a position in the church. I would much rather make a difference in somebody's life by influence than simply say, "Are you impressed with my title on my business card?" Nobody has gotten saved yet because I showed them my business card! I've given away hundreds of my business cards, and nobody has fallen on their knees and said, "I repent in sackcloth and ashes." My business card is a positional card. However, when I have handed unsaved people a Gospel tract and showed them the old Romans Road in the King

James Bible, a whole bunch of folks have gotten saved! The difference is influence power.

The Bible talks about this mega-power, this mega-influence of the early church. I'm not worried about the status of First Baptist Church of Hammond. I'm worried about our power, our influence. Christian, what kind of influence do you have when you go to the grocery store? What kind of influence do you have in your neighborhood? What kind of influence do you have in your home? The kind of influence First Baptist Church has changes lives; position does not change lives.

• **The second ingredient of a mega-church is mega-grace.** The word *grace* comes from the Greek word *charis* which means charisma, charm, generosity, or gracious. A mega-church is a very gracious, giving, and generous church. A mega-church gives their tithes and offerings. However, they go beyond what is required and give their alms. A mega-church runs bus routes and provides the money for those buses. A mega-church provides a Christian school for those bus kids. A mega church gives to Faith Promise and to the building fund. A mega-church gives and gives and gives. The mega-church says, "How can we give more so that we can get out the Gospel? Let's send missionaries to Jilin City in China and to Iraq and to the 116 countries that don't have a Gospel witness. Let's send missionaries to the world!"

• **The third ingredient of a mega-church is mega-fear.** The word *fear* is the Greek word *phobos* from which we get our word "phobia." A phobia is an excessive or persistent fear. This group of men who were leading the church in Jerusalem were very afraid that the church would lose its mega-power and its mega-grace. These men realized that the church would lose its influence and gracious generosity and kindness and charm and goodness if the church ever lost its great fear. This great fear was introduced in Acts 5, when Satan inspired a couple named Ananias and Sapphira to introduce a practice in the church that caused the blood of the apostles to run cold with fear that they would lose their great influence and their great grace. When Ananias and Sapphira committed this horrible, heinous crime against God, Peter said, "You have no idea what you have done! You have brought in a practice that, if allowed to spread, will destroy our power, our influence, and our grace."

The great fear of every pastor of a growing, soul-winning church is that the church could lose its influence and be snubbed by the Holy Ghost and no longer be used of God. Such was the church in Ephesus. Jesus said to the church in Ephesus, "If you don't fix that problem of your first love, I will remove your candlestick—the light—that shines in your church. You will lose all of your influence. You will be a big social club with a shell of a building called a church house. You may have lots of people attending, but you will have zero influence in the community and in the world."

Many mega-sized groups of people meet on Sundays around the globe. However, their influence around the globe is what matters in the mind of Christ, not just the number of the bodies inside that auditorium. If the number of bodies is the criteria, then Vatican City wins hands down. When the Pope gives some kind of address, more people come out to hear him than any other single gathering of a religious nature. The problem is those people do not make anyone a child of Heaven by their gathering together. This doesn't just apply to Catholics. It applies to any group: the Mormons, the Jehovah's Witnesses, or any Baptist group that might meet together and not do one thing about winning souls and getting people out of Hell.

A man from the Southern Baptist convention called one of our Hyles-Anderson College preacher boys and said, "We have literally millions of dollars sitting in our investment firms, and we would give you the money if you will start the churches. You boys from Hyles-Anderson College are starting the churches like the Southern Baptists used to start."

Of course, I advised the young preacher not to take any money from a convention; because after a while, whoever controls the purse strings could want to own and possess that in which their money is invested. The fact is, the criterion is not just the size of the church; it is the influence of the church. These apostles knew that as big as the church in Jerusalem was, it was not size that wielded the power. It was the influence of the Holy Ghost through that church. Jesus said, "...ye shall receive power, after that the Holy Ghost is come upon you...." Jesus didn't say, "After the crowd gathers together." It is the Holy Spirit of God Who gives me the power to preach and to influence people. The powerful influence of the Holy Spirit of God is exactly what fundamental churches need.

Holiness is a lost doctrine in our churches. The word *holiness* turns off most people. In a day and age of promiscuity and fornication with no shame, we have lost the doctrine of holiness. Boyfriends and girlfriends are necking and petting in lover's lane—some even in their parents' house with Mom and Dad present! A Baptist dad said to me, "I told my boy if I catch you fornicating, I'll kill you; but if you come to our house, I'll let you do what you want. I even give them my bedroom, Brother Schaap. What do you think of that?"

"If I were Scriptural," I replied, "I would find a spear and stab the two of them through and kill them like Eleazar did in the Old Testament. The Bible said that what Eleazar did was counted for righteousness to him and for the generations that followed."

In this day, sinners are patted on the back and told, "It's okay to fornicate. It's okay to have your gay lifestyle. It's okay to incite riots. It's okay to be immoral and ungodly."

Bless God! It is not okay! The growth of a mega-church is killed when the great fear is lost. A church has lost its great fear when sex becomes nothing more than humorous jokes told by the staff of the church, and fornication and adultery and immorality and ungodliness are nothing more than humor in the Christian schools. When a church loses its great fear, it loses its great grace. When a church loses its great grace, it loses its great power. When a church loses its great power, it loses its right to exist!

It is time for the men on the deacon board, the assistant pastors, the Sunday school teachers, every bus worker and bus rider, and the pastor to stand up on their hind legs and say, "I want the fear of God to permeate the pews of our church." When church members lose their great fear, my friend, the church loses the power of God.

The power of God is as obvious as the purity of the saints. The projectile force of my words is only as good as the holy life I live. I have known individuals who by themselves seem to have great influence and in singular acts of preaching a sermon, even at a convention, have seemed to be singularly blessed by God while living lifestyles of adultery and immorality, but they leave a trail of spiritual cancer that destroys the next generation. A man may get up and preach a powerful, profound sermon and be called the darling of his movement, but his sex sins and his immorality will poison and damn the next generation and stop the growth of the church.

The truth of the matter is, until there is a revival of holiness in the pews of Baptist churches, we will watch the Charismatics and even the Methodists pass us in their growth. It is a crime against God that in the 1970's every great soul-winning church was an independent, fundamental, Baptist church, but the holiness left. The great fear left! Running around, carousing around, and the humor of the bedroom, and the harlots permeated some of the centers of our leaders. We saw our movement fight and bicker and fuss! Much of the independent Baptist movement has lost its great grace. Why? Because fundamental Baptists have lost their great fear and thus their great power.

There needs to be a revival of holiness in the lives of every individual. The church is a family and a community of individuals, and the individuals of the pew must understand that we serve a holy God. He is called the Holy Spirit of God, the Holy Ghost of God, and the Holy Child, Jesus. Holiness is very important and is relative to church growth. As the church diminishes in its appetite for holiness, it loses its love for the lost. These worldly so-called Christian groups that are rocking and rolling and having their modern dramas—I wonder how their soul-winning program is.

Ananias and Sapphira made several mistakes that were costly to them and potentially destructive to the church in Jerusalem. They are the same mistakes that are often being made in churches today.

1. They kept back that which belonged to God. First of all, they kept back their bodies. The Bible says in I Corinthians 6:19, *"What? know ye not that your body is the temple of the Holy Ghost which is in you....?"* The church building is not the temple of God or the sanctuary of God. The believer's body is the temple of God. If Christ is in each Christian, then Christians are the temple of the Holy Ghost. Christian, you do not belong to yourself. A Christian's body belongs to the Lord Jesus Christ.

The word *holiness* means "separated apart to God." A Christian is to pull away from the world and present himself to God and say, "God, my body is Yours." Ananias and Sapphira kept back their bodies which belonged to God.

2. Ananias and Sapphira kept back the tithes and offerings. The Bible says, "Will a man rob God....?" (Malachi 3:8) One of our members who is a Hammond police officer told me that the word *robbery* does not mean "stealing." The word *robbery* means "to take personal property from another person unlawfully by using or threatening force or violence or intimidation." No wonder those couples who come to me for marriage counseling and refuse to tithe have a disastrous marriage. The Bible says in Malachi 3 that when a person does not tithe and give offerings, he invites the devourer to come into his home, The devourer nibbles away and devours that marriage. A marriage cannot be fixed if the couple won't tithe. Stealing the tithe and offering is stealing from the Lord.

3. **Ananias and Sapphira were the type of Christians who would have kept back their children.** Psalm 127:3 says, "*Lo, children are an heritage of the* LORD...." Parents have no right to play God with their children. God gives children to be trained by their parents for God and His will. The greatest opportunity First Baptist Church parents have in the world is to put their children in this church and in our Christian schools and have those children trained and pointed in the direction of full-time service for God. What a great privilege for parents to have a child want to serve God with his life.

The greatest tragedy in a mega-church is to have parents say, "Full-time service? There is no money in that."

The song writer said, "Take the whole world, but give me Jesus!"

I don't want the world's money! I don't want the world's fame! I want to be sold out for Christ. Full-time service does not mean just drawing a paycheck from the church. It means full-time serving God. Taking that which belongs to God is a serious matter. Suppose a man separates himself to serve God full time. Perhaps he came to Hyles-Anderson College. Perhaps he brought his family to First Baptist Church to learn how to serve God full time, and he believed God wanted him to serve God with his life. Time and circumstance have perhaps withheld the opportunity to pastor or go to a mission field, but it should not have permitted him to become inactive and lazy.

First Baptist Church is not a hiding place for those running from God. First Baptist Church is not Jonah's ship sailing from the will of God. First Baptist is not a church for those looking for a way to avoid serving God.

It bothers me when a First Baptist Church or school employee uses the nomenclature that he has a home church. What is the First

Baptist Church to that employee, a pretend church? Is First Baptist Church a church an employee uses as long as he draws a paycheck from the church? There are some employees who would immediately go "back home" if they lost their job in our ministry. It is time church and college and school employees put down their roots and make First Baptist Church their home church and stop robbing this mega-church from the holy character it deserves to have. If a teacher's ministry at Hyles-Anderson College is simply a job and he is part time in the church, then I would like for him to leave the job.

Hyles-Anderson College hires employees who are bus captains or division leaders who put in eight to ten hours of soul winning a week. Yet, after some are hired, the administration has a hard time getting them to go soul winning three hours per week. Those who draw a paycheck from the First Baptist Church ministry are not to slow down and become lazy and do less for God. Teachers who stand up in front of college students and tell them how to serve God full time should stop serving God part time. It bothers me when freshmen boys put in ten hours, and professional college teachers put in one hour. It also bothers me when First Baptist Church is nothing more than a temporary place of spiritual residence as long as a staff member has employment with us. I'm not hiring professional people. I'm not hiring hired guns. I want tender-hearted people who say, "First of all the church, then the other ministries."

A man who came to First Baptist Church and Hyles-Anderson College to train for full-time Christian service and after many years is still here in Hammond, should face the fact that he probably won't leave First Baptist Church. Okay, then why doesn't he teach a Sunday school class? How can a man sit in the pew and say, "Well, I was going to start a church. I was going to go to the mission field. I was going to... I was going to..." but all he does is sit in an adult Sunday school class and soak it in and soak it in and get fat, salty, lazy, and dead! First Baptist Church has a lot of horsepower in the pews. Some of our members need to get hitched up and start teaching a Sunday school class. With the process of refurbishing 5,000 to 10,000 square feet of Sunday school classrooms almost completed, teachers are needed for those classrooms.

Thousands of homes have been built in our Calumet region in the last five years. People in those homes don't even know that First

Baptist Church exists. They are sweet, open people, willing and hungry for the Gospel. Young churches by the dozens are starting up out there and saying, "Come to our church. Wear your blue jeans. We have drama and rock 'n' roll." Bless God! First Baptist Church members need to get their carcasses involved and let these new people know about the old church downtown. Get your carcass involved! It's a shame to say, "Since I can't start a church, I'm not even going to teach a boy's class."

4. **Ananias and Sapphira lied to God.** Many people lie to God about their marriage vows and get divorced. Several couples I'm counseling feel that the only solution is to write out the divorce papers. When a couple stands on the platform and promises God they will stay together "until death do us part," and they get a divorce. They have lied to the Holy Ghost. How about the spiritual commitment a teenager made when he came to Youth Conference or Pastors' School when he said, "God, I promise you I will do ___." If that teenager does not follow through with his commitment, he lied to God. It's time some Christians come to an old-fashioned altar and say, "God, I made a promise to You years ago that I would go soul winning or work on a bus route. God, I'm re-upping that promise."

5. **Ananias and Sapphira tempted the Spirit.** Galatians 5:17-21 says, *"For the flesh lusteth against the Spirit, and the Spirit against the flesh: and these are contrary the one to the other: so that ye cannot do the things that ye would. But if ye be led of the Spirit, ye are not under the law. Now the works of the flesh are manifest, which are these; Adultery, fornication, uncleanness, lasciviousness, Idolatry, witchcraft, hatred, variance, emulations, wrath, strife, seditions, heresies, Envyings, murders, drunkenness, revellings, and such like: of the which I tell you before, as I have also told you in time past, that they which do such things shall not inherit the kingdom of God."*

The Bible says there is a spirit inside of us and a flesh inside of us that are warring. When Ananias and Sapphira said, "We're going to hold back that which belongs to God, and we're going to lie to God," they caused a strife of the Holy Spirit in that church. Peter jumped all over that situation and said, "You are not going to bring that ungodly attitude into our church."

Today we face the spirit of fornication among our young people and the spirit of adultery. It is time that couples that are trying to get over their adulterous affairs stopped lusting after their former sin partner. It is time they got bathed in the holiness of God. It is time they came to the altar and said, "God, forgive the crookedness and the wickedness of my heart," instead of sitting back in their pew and being sorry they got caught.

God used Ananias and Sapphira as examples of two people who could have short-circuited an entire church. Two people who want to lust after each other and get together in the bed of adultery and defile their marriage vows and permit Satan to have an occasion against the church will short-circuit the great power of a mega-church. Don't ever think that an individual's immoral behavior does not bring direct bearing on the body of the church. The Bible describes the church as a body. If I take a hammer and hit my thumb instead of the nail, I have a sneaking suspicion that the rest of my body is going to go into convulsions. For some reason, the entire body goes into a ritual war dance. The feet start dancing, the face becomes contorted, the other hand grabs the hurt thumb and then words eject out of the mouth that are not to the praise and honor and glory of Jehovah God! (Although God's name is often mentioned!) Why doesn't the brain say, "Hey, hey, hey, calm down! That thumb represents less than one tenth of one percent of the entire square footage of this body"? The body does not care about logic because the body is convulsing in pain. It is time God's people understand that you cannot find a corner dark enough or distant enough to defile yourself without bringing a great, convulsive spirit to the whole church.

I personally know of churches that allowed the spirit of immorality to invade their churches, and because the leaders never dealt properly with the immorality, those churches never grew again. If there is not great fear to maintain the holiness and the spirit of a church, then that spirit of immorality comes in, and the Spirit of God is grieved.

When Brother Hyles went to Heaven on February 6, 2001, First Baptist Church did not feel like running buses and knocking on doors. A pain had occurred in the body that brought a grief through the spirit of our church that paralyzed this church. The pulpit committee wisely and prudently jumped into gear right away and voted in a pastor and focused on moving ahead. When a church doesn't move ahead, it will stop and die. For a long time the First Baptist Church was paralyzed by a major blow. The spirit of grief paralyzed all of us.

When a Christian is immoral, he paralyzes the Holy Spirit of God. When he climbs into the bed of fornication, he brings a spirit of shame and reproach to the church, he grieves the Holy Ghost, and the whole church body convulses with the pain though the members may not even know why. The foot does not have to understand why it is dancing to know that it is dancing. The hand does not have to logically, mentally comprehend the pain as it grabs the hurting thumb and squeezes it. It simply knows there is a pain in the body. There is a convulsing moment when an immoral deed brings a shame that makes the entire church wince though they don't even know why. Christian, do not ever think that you can divorce your actions from the corporate body called the local church. All the members pull together—all for one and one for all. The body is righteous together; when a member sins, the body hurts together.

Yes, when a Christian sins, the rest of the church tries to help them, but when the sinner pushes away and says, "I want my lust. I want my pornography. I want my Internet sex. I want my immorality. I want my ungodliness. I want to feed my mind with the sewer and septic tank of the world," he brings a shame to the church. Consequently, the Spirit of God says, "You do not have great fear. Therefore, you lose your great grace, your great influence, and your great power."

I have studied very carefully the last 30 years of the church-growth movement. That study reveals several churches that fell victim to their own size. Growing churches become vulnerable. Let me share several observations about these churches.

A. We must remember to love the sinner but hate the sin. As a member of First Baptist Church, we draw a big distinction between the sinner and the sin. When a sinner walks the aisle and says, "I've sinned, and I want to get right with God," I detest the sin, but I love the sinner. Christians cannot let the simplicity of the salvation of Christ deceive them into thinking that they can come to Christ and then turn right back and say, "Now I can live as I please." The Spirit of the Living God occupies the Christian's body, and He will convict.

Though it is not the pastor's job to make someone change, it is the pastor's job to remind his congregation that the Spirit of God lives in them. Feeding on God's Word will be a constant reminder that God expects each Christian to change. Fundamentalists are so afraid to face the fact that when a person becomes a saved born-again individual, God does not just insist, He commands and demands our holiness. I'm not ashamed to say that God does not only expect holiness; He demands holiness. I want to love the sinner and hate the sin.

B. We must not grow weary of high standards. Some ladies say to me, "I love your preaching. I enjoy your Sunday morning sermons and your Wednesday night Bible studies, but, Sunday night is a little rough." I have had others say to me, "I don't really care what you say, I'm going to dress the way I want to anyway."

Church members are ambassadors for their church as well as for Christ. When Christians grow weary of the high standards of morality and decency, they cause a church to lose its great fear, its great grace, and its great power.

C. We must not become careless with holiness. A Christian's attitude toward sin must be an absolute despising of it. The Bible says in II Timothy 2:22, "*Flee also youthful lusts.*" Run from it! Don't dabble in it! Don't play with it! Don't analyze it! Run from it! Joseph fled from Potiphar's wife. King David got into serious trouble when he did not look away and flee.

When the unclean spirit defiles the church, it paralyzes the growth of that church. Stay pure. Keep your humor clean. Keep your private life clean. The growth of a mega-church cannot be divorced from how the church members live privately. A church cannot grow when its members go to the beach and strip half naked or have mixed swimming parties.

It broke my heart when I heard about some of our college kids who went to a mixed swimming party at a motel swimming pool. Those kids call themselves First Baptist Church members and Hyles-Anderson College students. Shame on them! Our church high school kids need to stop dressing improperly and going out to the beaches and acting like animals and playing their hip-hop and rap music and getting their passions inflamed. In the name of Jesus Christ of Nazareth, why don't Christians get a dose of holiness!

The goals I have for First Baptist Church are directly related to the holiness of the members of First Baptist Church. Our church won't send out 1,000 missionaries if there are a bunch of whores and harlots in our high school. We will not reach 116 nations who have never heard the Gospel if we have members who are lusting and immoral.

There should be a revival in the heart of every man, woman, boy, and girl that says, "God, I want a revival of holiness. I want great fear—excessive, persistent fear—that I might never be the one to short-circuit the great grace and the great power of a great church."

The song says, "It's me. It's me, oh Lord, standing in the need of prayer." If every church member would take that attitude and say, "God, let me watch carefully how I live before You in private and before the world in public so that the great grace of God and the great power of God can keep our church the mega-church it was, is, and should be."

CHAPTER SEVEN

The Sin of Imbalance

"And to the angel of the church in Pergamos write; These things saith he which hath the sharp sword with two edges." (Revelation 2:12)

IN REVELATION 2 and 3, seven churches are addressed personally by the Lord Jesus Christ. These churches are given very practical advice about their condition—their strengths as well as their weaknesses.

In the previous chapter, we discussed the ingredients of a mega-church which are great fear, and great grace, and great power. It is terrifying to those who understand the purpose of a church to watch anything to come into a church that would upset the balance or the equilibrium of a church that keeps everything running just right.

When Adam and Eve sinned in the Garden of Eden, they introduced into their bloodstream a potent toxin that slowly poisoned the body, bringing aging and death to a body that did not have to die. That body could have lived eternally along with the soul and spirit. When God breathed life into the body of Adam, there was no aging process set in motion. There was no decay process. There was no cancer. There were no heart attacks. There were no maladies. There was no problem that could come to that body that would age it. The hair would not turn white or turn loose. The shoulders would not sag and droop. The body would not get rheumatism or arthritis. There would be no aching joints or broken bones. There would be no need for vitamins. The body was created in a state that could have perpetually lived.

Have you ever noticed those people who are robust and who take care of themselves? Their soul gets to a certain age and never seems to get much older! They act much like youthful children. Brother Hyles talked about the childish, juvenile adult whose soul is ageless. Grumpy old souls are not grumpy because their soul is aging; they are just acting old. The physical body and the circumstances of life should not determine the state of a Christian's soul. Instead, the work of God, the Word of God, the promises of God, and the hope of eternal life in Christ Jesus should affect the Christian's soul. Brother Hyles enjoyed telling the following story about Dr. John R. Rice.

Brother Hyles and Dr. Rice were preaching together at a conference. When it came time to leave the church and go to lunch, no one could find Dr. Rice. After Brother Hyles and others looked all through the church and school but could not find Dr. Rice, they went outside to look for him. There on the children's playground was Dr. Rice, a man in his 70's, playing hopscotch with some children.

There is a certain youthfulness in each person that does not ever have to age. Man's spirit is robust as he walks with God and is filled with God's Spirit.

I have often used a balloon to illustrate the spirit. If the balloon is filled with air, you can push it down, and it will spring right back up. If you give it a hard whack, it will bounce right back because it is filled with air. A Christian's spirit that is filled with God's Spirit is as resilient as a balloon. The spirit never dies or decays or ages—it is eternal.

God breathed eternal breath into an eternal body, and man became a living, eternal soul. However, the body began to die when something from the outside was introduced into it. The fruit of the knowledge of good and evil was not some mystical aura or some bizarre relationship into which Eve entered. Eve ate something, and the eating of a particular fruit brought a toxin into the body that poisoned the blood. As a result, the body began to die.

The church is the body of Christ and has been promised divine perpetuity, meaning the church does not have to die. The local church body like First Baptist Church of Hammond does not have to die. I know of churches that lived five years and died. I know of churches that grew as big as First Baptist Church and now no longer exist. However, the local church does not have to die if it does not want to die. According to Acts 20:28, the church was bought with the blood of God. The blood of God is not tainted blood. The great fear that good men have about local churches is that somebody will ingest or bring into the body a poison that could corrupt the church with a spiritual, emotional cancer from within and rot a church until it is corrupted.

Let me illustrate. Dr. Tom Vogel, the academic vice president of Hyles-Anderson College, recently noticed a board in his house that looked weak. He pulled up the board and inspected the floor joists underneath. He checked the floor joist with his hand and was able to push his finger all the way through a joist. Carpenter ants had infested that area of his house and caused many thousands of dollars of damage. A secret silent invader had crept into that house and had eaten away the support.

That is why in Acts 5, when Ananias and Sapphira introduced unholiness—an evil potent toxin—into the church, Peter was so zealous to root it out. That is why God was willing to kill those two people. God knew that He had to kill the cancer that had been ingested into the church body that would defile the entire body lest the church in Jerusalem decay and die.

These seven churches in the book of Revelation all died. Jesus told each church that if it did not root out the poison that was in its bloodstream, they would no longer be a thriving growing church.

One of the great doctrines that is seldom preached in our pulpits is holiness. What exactly is holiness? This word "holiness" is sometimes used in very dead dying churches that are skeletons of what they once were. These dead congregations get up on Sunday mornings only at their one-hour worship service and sing, "Holy, holy, holy. Lord God Almighty..." with no concept of what holiness is. These churches rock 'n' roll on Saturday nights and bury their members with a funeral dirge on Sunday mornings.

One Saturday evening, I was briefly listening to a youth program on a very powerful so-called Christian radio station in our area. I have never heard such heavy metal and hard acid rock music in all my life. The next Sunday morning, out of curiosity, I tuned in the same station. I thought for sure that God had died, and the whole world was in mourning! These churches talk about holiness and have no idea what they are talking about. Most Christians have no concept of what holiness is. Some churches are called holiness churches, but their young people live like the Devil, and their women walk around in their immodest dress. Holiness is a foreign language to the average Christian.

Holiness is such a broad powerful word. I have heard many Baptist preachers say that this country could be fixed if every Baptist pastor would rise up in his pulpit and preach a year-long series on holiness. The truth of the matter is, that statement is not far off the mark. The doctrine of holiness is not singing "Holy, holy, holy," and it certainly has nothing to do with calling an individual "his holiness" as the Catholics call the Pope. Holiness has absolutely nothing to do with boring, dried-up music.

Rather, holiness is a wonderful concept. In fact, there are creatures in Heaven like we have never seen on this earth that have several eyes and wings and feet that are perpetually saying, "*Holy, holy, holy, Lord God Almighty, which was, and is, and is to come.*" (Revelation 4:8d) I love that picture.

The word *holiness* or *holy* comes from the same root word as our word "whole." If someone is a holy man, we sometimes think of him as having a pious look on his face and never having any fun. If someone mentioned going to the amusement park to this holy man, he would probably throw his King James family Bible at that person. Most people's idea of a holy person is that he is boring and spooky and syrupy, but that has nothing to do with holiness whatsoever! A holy person is a complete person—a whole person.

The word *holiness* comes from the same word from which we get our word *integer*, which means "a complete or whole number," not a fraction—not ¼ of a person, but one whole person. A holy individual is a balanced individual.

The first church addressed in Revelation is the church of Ephesus. Notice Revelation 2:2, 3 says, "*I know thy works, and thy labour, and thy patience, and how thou canst not bear them which are evil:*

and thou hast tried them which say they are apostles, and are not, and hast found them liars: And hast borne, and hast patience, and for my name's sake hast laboured, and hast not fainted."

Ephesus was a commendable church. God talked about the church's wonderful attributes. God said, "You are the most doctrinally sound church I have. You know your doctrine so well. You recognize false cults and religions, and you are masters at scripturally destroying the cults. You are masters at pointing out error from truth. I commend you for that."

God continues in verse 4, *"Nevertheless I have somewhat against thee, because thou hast left thy first love."* God is talking about balance. He admires some attributes about this church in Ephesus. On one side, the church had a very profound understanding of the Scriptures. The members knew the Book and stood for the Book. On the other hand, something about this church bothered God a great deal. In fact, it bothered God so much that He told the church if this problem was not corrected, He would not look at their good and ignore the evil. The good of that church did not balance the bad. The evil had to go. Ephesus had a lack of first love. The people had a cold heart. They had left their first love—their zeal, enthusiasm, and freshness. They had left the fun of watching a new convert come down the aisle.

The point of this chapter is not to deal with the specific problem of this church or the other six churches. The point is that the church of Ephesus, as well as the other six churches, was imbalanced. The church was unholy. On one side of the equation, the church had the right theology; on the other side, they had no love. Ephesus did not balance their hard theology with hot passionate love. God told them that if they didn't watch out, theology would kill them. They would become a cold, boring, dead, unproductive, and dying church. The imbalance of theology and passion was killing the church in Ephesus.

Jesus commended Ephesus for their theology and their doctrine and discernment and scriptural integrity, but then rebuked them for leaving their first love. The members no longer took the Scriptures and told an old rotten sot how to get saved. The Bible is good for nothing if you are not using it to get some soul out of Hell.

The church in Ephesus was an unholy church (not like we think of unholy with adultery and fornication) because it was an imbalanced church. A church must have the right theology. Take the King James Bible out of the First Baptist Church, and it will die. Take soul-winning zeal out of the First Baptist Church, and it will die. A church must have both.

When Brother Hyles went to Heaven, the First Baptist Church membership did not make the common mistake that is made by most big churches. They did not bring in a preacher who was different from Brother Hyles. For some reason, a pendulum swing often occurs in most big churches. The church will say, "Well, our previous pastor was a zealous soul winner; now let's get a deeper-life, doctrinal preacher." Or many of those churches go from a deeper-life, doctrinal preacher to some wild-eyed zealot who doesn't even know the Bible has 66 books. Either swing will kill a church.

When studying the Bible, a Christian had better have a love for God to use the Bible, or there is no sense in studying the Bible! The local church is not supposed to gather around the Word and study and study and study and study. The church is supposed to study the Word and then use the Word. In II Timothy 2:15, the Bible says, "*Study to shew thyself approved unto God....*" Christians are supposed to study the Bible, then go out on the streets, and show the lost world how to be saved.

I tell our Hyles-Anderson preacher boys that they better sit and learn and hang on every word in their theology classes. Students are supposed to study so they can show something. Not only had preacher boys better learn in their doctrine classes, they need to take what they learn and use it on a bus route. However, some college students do nothing but bus route work and leave off studying in doctrines class. The Bible states again and again that we must observe to do. Christians are to watch and learn and do something with what they watch. Without balance, unholiness enters.

Jesus addresses the church in Pergamos in Revelation 2:13, "*I know thy works, and where thou dwellest, even where Satan's seat is: and thou holdest fast my name, and hast not denied my faith, even in those days wherein Antipas was my faithful martyr, who was slain among you, where Satan dwelleth.*" The word *seat* means "government authority." Satan had put his demonic governor's headquarters in the city of Pergamos. Jesus asked, "Did you know that your church happens to be in the headquarters for the kingdom of darkness?"

History tells us that Antipas, a member in the church of Pergamos, was forced by a Roman centurion to bow to a bust of Caesar and say, "Caesar is Lord."

Antipas refused and said, "No, Jesus is Lord."

The Roman centurion told him again to bow his knee to Caesar. Antipas said again, "No, Jesus is Lord."

The centurion said, "Antipas, the whole world is against you."

Antipas said, "Antipas is against the whole world."

A large hollowed-out container was brought; Antipas was put inside, and the container was placed over a roaring fire. Antipas was roasted alive.

Jesus said, "I know my martyr Antipas. He stood for the faith." Jesus commended the church in Pergamos for taking a tremendous stand. Jesus told them that their faithfulness was legendary in Heaven.

Jesus then added in Revelation 2:14-16, "*But I have a few things against thee, because thou hast there them that hold the doctrine of Balaam, who taught Balac to cast a stumblingblock before the children of Israel, to eat things sacrificed unto idols, and to commit fornication. So hast thou also them that hold the doctrine of the Nicolaitanes, which thing I hate. Repent; or else I will come unto thee quickly, and will fight against them with the sword of my mouth.*"

Jesus was saying, "Pergamos, I admire your faithful stand and your loyalty, but you are about to become My enemy because you have also introduced license. You are so proud of taking a stand that you are allowing yourselves to indulge in sin."

The average man goes into pornography because he is such a good faithful husband to his wife. He looks at pornography as a little bit of sugar and spice—a treat for being such a good man. The average man with whom I counsel about pornography is not a pervert. He is a godly, faithful, hard-working, loving, and affectionate husband. His wife is always stunned. This man uses pornography as a little bit of reward for being such a fine, upstanding man.

God says, "You think because you have the right to stand for Me that you also have the right to sin for yourself." That kind of dichotomy, that kind of duplicity, that kind of double standard brings down the judgment of Almighty God! It is the sin of imbalance. A Christian never lives so good that he can allow himself to do wrong. NEVER!

Jesus was telling all seven churches, "Let Me show you the imbalance that is bringing unholiness and ultimately damnation to your church."

The brilliant ploy of the Devil is that he did not destroy any of those churches; Jesus did. Satan just stands by watching as the pastor preaches and the people listen, and then he watches the church get imbalanced. Satan just sits back and watches Jesus Christ say, "Enough is enough." Satan does not kill the local church.

The church members kill a local church when they somehow think that if they are doctrinally sound, they do not have to care about the heathen in Africa. If doctrine does not compel a Christian to reach the nations, I do not care about his doctrine. If a student attends a Christian college that does not warm his heart to go reach the lost, then he is not learning real doctrine.

If I had my way, I would require every young man to spend his first two years in the dormitories so that he can learn to walk with God alone. A college boy needs to find out that the God of the Bible is big enough for him. He needs to call on the Lord God Jehovah and find out that the God of the Bible is his God and the Christ of the Bible is his Christ. He does not need to run home to his mama or to his daddy's wallet. The imbalance of a student dabbling in the classroom and never really getting fully involved in a ministry and never fully giving his heart to Christ will produce a cold, dead, half-indoctrinated, unholy Christian—an imbalanced Christian.

As First Baptist Church continues to grow, it must grow in balance. There must be good, solid, sound Bible teaching and preaching. We have to teach the King James Bible and why it is the right Bible. We must teach our members how to rear their children and how to build their marriages. We must get in the Scriptures and build ourselves on the solid Rock, Jesus, and the Word of God. However, First Baptist Church is also going to crank it up on Sunday nights and emphasize that the world is going to Hell, and that Heaven is real with a Saviour Who makes all the difference! Church members must keep their hearts hot. If learning does not increase love, a person will bring in license to sin. Churches become unholy because of imbalance.

Soul winners, how much Bible do you read? Bus workers, how are your grades in college? Sunday school teachers, how much time do you spend in the Word of God? Those of you who produce and walk souls down the aisle, do you know the Bible? If all a Christian does is give it and give it and give it and never take in the Word of God, he will eventually stop giving it and will die.

You may be a scholar that loves the Bible and knows all about the JEDP theory and why it is wrong. You may know the Graf-Welhausen theory and why that is wrong. You know all about the *Textus Receptus.* You know all about the Scriptures and the history of the King James Bible. However, when is the last time you personally won a soul to Christ? How big is your bus route? When is the last time you walked a sinner down the aisle? I know people who are brilliant in the Scriptures, and yet, they cannot win one soul to Christ.

One of my favorite Bible teachers in another Christian college I attended said to me after I had won 15 people to Christ at a state university, "You got 15 people saved? How do you do that?"

I thought, "What am I doing in a school where the top Bible teacher is asking a sophomore boy how to win souls?" Something was wrong with that picture! Hey, college teacher, are you letting the college boys show you up?

The unholy churches died because of imbalance. A holy church is a balanced church. The seven churches in Revelation were guilty of the sin of imbalance.

1. We must balance zeal with knowledge. In Romans 10:2, Paul laments that his nation Israel is not saved. He states, *"For I bear them record that they have a zeal of God, but not according to knowledge."* Notice the imbalance there: zeal without knowledge.

2. We must balance hearing with doing. In James 1:22, we are warned, *"But be ye doers of the word, and not hearers only, deceiving your own selves."*

3. We must balance marriage and ministry. When I was a college student, I heard guest speakers on occasion try to emphasize the importance of giving 100% to the Lord's work. They would make statements to prove their point. However, that authentication indicated they were also willfully neglecting their families and spouses. I decided, as a young preacher, that it was not necessary to choose between building a strong marriage and building a strong ministry. I believe it is not only possible, but necessary, to build both at the same time. I Timothy 3:5 states, *"For if a man know not how to rule his own* *house, how shall he take care of the church of God?"* Again, notice the balance.

4. We must balance vision and faith. It is very possible for a leader to let his own vision outdistance the faith of his followers. In our own situation here at First Baptist Church, it would be unwise for me to tell our congregation all that I believe the Lord would have us to do in the next quarter of a century. My vision is frightening. However, I tell them enough of my vision to encourage and stretch their faith for the next couple of years.

5. We must balance our reaching the poor with financing the ministry. I love the bus ministry. I was a bus captain in a poor city for 11 years. I absolutely love the bus ministry, but honestly, it was a huge financial drain on my pocketbook. The bus ministry costs money—much money. Here at First Baptist Church we spend over $1.2 million each year to run our buses. Those bus kids don't give money in the offering plate. Now, they might grow up in 20 years and become tithers and deacons and leaders, but a church can't build entirely on a bus ministry and stay healthy financially, unless it is being supported outside the membership. We teach our preachers to build their churches on the middle-class, mortgage-paying, car-payment-paying segment of society.

6. We must balance soul winning and service. Every Christian should be a soul winner. And as souls come to church and become involved, they need teaching and training and fellowship and friends and support. Many are addicted to sinful habits and need counseling. Many of them have broken or bruised relationships, their children need Christian schooling, and much more. That is why we have soul-winning ministries seven days a week, and on some days, several soul-winning opportunities are available. We also have 27 youth baseball teams in our church, men's softball, golf, and basketball, ladies' sewing, Women's Missionary Societies, boys' and girls' service clubs, a full music program, six Christian schools, and a Christian college, and much, much more. We balance getting the lost and training the lost.

There is no area that does not need careful watching lest it become imbalanced or unholy. An imbalanced Christian is a potentially dangerous Christian, just as an imbalanced tire could become dangerous on the highway. One of the great fears I have as I study the present "large-church movement" is this matter of imbalance. I see many churches focusing on seeker-sensitive issues at the expense of doctrine and proper church procedures. I see churches adopting very worldly music and entertainment at the expense of coming out from them and being separate. I see "bigness" imbalancing "godliness." I see methods of church growth imbalancing a simple love for all mankind and a love for the "one" lost sheep. I see the emphasis upon "come as you want" unbalancing *be not conformed to this world,*" and, "*be ye transformed.*" I see compromise becoming a very important concept in the church that is supposed to be built on the "Rock" of the unchanging Jesus Christ.

I also know that the word "balance" can be used by lazy, uncreative, and uncompassionate people to hide behind. I do not believe balance equals laziness. Just ask my church staff what I believe about laziness. I also believe, however, that it is possible to run a bus ministry and have the cleanest buildings in town. I believe it is possible to grow a large mega-church in a downtown area without compromising our music, our standards, our preaching, or changing our Bibles. As one great preacher of the past generation has often said, "Straight down the line! Never vary!" Great advice!

CHAPTER EIGHT

Cancers in the Growing Church

"Be watchful, and strengthen the things which remain, that are ready to die: for I have not found thy works perfect before God." (Revelation 3:2)

THE SEVEN CHURCHES described in the book of Revelation were located in Asia Minor. These churches at one time had been, or were at the time of the writing of Revelation, thriving, growing churches. There were many, many more churches in the world at this time. However, these seven churches were given as example churches.

There are some mistaken interpretations of this text. One interpretation that is prevalent in fundamentalism says that these seven churches are actually seven different time frames within the entire history of the local church from its early beginnings with the ministry of Christ until the Rapture when Jesus Christ comes and takes His born-again saints to Heaven.

For several years, I taught the book of Revelation at Hyles-Anderson College. I spent hundreds of hours in study of the book of Revelation and read many commentaries written on the book of

Revelation. I don't agree with this interpretation of the seven churches. Let me explain why I think this interpretation is a dangerous one.

The church of Ephesus was a very large, thriving, growing, and seemingly healthy church. In the Scofield Reference Bible, Mr. Scofield explains this interpretation of the different stages of the seven churches. This interpretation states that the church of Ephesus was the early stage, commonly called the apostolic age, immediately after Jesus Christ ascended to Heaven. Nothing in the Bible says that the church in Ephesus was the church at the end of the apostolic age.

After Revelation 2:7, Mr. Scofield writes, "The message to Smyrna. Period of the great persecutions, to A.D. 316."

I'm not sure where Mr. Scofield got his information. His statement sounds intelligent, but it's not in the Bible. I let the Bible interpret itself. I don't let a history book be my hermeneutics (the principles of how to study the Bible) teacher. I don't let a history book tell me how to interpret the Bible. I let the Bible tell me how to interpret a history book.

After Revelation 2:11, Mr. Scofield writes, "The message to Pergamos. The church under imperial favour, settled in the world, A.D. 316 to the end." After Revelation 2:17, he writes, "The message to Thyatira. A.D. 500-1500: the triumph of Balaamism and Nicolaitanism; a believing remnant." Mr. Scofield goes on describing what he believes to be different church ages. His heading at chapter 3 is, "The message to Sardis. The period of the Reformation; a believing remnant." I believe Mr. Scofield was a very good man, and I do not want to accuse him; yet, this teaching can be dangerous.

Some people say that these seven churches in the book of Revelation are snapshots of seven time periods varying in length. It seemed that no matter what commentary I read, the commentary stated that the present age is the Laodicean age. I picked up a commentary that was written around 1000 A.D. The writer said that because of the sorry condition of the church and its compromise, we know we are living in the Laodicean age. Many preachers believe the world is now in the Laodicean age because Christians are not what they are supposed to be.

I have a sneaking suspicion that Christians have never always been what they should be. Peter probably wasn't the Christian he should have been when he denied the Lord Jesus Christ. All the other disciples when they fled at Calvary probably weren't the Christians they should have been either. Christians always have been succeeding and failing, succeeding and failing, succeeding and failing—ever since the first Christian was called a Christian at the church of Antioch.

One of the dangers of this teaching is that if we are in the so-called Laodicean age, then the age of great growth is over; we are simply trying to hold on until Jesus returns any moment. That teaching puts the emphasis upon doing little and not building great ministries and not seeing multitudes saved. I am not interested in sitting around seeing if I can hang on 'til the end. I want to build something for God. I want to reach the world with the Gospel, and I believe with every fiber in my body that anyone who wants to believe God and work hard can do just that!

These seven churches are not seven time zones telling us God's chronology of the local church. They are not seven snapshots of eras of church history. No, they are seven snapshots of seven churches that existed in Bible days, and God chose those seven churches to typify what all churches can be at any given time.

First of all, I believe God is saying that any church, at any given stage of its life, could be typical of any one of those seven churches in Revelation. First Baptist Church could be a church of Ephesus at different times of its life or could be a church of Philadelphia or any of the other churches at different times of its life. These seven churches are representative churches of all churches, representing what all churches have been, what all churches are, and what all churches could be.

First Baptist Church of Hammond has been a pattern for many other churches. Many churches have been started, grown, peaked, declined, and now no longer exist. Those churches have gone through all seven stages in five to twenty-five years. Since its founding in 1887, First Baptist Church has gone through several phases. For instance, the church in Philadelphia was a very young, aggressively growing, and fragile church. When First Baptist Church was founded under Brother Allen Hill, it was a Philadelphian church.

The church at Smyrna was a persecuted church. First Baptist

Church has gone through different time periods of great persecution in its history. So, while the First Baptist Church was going through persecution, it could have been defined as a Smyrnian church. The church in Thyatira was the fastest growing church of all seven churches. The Bible says, *"I know thy works… and the last to be more than the first."* (Revelation 2:19) The church in Thyatira was growing faster at that time than during any time period of that church's history. I believe the First Baptist Church was a "Thyatiran" church after Brother Hyles came to Hammond in 1959 when it became an exceedingly zealous church and became the world's largest Sunday school in 1972.

I was recently talking with an architect about our new auditorium and was giving him some numbers. He said, "Go over those again."

I repeated what I had told him about First Baptist Church's being the world's largest Sunday school and having the world's largest bus ministry, the world's largest independent Baptist college, etc." He put down his pencil, scratched his brow, and said, "You've lost me. I've never heard so many 'world's largests….' How many people do you baptize a year? I'm in a Baptist church, and I have never heard numbers like those."

I told him, "On a low year, we baptize about 7,000 to 8,000. On a big year, we baptize 12,000 to 15,000."

"No, you don't," he incredulously said.

"Yes," I said, "we do."

He looked at me and asked, "Do you know what you have here? You've got the world's most incredible church."

"Yes, we do," I agreed.

A Thyatiran-type church is one that is just growing and abounding. There are times when the growth settles down and the church fights sin.

Sometimes issues arise in a church. I remember well a time when Brother Hyles paid his respects to a couple of church members who were bringing damnable heresies into the First Baptist Church. During his sermon, Brother Hyles looked right at a man and put him in his place. He said, "You're preaching heresy in my church!"

Brother Hyles once went out to the college and burned the ears of the faculty and staff and students! Brother Hyles spoke to the college chapel, and when he walked out, no one breathed for about 60 minutes. Brother Hyles let those have it who were spreading heresies, such as believing that a Christian could lose his salvation or live days and days without sinning and have a perfected nature. The church of Pergamos was infected with the doctrine of Nicolaitanes and the doctrine of Balaamism.

Hyles-Anderson College is an independent Baptist college. However, our students come from over a dozen different denominations. Those students are welcome to come, but they know that Hyles-Anderson College and First Baptist Church are independent Baptist. Students may disagree with our doctrines, but they have to keep their mouths shut if they want to stay at Hyles-Anderson. Sometimes students get in the dorms and talk about their pet teachings and pet heresies, such as speaking in tongues. Sometimes, because of issues such as these, First Baptist Church goes through a "Pergamosian" stage.

Not one of the seven churches in Revelation exists today. That tells me that the warnings that Jesus gave in Revelation chapters 2 and 3 came to pass. Jesus addressed His comments to the pastor of each church. The Bible says, "*Unto the angel of the church of Ephesus…*" and so on. The word *angel* comes from the Greek word *angelos* which means "messenger." The messenger of the church is the pastor.

For 41 years, Brother Hyles was the "angel" of First Baptist Church. Through the entire history of the First Baptist Church, there have been 14 different "angels," and I am now the fifteenth "angel" at First Baptist Church. Jesus wisely knew how to fix a problem by going directly to the person who has the power to fix the problem—the pastor.

Jesus said, "There are some things I like about your church, but you have a cancer in your church." Five of the seven churches had significant problems, and the other two had slight problems. They all had a weakness—a cancer. Jesus said, "If you don't take care of the cancer, it will eat at you and rot your church from the inside out; a day will come when you will no longer even be in existence."

First Baptist Church never has to die if it does not want to die. How many times have we heard Brother Hyles use the word "perpetuity." Brother Hyles taught that the local church has been promised divine perpetuity, which means the church can perpetually live on and on, if the church so chooses.

Jesus said in Matthew 16:18, "...I will build my church; and the gates of hell shall not prevail against it." The "gates of hell" represent two different things. First, gates in the Bible always represent city hall—the place of the government and political powers. Jesus said, "No authority of hell, no political king out of hell, and no demonic power can bring down my church!" Secondly, the "gates of hell" are holding in the sinners. Nothing can keep a church from doing what it ought to be doing. The church ought to be walking up to the gates of hell, kicking them open, and saying to all the lost sinners, "Hey! You're all in bondage. Let's get out and go to Heaven!"

Jesus said, "I'm going to build My church, and nothing can stop it—except the church itself."

Churches don't die from external pressures; they die from internal corruption. They die from internal poisoning and not external pressures.

First Baptist Church has a wonderful relationship with our mayor and his staff and workers at city hall. However, if the mayor and I did not get along well, that would not stop our church from functioning. First Baptist Church has a good relationship with our local councilmen, and we work hard to keep those good relationships. However, nobody externally can stop First Baptist Church from doing what we ought to be doing.

Sometimes external pressures do bring collapse of a church because the inside was rotten. A big, old tree can stand for years, and then a big gust of wind brings the tree down. The wind didn't really bring down the tree; it was the corruption inside. The wind just revealed the weakness of the tree. Sometimes external pressures can be profound, but if the internal cancer is not there, a church can stay strong as long as the church members want to stay strong. Our generation has an opportunity to pass on to another generation an heritage that there can still be an aggressive, growing, soul-winning, sanctified, filled-with-the-Holy-Ghost Baptist church—a church that is set apart for the purpose of winning souls and holding forth the Word of God. That is the choice of a church.

For a church to continue to have divine perpetuity, it is wise to look at some of the cancers that destroyed other churches—not to

criticize or belittle these churches or to point a finger at them—
rather to do some soul searching and asking ourselves, "Is it I?"
Christians should do an analysis of their own hearts and say, "Lord,
are You showing us a little cancer we may have in our own lives and
our own church?"

By looking at the cancers in these seven churches in Revelation,
we can put up a guard around our lives and our churches; just like
China did when it discovered the SARS disease spreading throughout the country and being carried to other countries. Many countries
launched programs to control the virus; and after several months,
the virus was controlled. When a forest fire is raging, it comes to a
point where the fire is out of control. The firefighters finally gain the
upper hand and contain the fire; the fire is then diminished and
extinguished, and eventually comes new growth. By discovering the
cancers in the seven churches in Revelation, these cancers can be
contained, controlled, extinguished, and cut out. Then a church can
reproduce and grow and grow.

Let's look at what the Bible says about the cancers in these
churches in Revelation. In each of these seven churches, something
was out of balance. One of the most dangerous things in an organization is for it to be out of balance. Have you ever seen a washing
machine out of balance? If you hang on tight, you can dance with it!
Imbalance can happen in an organization. Before you know it, a
whole lot of folk are upset with other folk, and the organization starts
"dancing" away from where it should be. Balance is the key. Each of
the seven churches had a strength; each church had a weakness.

1. Ephesus. (Revelation 2:1-7) According to Revelation 2:1-
3, the strength of this church was its doctrine. The church at
Ephesus was a hardworking church which had labored to maintain
its doctrinal integrity.

However, according to Revelation 2:4, the weakness of the
church in Ephesus was its diminished devotion. A church's devotion
must balance with its doctrine. A church must believe right and have
the right Bible, the right plan of salvation, the right Gospel, and the
right doctrinal statement. Many churches across America have the
same doctrinal statement as the First Baptist Church of Hammond
but their devotion ran out a long time ago. The only thing some
church members are devoted to is Monday night football or the

bowling league or the softball league. First Baptist Church has a few men who only come to church in order to fulfill the required number of church services they must attend to be allowed to play in our softball league. These men are not devoted to our church; they are devoted to softball.

A Christian's devotion to Christ must match his doctrine. A balance must be maintained. Some church employees or college employees attend church because they have to fill out an activity report. If you asked those same people to sign our church's doctrinal statement, they would gladly sign it. However, doctrine must have devotion—a passionate love that drives it so that doctrine is put into practice. Having a piece of paper that says, "I believe the Holy Scriptures were inspired by God and are divinely preserved in the King James Bible" is meaningless if a Christian doesn't take the King James Bible and read it and use it to tell someone how to get saved!

2. **Smyrna.** (Revelation 2:8-11) The strength of this church was faithfulness. Jesus said, "You folks have been under the incredible pressure of people who are trying to destroy your lives. They have taken your human possessions." These Christian people in Smyrna were being murdered; yet, they were faithful.

The weakness of this church was their fear. Their fear and faith were not in balance. There are young men in high school and college concerned with "What am I going to do with my life?" Many of them will bolt into sin rather than serve the Lord Jesus Christ because of one little four-letter word—F-E-A-R. Most of them love Christ and are faithful to church, but they are afraid. Still, many Christians have that same fear but overcome that fear with their faith. Such is the case of our China Mission Team. Some of these dear people walked away from high-paying jobs with six-figure incomes; yet, they gave it up for a few hundred dollars a month to go to China. These people taught in our Sunday schools and some of them in our Christian schools. They have the same fear each Christian has; yet, they overcame that fear with their faith and are now in Jilin City, China, teaching boys and girls. These missionaries said, "Yes, I too have fear, but I have an equal or greater amount of faith than fear."

I believe the number-one reason that good kids go bad is because they have been called to full-time Christian service as a young child, made the decision to serve Christ full time, but through the years, they started getting scared that they might really have to follow through with their childhood decision. Those fears began to imbalance and counterbalance their faith. These are kids who believe the Word of God and read the Bible and memorize the Bible, who pray every morning and night, who go to a Christian school, and who love Christ, but they are kids who are terrified that they might have to serve God. I believe the number-one reason kids in a church like First Baptist Church leave the will of God, break their parents' hearts, and run off into the dens of fornication and defilement and sexual promiscuity and immorality and pornography and alcoholism is not because they are not saved. No, I believe they are saved. Sin is the number-one escape for people who are scared they will have to go through with the decisions of serving God.

Laymen sometimes have a hard time understanding the testimony given by most preachers who stand in front of a large crowd. Those preachers often say, "You have no idea what I was like when I was a little boy." None of my church members knew me as a little boy. They did not see me when I cried every single day in first grade, second grade, third grade, and fourth grade—terrified to leave home to go to school. I stood off to the side during recess, sucking my thumb and watching my older sister play kickball.

The teacher would approach me and say, "What is wrong?"

I was just scared, mortified with fear that was totally unfounded, unwarranted, and unjustified. No bullies picked on me. I was just terrified that I was away from home. I've often thought, "Lord, why would You take somebody who couldn't even stand leaving home and put him in front of thousands of people and make him preach?" I was terrified of anything to do socially. There was a reason I was a really good boy and never got in trouble with a girl—I was terrified of girls! I never asked out a girl. I attended a public school full of pretty girls, but I was terrified of them.

How many times did Brother Hyles talk about his inferiority complexes and insecurities? That insecurity is very common. There are so many Gideons in this world. God has a habit of picking people like Moses, who was terrified to speak and stuttered when he spoke. Some of the greatest men in the Bible were terrified of serving God, but they went through with it anyway. Their faith overcame their fear.

First Baptist Church must overcome its fears. The day came when Brother Hyles no longer walked into the pulpit of the First Baptist Church. The church had to make a decision: Would we let fear captivate us and paralyze us as so many other big churches had unfortunately done, or would we match those fears with our faith and as the songwriter admonished,

> Rise up, O men of God.
> Have done with lesser things.
> Give heart and soul and mind and strength
> To serve the King of Kings.

We had our fear conquered by our faith. That is balance!

All Christians have fears. Many junior high and high school boys are full of mischief. They run to their girlfriends. They are scared to death to run to God because God has called them, but they are not like Samuel saying in I Samuel 3:10, "...*Speak; for thy servant heareth.*" Instead, they put on their headphones because they don't want to hear the voice of God. A boy spends time with his girlfriend so that her pretty face keeps him from thinking about the voice of God. That is why those same boys do not want to go to Christian youth camp. That is why they do not want to have their devotions. That is why they do not attend Teenage Soul Winning. They are scared to death! That's why they do not listen when I preach. They feel that if they can tune out the preacher, then God can't get in. God said to a church and to individuals, "If you let your fear outweigh your faith, then you have a cancer inside that will corrupt you. In a generation your church will be gone."

3. **Pergamos.** (Revelation 2:12-17) The strength of this church was their loyalty to the name of Christ. However, people who are extremely loyal to Christ often indulge in license. They take little liberties and little sins as rewards for their strong stand for Christ. Again and again I find in my counseling sessions that the perverts are not the ones who are in trouble; rather, it is the pure-minded, godly, righteous people who get in trouble because they say, "I've stood so firm for Christ. I've given so much. I've tithed so much. I give offerings. I've done so much for God. What harm will it do to me to take one look at a dirty magazine? What harm will flirting a little bit with another man's wife do to me? I'm not going to have an affair; I'm not

an adulterer. I'm just going to take a peek at an X-rated video. I'm not a pervert, God." These loyal Christians try to get by with these so-called little sins that devour marriages and corrupt the church. A Christian cannot allow his loyalty to be over-balanced by his license.

4. **Thyatira.** (Revelation 2:18-29) This church had great passion and was growing faster than it had ever grown in its history. I have never seen God do anything great without using a man of great passion! Never! I also do not know of one man of passion in the Bible who did not have a perversion. I have studied every great leader in the Bible. The same David who said, "Is there not a cause? I'll lift the head off of that big Goliath. Come on, big boy. I've got a little sling, and I'm going to take off your head and feed it to the buzzards!" also said, "Who is that woman over there bathing? Go get her for me." David had a perversion.

The same Samson who said, "Come on, you thousand Philistines. I've got the jawbone of a jackass in my hand. I'll kill every stinking one of you!" also said, "I want Delilah. Go get her for me."

A Christian who has the drive to do something great for God must make sure that drive is very, very controlled. Those who have the chutzpa to build a great ministry, those who have the drive and the passion to say, "I'll build a Sunday school class. I'll build a bus route," must keep passion in check. Some of the greatest bus workers are now out of the ministry, out of church, and not serving God. Some of the greatest, driven graduates of Hyles-Anderson College sometimes end up being the most disappointing. Those who have a great passion and great drive to rise up above a lazy crowd must make sure that their passion is held in check.

Since many passionate leaders in the Bible had a perversion, how can a passionate Christian keep perversion out of his life? The most important way I can keep from becoming perverted is to stay faithful to my wife. The moment I start thinking that my ministry is more important than my marriage, I become a pervert. Those who are driven and have a passion to do something great, who hunger for more preaching on how to build a church, who hunger to build their Sunday school class, must never fall for the lie that says you must choose between your marriage and the ministry. Some men come to Hyles-Anderson College and neglect their marriage while they are building a big bus route. When the ministry leaders here see some college man really getting fired up, he should ask him, "Are you staying fired up about that woman you call your wife?"

It would be a great shame for a man on the church staff if he did not reach his potential. It would be a greater shame for him to start on that rise to reach his potential, and for the Devil to snag him as he neglects his wife and brings shame and reproach to the cause of Christ. I'm not interested in building a big church at the expense of good marriages and at the expense of children. Parents have no guarantees that their children will turn out right, but I don't ever want a child to point his finger at Dad and say, "You are the reason I am living like the Devil because you never had time for me!"

If a child does not turn out for Christ, let him be able to go to God and say, "I no longer want to believe in You, but my dad is not at fault." Christians must not give the Devil or the community or the kingdom of darkness a place for perversion to excuse their passion for God.

Christianity needs men of passion. The risk is worth it. If I scripturally stay right with my wife and with my other relationships, stay right with my God, and don't give place for passion to be perverted, I can stay passionate and walk guard and say, "That is not going to happen in my life."

A prophetess on staff at the church in Thyatira was seducing the leaders in the church and committing adultery with them. God said, "Your church will be dead in one generation." Sexual sins poison fundamental churches. I can't emphasize that statement strongly enough. Christians have pumped too much of Hollywood's hell into their heads, and some of them actually think it is acceptable to have an adulterous affair. It is never acceptable to have an adulterous affair! It is out of Hell! Those who are guilty of sexual sins will poison the church.

Go ahead, Christian. Have your passion for God, but don't let perversion grab that passion and steer it toward perversity. Keep the fires hot at home! Shut off that stupid television once in a while and spend some time smooching with your spouse. If a man likes television more than he likes smooching, he is weird. I've watched television, and I've tried smooching. Bless God, television is not even close! If a man would rather go to a ball game with his buddies than take a walk around the block with his wife, he has fantasy problems.

I like a good ball game, but I love holding my wife's hand and taking a walk around the block, watching the sun go down and saying, "Let's get lost in the woods, baby, and do some nature hunting!" Too many men are eager to get excited with their wives before marriage, and then treat her like she is a lifeless mannequin after saying, "I do." Couples, you need to cool it down while you are dating and heat it up after you say, "I do."

First Baptist Church will not be built by sacrificing the marriages of our members. We are not going to put our marriages on the altar of indulgence and self-satisfaction and selfishness. I am not willing to sacrifice my marriage. Jesus Christ does not demand your marriage for His ministry! If marriage is a type of the union between the Christian and Christ, then if a Christian is sacrificing his marriage for the ministry, he is saying that he does not need to be yoked up together with Christ for the ministry. That's a lie out of Hell!

Fundamentalism needs a revival of husbands who love their wives. In churches like First Baptist Church, it is amazing in one week's time how many adulterous affairs a pastor has to counsel. Adultery is a sin against God. It is a sin against the church. It is a sin against the Bible. It is a sin against marriage. From the pulpit, I have seen women looking around like they are looking for adultery. Women, get your eyes on your husbands! Christians will criticize me for preaching this way from the pulpit, but then they go home and watch adultery on television. Christians have no problem at all watching a good-looking man and a good-looking woman crawl into bed together on a television screen. It is amazing how many Christians know all about the talk shows and Jerry Springer and all the smut and perversity of the world as the sewers of Hell run through their brains blatantly suggesting to them it is acceptable to fantasize about another's spouse.

Christians are getting on the Internet and flirting with mystery people on a glass screen. Since I began pastoring, a week has not passed that I have not counseled with someone who has left his marriage because of the Internet. Those Christians are bringing damnation to First Baptist Church and reproach to the name of Christ and shame and reproach to everything that is good and godly in this country.

Recently, the Supreme Court called God a liar and said that

homosexuality is acceptable. That decision is a wicked sin against God. However, those Christians who fantasize about having an adulterous affair have no right to lift one eyebrow about the Supreme Court's decision! Whoremongering is whoremongering is whoremongering! Flesh is flesh. Just because sodomy sounds so repulsive to red-blooded American men does not make adultery better. It doesn't make pornography better. It is time for red-blooded men who get hot under the collar to get hot under the collar for their wives. Shut off that stupid television! Shut off that stupid Internet! Find your spouse again and replay the honeymoon. Stay hot and stay happy with your spouse. The church does not need those who have a passion and those who do great things for God to become perverts in the ministry and place a generational curse on the ministry.

First Baptist Church should be the holiest place in Hammond. First Baptist Church members ought to be the cleanest group of people in the world. I love those sinners who come to First Baptist Church. There is a balm of Gilead here. There is forgiveness at Calvary. However, I am not interested in a bunch of people coming to the altar and saying, "Okay, I'm going to make a pretense; but as soon as I get home, I'm getting those magazines out again."

A Christian's holiness must be more than just an act. Other people should be able to look at another Christian and say, "That's a righteous husband," or "That's a righteous mom," or "That's a righteous dad." Dads, your kids ought to be able to look at you and say, "He's not a perfect father," but never let them be able to say, "He's a perverted father." Be holy! Be pure!

Sometimes I sit in my office or lie on my face by the hour, and I can't even talk to God because I'm so stunned by some of the perversity I hear in counseling sessions. This perversity includes sins and crimes against decency and righteousness that are filthy and disgusting. Our nation is in trouble. I have always preached that when a nation makes laws to protect sodomites, that nation is in trouble with God. God bless Mr. Rehnquist, Mr. Scalia, and Mr. Thomas who had the moral fortitude to stand up and say, "This is not right." Those other six justices are in trouble with God.

A nation cannot make a law that says that the Bible is not wanted. Neither can a nation adopt laws that say, "God, we don't want to talk to You. You're not welcome in our schools." The Supreme Court made that statement to God in 1963. Now that Court has gone way beyond that law and said, "Not only is the Bible not welcome, but the perverts, who are condemned by the Word of God are protected by the law." Romans chapter 2 declares that a nation that is guilty of upholding sodomites is in trouble with God.

I am a man of passion. My wife has often described me with the word "passion." I have a passion for God that is indescribable. I love God, and I would do anything for Him. However, studying men of great passion has caused me to build huge walls around my passion and to say to God, "God, I'm not going to be one of those men who fall into perversity." The answer is partly my wife and partly my staying within a schedule of righteous living that allows my passion to stay focused on God. If a person points that passion at anything, it becomes the object of his desire.

Some Christians have a passion for the material goods of this world. They have used their passion that could win the world for Christ and focused that passion on acquiring material goods. They have wasted their passion. Some have taken a passion for the mission field and wasted it on material goods. Others have taken a passion for the pulpit and wasted it on perversion. Many have taken that energy and have prostituted it away from God.

The only hope this old country has is for righteous congregations like First Baptist Church to lay aside their perversity and say, "God, for the sake of my nation, I will walk holy before my God and before my children." A revival of clean, decent, holy living needs to be in every home, in every church, and in every heart.

Mr. Scofield was a good man who now knows his interpretation of the churches representing different church ages was wrong. I am sure that Brother Hyles has corrected Mr. Scofield on this fallacy of teaching!

CHAPTER NINE

Balancing the Past with the Present

"And unto the angel of the church in Sardis write: These things saith he that hath the seven Spirits of God, and the seven stars; I know thy works, that thou hast a name that thou livest, and art dead." (Revelation 3:1)

WHEN I WAS a freshman in college, I was enraptured with the teaching of theologians regarding the seven different church ages, and I thought it was very intriguing. However, as I studied the Bible, I found this teaching was a bunch of baloney. I was relieved when I found out Brother Hyles thought this teaching was a bunch of baloney, too! I felt vindicated. Every theologian I have ever read states that he felt he was living in the Laodicean Age, whether that theologian lived 1,000 years ago or is presently living.

One reason I believe theologians teach this is because the Laodicean Age was a compromised age, and it appears that Jesus is just about ready to return. It appears that not much church building can go on. My personal opinion is that theologians write that because they are too cotton-pickin' lazy to go out and knock on doors and build bus routes. Or maybe these theologians tried building a church and failed, so now they would rather tell everyone that building a church can't be done. They write books instead!

This business of church ages is not in the Scriptures. The reason I do not like or believe this theory is because my heart is set on church growth, not on church excuse. I'm not looking for an excuse as to why First Baptist Church of Hammond cannot go to the next stage of growth. During the fall of 2003, First Baptist Church started 17 new adult Sunday school classes. Our goal with those classes is to multiply and divide and then multiply and divide. In the next five to ten years, I would like to have 100 new adult Sunday school classes in our church.

If I believed that we are living in the "Laodicean Age," starting new Sunday school classes would be the stupidest thing I could ever do. If I believed we are living in the Laodicean Age, I would just get comfortable in my pulpit and tend the flock God has given me and let the law of attrition peel off church members as they die or move away until eventually the church could meet in the two center sections of the auditorium and talk about the glory days of the past and the good old days when Brother Hyles used to be here. What wonderful days all the way from Reverend Hill to Brother Hyles—weren't those the glory days! Now we'll just kind of coast along.

No! I'm not a coaster! I've got too much drive in me to coast. I want to do something for God! As I look at the Bible, I find that God wants to do something also.

We must look at these seven churches and figure out what went wrong with them because none of those seven churches exists today. If they no longer exist, that means that something, some disease got into those churches and killed them. When a cancer invades a church and grows in that church, it rots the church from the inside out until it collapses.

Our neighbor had a giant tree fall over in our yard recently during a wind storm in our area. That tree had been rotting on the inside and eventually collapsed because the external wind revealed the internal disease. Just like that tree, these seven churches in Revelation had an internal disease that collapsed them.

Previously, we discussed some of the diseases of these churches. A type of imbalance was the cancer in all of these churches. A church out of balance eventually crashes. If one wing is removed from an airplane, it will eventually crash; both wings are needed for the plane to fly. Every person, every church, every marriage, every relationship must have the two wings of balance. For instance, you must have love in a family, but with love you must have discipline. All love and no discipline will produce spoiled rotten children. All discipline and no love will produce bitter, harsh, unfeeling, inconsiderate and almost rebellious children.

These seven churches in Revelation show us the imbalance that created a catastrophe and eventually brought about the downfall of each of those seven churches. In Ephesus, they had a difficult time balancing doctrine with devotion. They were very theological, but they didn't have much of a heart for God. They had left their first love and were an uncaring, unloving, unfeeling church that was right on the target with their statement of faith.

The church in Smyrna could not balance their faith and fear. They were terrified of losing their church and terrified of losing their lives. They lived in constant fear. One of the greatest tools the Devil uses to keep a Christian from serving God is the tool of fear. College graduates are afraid to start a church, afraid to go to the mission field. It takes courage to go the Congo. It takes courage to go to Jilin City in China. It takes courage to go to Mexico. It takes an individual who says, "I am willing to overcome my fear."

The word *faith* means "overcoming your fear." Faith is strapping those skis on your feet and going down the hill when your heart is pounding, your throat is dry, and you have no idea what is at the bottom. God says that you have to balance fear with faith—not foolishness, but faith.

The church in Pergamos was a loyal church, but with that loyalty, the people were taking liberties with sin. They felt that God wouldn't mind their license to sin because they had been loyal to Him.

Thyatira had passion for God which became a perversion. The staff was guilty of adultery.

The imbalance of the church of Sardis was the past versus the present. Jesus said, *"Thou hast a name that thou livest."*

First Baptist Church of Hammond has enjoyed a tremendous name through the years. What a name with 41 Pastors' Schools! What a name hosting our 31st annual Youth Conference! What a name in 1972 being called the "World's Largest Sunday School" and holding that title for many decades! What a reputation when Brother Hyles was pastor for 41 years and 5 months!

What *"a name that thou livest"* with Hyles-Anderson College, the largest independent Baptist college of its kind in the nation. What *"a name that thou livest"* with turning out 300 missionaries, more than any other Christian college of like kind. What *"a name that thou livest"* with 700 senior pastors pastoring as graduates from Hyles-Anderson College across the country. What *"a name that thou livest"* with over 1,000 preachers preaching in pulpits around the globe. What *"a name that thou livest"* with our school teachers who have seven positions available for every one graduate from our college. *"Thou hast a name that thou livest."* First Baptist Church has the world's largest bus ministry under the leadership of Dr. John Francis and Dr. Roy Moffitt. Nobody else comes close.

I was talking to a man about our church recently. He said, "Name your top men." I gave him the names of my men who are great producers and loyal helpers in our ministry.

He then asked, "What kind of man do you have in your bus ministry?"

I said, "I could pick up the phone and make one phone call and have 5,000 more people next Sunday." What *"a name that thou livest"*!

First Baptist Church has all these wonderful conferences. We host the Christian Womanhood Spectacular, the largest fundamental ladies' convention. We have an Educators' Convention. We have Pastors' School every March. Our files are filled with letters about these conferences' changing the lives of Christians. I received a letter from a man who said, "I'm not even a Baptist, but I came to Pastors' School, and my church has grown from 150 to 350 in the 12 weeks since I attended Pastors' School. People ask, "What is going on with your church?"

I tell them, "Go to Hammond the third week in March, and you will find out what I found out." *"Thou hast a name that thou livest."*

The influence First Baptist Church has, the missionaries and preacher boys we have, the college and the Christian schools we have, the preaching the First Baptist Church congregation heard under Brother Hyles' ministry—all these show that we were spoiled rotten and spoon-fed by a master pulpiteer. First Baptist Church has soul-winning organizations like Phoster Club. Hundreds of churches have Phoster Clubs because of the influence of First Baptist Church of Hammond. Hundreds of churches have Fishermen's Clubs because of the example of First Baptist Church of Hammond. We have been privileged to be copied across the world. Truly it could be said about the First Baptist Church of Hammond, *"Thou hast a name that thou livest."*

Wow! Hasn't First Baptist Church enjoyed a good life? How many times has the altar been jam packed! For over 44 years, there has not been a Sunday in First Baptist Church when someone has not been baptized in our baptistery. In 2002, twenty thousand folks walked an aisle at First Baptist Church trusting Christ as Saviour. That number doesn't include the 8,000 to 10,000 saved on special days like our Teenage Soul-Winning marathon. It doesn't include the 29,000 people our teenagers won to Christ on the streets in 2002 or all of the souls won by college kids while visiting on their bus routes on Saturdays. That number doesn't include the folks won to Christ by the Phoster Club or the Fishermen's Club or the Gospel League Home ministry and the homeless ministry and the nursing home ministry and the truck stop ministry and the sailor ministry. That number does not include the 48,000 who professed faith in Christ on one day in multiple services.

First Baptist Church has a great past. We have a past that Charles Spurgeon's Tabernacle once had. We have a past that the First Church of Oberlin, Ohio, had under Charles G. Finney. We have a past that Moody Memorial Church had when D. L. Moody graced their pulpit. Yet, if I know history, I believe First Baptist Church of Hammond has had a greater past than all three of these churches together. Charles Spurgeon baptized 700 in a great year. First Baptist has had days when we baptized 5,300 in one day. What a phenomenal past!

When I became pastor of the First Baptist Church, it became apparent to me that God was not going to allow First Baptist Church to fall victim to the historical blunder of great churches dying. When the pulpit committee called me and asked me to consider the pastorate of First Baptist Church, I asked them, "Why did you choose me?"

The men answered, "It's because of what you said."

I said, "Well, I've always said, 'Only a fool would take the pulpit of the First Baptist Church.' "

Terry Duff, one of our deacons, slyly remarked, "That's why we are asking you, Brother Schaap."

Shortly after becoming pastor, I looked over the audience and saw a large group of people in the back with no place for them to sit. We had to open up the mezzanine section, which in the past had been closed off during the summer while our college students are gone home. We had to put out extra chairs even in the summertime. When I realized our church was not dying, but was actually growing, I got more scared because I thought, "What does that mean for the future?"

Where are we going to go if this church grows? Where are we going to put everybody? That means a new building. That means money. That means fund raising. Suddenly, I understood what Brother Hyles meant. He said that when First Baptist Church became the "World's Largest Sunday School" and he needed advice, he realized he had no one to whom he could go because no one else had a church larger than ours, so I have no one to whom to go.

Many times I fall on my face and say, "Tell Brother Hyles I know exactly how he felt. I don't know to whom to go to ask, How do I take this church to the next level of growth?" I've told the Lord that if First Baptist Church is going to grow, I want to be sure no cancer stops the growth process. I don't want to mix something wrong in the ingredients that would kill this church for the next generation. I'm not interested in building our church for my generation, only to kill it for the next generation. I believe, should the Lord tarry His coming, First Baptist Church should live on and grow and live on and grow for decades to come. We must be careful not to be infected by the same cancer as the church in Sardis: an imbalance of the past and the present.

The past is a wonderful tool; however, if it is not a tool, it will preoccupy the Christian's life. Many decide to park themselves in the past. Many church members decide to park in their past. They remember the glory days when they produced in the church. They remember the days when they were teaching a Sunday school class or running a bus route and when they brought scores of visitors for Fall and Spring Programs. They remember the past when they were helping to build what we now look at as the glorious past.

Dr. Bob Marshall gave me a book written in 1973 which listed the top churches in independent, fundamental circles. The list did not include all of the largest churches. However, they were churches that were coming on strong and making a mark on fundamentalism. These were the churches pastored by those men who preached at the Sword conferences with Dr. Rice and Brother Hyles.

After I read it, I said, "Brother Bob, I wonder how these churches are doing today." One of Brother Marshall's staff members called these churches to find out how they were doing 30 years later. Let me share those results.

In South Carolina, there was a church that was running 504 in 1973. They are averaging 1,500 now with the same pastor. That fact is exciting and encouraging to me.

A church in Georgia was running 2,109 and now averages 400. In Florida, a church which averaged 3,400 in 1973, now averages 2,200. Another church in Florida went from 2,300 to 700. A church in Ohio which ran 1,900 in 1973 merged with another church, and the two of them combined are averaging 700. Another church in Ohio averaging 2,000, now averages 500. A church in Kentucky running 1,800, now runs 300. A church in Maryland running 1,655 in 1973 now runs 500 to 800. A church in Texas running 1,745, now averages 1,500. A church in Ohio running 800, now runs 50. A church in North Carolina running 1,200, now runs 700. A church running 3,000 in Michigan, now runs 150. A church in Colorado running 2,600, now runs 600. Another church in Ohio running 1,000, now runs 500. A church in Tennessee running 650, now runs 1,200. Of those 15 churches, only two of them are doing better than they were 30 years ago, 13 of them are doing worse. I don't want that ever to happen to First Baptist Church of Hammond.

Several years ago, I took some contest winners to Oberlin, Ohio, to visit Oberlin College and the great First Church of Oberlin where Charles Finney pastored in the 1800's. Oberlin College is the prettiest campus you would ever want to see. The church was a gorgeous little church and seats about 1,600. On the main floor was the actual pulpit with the actual Bible from which Charles Finney preached when he was the pastor. We chatted with a couple of staff members who came into the auditorium. They were very kind and friendly.

They gave us a beautiful booklet which recorded the glorious past of the First Church of Oberlin and the great heyday of Charles Finney called, "*The History of the First Church*."

I asked, "What did this church average in the days of Charles Finney?"

One man said, "Charles Finney packed out this place, and it seats 1,600. Hundreds of people were saved."

I asked, "What does the church run today?"

The man answered, "Oh, on a good day about 70."

I talked with the men who were with me and said, "How does that make you feel when you realize a church has nothing but a *"name that thou livest?"* How would you like to be those 70 people who attend church here and realize that you are sitting where history was made?

We knelt around the pulpit and put our hands on Charles Finney's Bible, and we asked God to use us in a mighty way. I said, "God, do it again. Please raise up great preachers in this group here."

We walked on down the campus and came to a huge auditorium built in honor of Charles Finney by his son. I walked inside the auditorium, and several college ladies were sitting behind folding tables. A sign was posted on the table that said, "Register here for the National Organization of Women Conference." Above those ladies was a bust of Charles Finney on a shelf. I walked up to the girls and shook their hands. I asked, "What's going on here today?"

One of them said, "The vice president of the National Organization of Women is speaking. Can we help you or answer any questions?"

"Sure," I said as I pointed above her head. "That bust of that man on that display shelf above you, who is that?"

One of the girls read the sign below the bust and said, "Charles G. Finney."

I asked, "Do you know who that is?"

"He was the founder of Oberlin College," a girl said as she looked at another girl, and then asked, "wasn't he?"

The other girl said, "He was the leader here."

I asked, "Do you know anything about him?"

One of the girls laughed and said, "We've heard some stories. Do you want to hear them?"

"Yes, I would," I answered.

"He was a real fundamentalist, conservative kind of a nut," the girl continued. "They had really weird rules on this campus back in those days."

"Like what?"

"Girls couldn't even go in a boy's dorm back then," she declared.

"You've got to be kidding," I responded.

"Not only that," she said. "You couldn't even hold hands."

"You've got to be kidding!"

"We knew you would think it was crazy," she said. "Have you ever heard of any place like that in the world?"

I looked at the other fellows with me and said, "I don't know. Have you ever heard of any place like that?" We kept playing dumb, and they kept telling us more and more.

My group then headed toward the bookstore in the Student Union area. We walked inside the student union, and above our heads, a huge banner was hanging that said, "Gays and Lesbians Speak Out." I walked inside the student union, and all around the room were couples of guys. Inside the bookstore, I stood near two fellows who were breaking up. It was the sorriest conversation I have ever heard in my life. I stood there looking for a barf bag in which to vomit. One was stroking the hair of the other guy and saying, "I'm really going to miss you. This has been a sweet, wonderful relationship."

I stood there thinking, *"This is a college that Charles G. Finney operated."* My heart burned. I felt like Paul when he was at Athens as his spirit burned inside of him, and I wanted to stand up and say something. I called my group together and said, "I can't believe this is happening."

We were leaving the steps of the First Church, and Brother Bob Marshall came running up behind me and said, "Fellows, I just talked to a sophomore man. As he was going up the steps, I stopped him to chat with him and won the fellow to Christ. Let me tell you his story. When I asked the fellow 'If you died today, would you go to Heaven?' tears burst from his eyes. He grabbed me and said, 'Mister, do you know how to get saved?' I said, 'Yes, I do.' That sophomore had been on campus for two years and had asked every student and every professor how to go to Heaven. He said, 'I'm so scared of going to Hell.

I want to know how to go to Heaven when I die. Can you tell me?' Not one student or professor could tell him how to go to Heaven."

Can you imagine the day at Hyles-Anderson College when not one professor or student would be able to tell a sophomore how to go to Heaven if he wanted to get saved. That sounds almost ridiculous. However, churches and colleges and ministries get imbalanced. They allow the past to become the grand, old glorious past, and they are not making a wonderful, glorious hot present.

If First Baptist Church wants to have *"a name that thou livest,"* we could sit back like the First Church of Oberlin and Charles Spurgeon's Tabernacle and like the Moody Church. When my dad was here to visit one time, I took him to Moody Church for a tour. There was a rock concert going on with a bunch of teenagers dancing around like animals in frenzy. We left the concert and walked down the halls to an old storage room. We could see through the window a picture of D. L. Moody. A janitor came walking by.

I asked him, "Is that a picture of D. L. Moody in there?"

The janitor answered, "Yes."

I asked him, "Are you going to do anything with that picture?"

He said, "No. Nobody wants anything to do with that guy."

Back at Oberlin, I took the fellows to a huge monument that was built in honor of the Chinese missionaries and the thousands of Christians that had been slaughtered when Communism took over China. We walked over to the monument and had to clear away the beer cans from off the monument to find a place to sit down. Dozens of half-filled beer cans from an obvious party the night before littered the place. I thought about the statue of Brother and Mrs. Hyles at Hyles-Anderson College and feared the day would come that there would be beer cans around their statue.

How does that decay happen? Good, godly people build a great past and then, as a monument, they just look at that past and say, "Wow! Look what we did. Look at the bus ministry we did build. Look at the Fishermen's Club we had. Look at the monuments we did have. We were the world's largest Sunday school. We did have the world's largest bus ministry. Those sure were great ministries we used to have." The past becomes a huge monument—a beautiful, faded picture that we can bow down and worship. Or a Christian can say, "The past is not to be worshiped. The past was to school us in how to build a great present."

One day my family was cleaning out and remodeling our basement. We found several trophies won by my daughter and son. I asked my children, "Do you want to keep these?"

Both of them looked at the trophies and said, "No. Wonderful memories, but that's not where I want to live."

I felt more sentimental getting rid of the trophies than Jaclynn and Kenny did. The past becomes a monument with tarnish. The colors fade.

First Baptist Church of Hammond is very close to having the same thing happen as happened at Oberlin and Spurgeon's Tabernacle and Moody Church if our members "used to." I'm not interested in how we "used to." I want to know how we did this past Sunday morning! I don't want Brother Hyles to be a memory. I want people, for years, to walk in and say, "Thank you, Brother Hyles, for building First Baptist Church. We're keeping it going, bless God!"

I don't want sophomores learning how to get saved! I want sophomores bringing converts down the aisle! It is never the time for church members to sit back and take it easy.

I don't like reading history much; I like making it. I do enjoy reading some history; however, ten thousand times more than I like reading history, I want to do something today that people can study later on. I want to build something! I want to grow! I want to say to Brother Hyles, "I did learn something from you."

Our church has a Pastors' Hall of Fame which has pictures of the 14 pastors of the First Baptist Church. Each picture has a description of the ministry during that pastor's term. Those men taught me something—not just to go out to their picture and bow down to them. They are pastors who said, "I've got an opportunity, and I'm going to do something with it."

1.   **The past is either an asset or a liability.** The past either condemns one or builds one's confidence. Past success condemns present failure. Past failures rob one of the confidences he needs for the present. If a Christian has a failed past in his life, more than likely he is sitting down and sucking his spiritual thumb believing that he is finished and can never do anything great again for God. What a miserable use of the past!

Many of our mission men have learned from their past of getting drunk and smoking dope. Recently, two of our mission men ran across the street and stopped me. One said, "I want to share something with you that I got from my Bible, Brother Schaap." The other said, "I had a prayer answered, Brother Schaap." Those men are learning from their past.

A couple with a wrecked marriage sat in my office the other day. They displayed feelings of distrust, anger, fear, worry, and contempt for one another. The man stated, "I messed up before. Why can't my wife leave it alone?"

I said, "This is the baggage that comes with sin."

God judged your sin at Calvary, but the baggage that comes from rotten living is the baggage you carry with you with fear and distrust. I wonder if that man has learned anything from it. Has he learned anything beside the fact that his wife doesn't trust him? Has he learned how to walk more carefully? Has he learned how to walk holy and purely and honestly and righteously so his wife will trust him? It's amazing to me how many people live in the past, suck their spiritual thumb, and say, "I blew it. God can never use me."

They need to get that stupid thumb out of their mouths, stand up, dust off that crummy residue of remorse and guilt and start marching on to the present.

A Christian cannot sit back and let sin conquer him every day with his remorse and guilt and regret. He has to get on his hind legs and do something for God! Those people in the Congo don't care about a person's past.

A young man said to me, "I made a big blunder, Brother Schaap. I probably can never be used of God."

I said, "Did God call you to preach?"

He said, "Yes, Sir, but I made a big mistake."

I said, "The people in Jilin City, China, don't give a flip about what you did. You're going to suck your thumb and let the world go to Hell because you made one stupid mistake?! There are 280 million Americans that might not let you preach to them, but 96% of the world's population does not care if you fornicated during some sinful moment during your dating life. Get out there on the mission field!"

What that fallen preacher wants is his pulpit he forfeited. He wants all the fame and glory that he thought he had before he took a tumble in sin. That past is like a chain about his neck saying,

"That's when I really had the power of God."

He must stop fretting and say, "It's over. What can I do now?"

When a preacher makes excuses about his past, what he really wants is an American pulpit and a church who will give him a fat-cat salary so that he can be a big shot again. That preacher needs to humble himself, remove himself from his past, and get busy in his present!

The past is done. I have a God who doesn't say, "I was what I was." No, He says, "I am that I am!" God is a God of today. The past is meaningless and worthless relative to today's opportunities. Some Christians need to visit their past and say, "Trophies of the past and great successes of the past are going to the dumpster because I am not going to live in the past anymore." The past is not simply for memory's sake.

Mama, your little boy who is now 25 years old is no longer a junior-age boy sitting on your lap saying, "I'm going to marry you." No, he is now a man. The past is not for memory's sake; the past was a school that parents used to build that man.

If a Christian lives in the past, he will waste his present, and thus, give a horrible past to those he meets in the future. If the past was so good, then why are some people so cotton-pickin' selfish and ruining the future's past? The future generation looks to our generation and says, "Would you give us something? Would you give us something called 'our past' that we can enjoy also?"

If I park myself in the past and say, "You don't understand how great it was in my days. You should have been at First Baptist Church back in the days of Brother Hyles. You can't imagine what it was like when I was in high school. I set all the records. I have trophies. I hit home runs." Then what am I giving to the future? Our generation's present is passed on to the future which is the past of the future generation. When our present is done and we have wasted our lives sitting in the past, the future comes back and says, "I'm ready to receive from you the past." However, there will be nothing to give the future—nothing but wasted years.

If First Baptist Church lives in its past, the children who are now two or three years of age, who did not know Brother Hyles, will not have a past and say, "Wasn't it great under Brother Hyles' ministry?" because they weren't under Brother Hyles' ministry. Some members want to sit back and suck their thumbs and say, "It will never be like the old days again."

The future generation does not have any old days. Those members are killing the future generation's past. The future generation's past will be filled with a mother who never let them grow up or a dad who always talked about the good old days. I refuse to do that to the future generation. I have to do all I can now, preach the sermons I have now, win the souls I can now, build the bus route I can now, love the people I can now, give myself now; so when the future comes, I can say, "I'll give you the same Bible Brother Hyles gave me. I'll give you the same truth Brother Hyles gave me. I'll give you a great past because your past is my present, and I'm going to give you something worth having."

2.   **The past is not a trophy to display, but a character to live.** What did I learn from all my days growing up, from all my wonderful feats of accomplishment or my mediocre living or my sin? I learned a character that I can take into the present and do something with that character. If all that a man learns from basketball, baseball, and football is a dust-covered trophy that Mama saves as a keepsake in his room, he is a flop. What a waste of Dad's money for basketball shoes! What a waste of Dad's getting off work early to watch the games! What a waste of a coach who sacrificed and loved and invested in that player!

How about the character to show up on time? How about the discipline to pull together the team? How about the work ethic? How about the "We're-down-in-the-ninth-inning, but-we-can-rally-and-win-this-thing" spirit. What did that teenager learn back there in his youthful days? How to chase the cheerleaders? What did he learn back there? How to tell dirty stories on the bus? What did he learn back there? How to waste time for mom and dad and realize later on when it is too late how good he had it back home? All the effort of the past is usually nothing more than trophies and plaques that become dusty and eventually end up in the garbage. Most people learn nothing from the past other than trivializing the present and thus robbing the future.

3.   **The past should be a spark plug, not a boat anchor.** Many a mother tries to pull her boy from the present back to the past while ignoring her husband in the present. Her husband sits there and says, "Thirty years ago, I had an affectionate woman. Thirty years ago, we

had romance and puckering up time. Thirty years ago, I took her for a ride, and we wound up in lover's lane having the time of our lives. What have we got now? Our son's room, 20 years later, is still preserved like it was the day he left for college."

When my daughter got married, within two weeks her bedroom became a laundry room! My wife and I didn't rear our daughter for a trophy. We reared her for her husband. We reared her for the work she is doing—teaching piano at our schools. We reared her for the Sunday school class that she and her husband teach. I reared her to make an eternal difference in the lives of young kids. I didn't rear my kids for a trophy!

Those women who live in the past will also relive their lives in the grandkids. Men are the same way. A man's football career was cut short because of a broken leg or bum deal or maybe because he wasn't as good a player as he thought he was.

Let's be honest. Most men's exploits are just a bunch of hot air. Very few people were ever as good as they think they were and usually a whole lot less than what they tell they were. A dad says, "Back when I was in high school...." That dad is living in the past, trying to bring his boy back there and say, "Why aren't you like your old dad? Your old man had it."

Parents need to walk out of the past and get in the future where their kids are. Some need to look at their 25-year-old son or daughter and say, "Excuse me, I forgot you grew up. I'm proud of you, and I believe in you. I'm here if you need me. However, we are going to go on with our lives."

I have as great a past as any man could want. I have great parents. I had grandparents who doted on me, loved me, and taught me. My dad taught me to work, taught me a trade, and taught me integrity and honesty.

Somebody asked me the other day, "Why do you think First Baptist Church is doing so well financially?"

I believe it is partly because my dad taught me how to handle money and how to be wise with money. I was won to Christ by my sister when I was five-years-old. I have a mother who prayed me into the ministry. What a heritage! What a past I have! I still don't know what beer tastes like. However, I am not going to live in my past. I will go on. Some don't have as good a past as I do. Good past or bad past, each person still must go on.

First Baptist Church has a great past, but it must go on. I will go on. My past, I'll place behind me. I've got a present I must live, which will be somebody's past when I turn it over to them. I want to give to the future generation the best past that I can give to them.

When I look at Brother Hyles' picture, I think, "What a past!" For three years, every Thursday for three to four hours Brother Hyles taught me how to pastor this church. After I got engaged on June 1, 1978, he met with me once monthly for a year to tutor me on how to be a good husband. Precious memories—memories of being scolded, nurtured, lectured, taught, instructed, preached to—what a past!

I remember walking down Baptist City streets and praying, "God, I'm going to ask You for the most selfish, ridiculous request. Everyone wants this, but I'm going to ask it of You. All these college preacher boys would love to get to know Brother Hyles. I don't even know what I'm asking, but could I get to know Brother Hyles in an unusual way like nobody else knows him."

I used to sit at the Hyles' table eating, and while watching Brother Hyles eat, I'd think, "God, I get to eat at the table with the man I wanted to get to know." God has spoiled me with a wonderful past, but I must leave the past and go on to the present.

I am going to hand over my present to the future someday, and I want my future to look back and say, like I did about Brother Hyles, "What a past Brother Schaap gave me." I want the little children to exclaim, "Wow, was I ever lucky to go to First Baptist Church of Hammond!" I want little boys who become 45-year-old men to one day say, "What a past I had." And then I want those men who are now little boys to one day look at their past and say, "I had a great past, but now I must walk away from it because I have a future to live."

In Revelation 3:10, the Bible says of Sardis, "... *thou hast a name that thou livest, and art dead.*" Why were they dead? Because they were living in the past and not the present. What a Christian used to do is not important! What is he doing now? An older Christian may have to run a little slower and not put in as many hours as he once did, but his focus should be the same. The mistake Christians make is they change their focus and their speed.

Brother Johnny Colsten, my associate pastor, is numb on the

entire left side of his body from a stroke. You wouldn't know it because he works seven days a week. He's in his middle sixties. Many men like him become too busy or too old for their bus route, but it's amazing how they have time to go fishing. They're not too old to fish 12 to 14 hours a day. It is amazing how much energy people have left to sin, but not enough energy to teach their Sunday school class.

I saw an older, white-haired man driving a fancy sports car. He had a lady next to him that looked like she was about 25 years old. He had his wrinkled, feeble arm around her. I thought, "He has enough energy to do that. However, if you asked him to come to church, he would probably say, 'I just am not strong enough or well enough to come to church.'

Older folks, you may not have as much gas in your tank, but your vehicle should be headed in the same direction. Mary Ruth Harrington, an 84-year-old lady in our church, is still teaching a Sunday school class every Sunday!

Say, Christian, why don't you get out of the past and build a great present so that the future can thank you for giving them a great past.

CHAPTER TEN

Quantity Vs. Quality

"...For thou hast a little strength, and hast kept my word, and hast not denied my name." (Revelation 3:8)

GOD TOLD THE church in Philadelphia that they did not have much, but they did have something. They didn't have a lot of strength, but they did have a little strength. God said, "You're not a big church like the church in Ephesus. You're not a super aggressively growing church like the church in Thyatira. You're not a well-known church like the church in Pergamos. You are a church that only has a little strength."

In verse 11, God gives some instruction about what they had: "Behold, I come quickly: hold that fast which thou hast, that no man take thy crown." That word crown comes from the Greek word stephanos which means "a mark of royalty or a symbol of honor."

Verse 12 continues: "Him that overcometh will I make a pillar in the temple of my God, and he shall go no more out: and I will write upon him the name of my God, and the name of the city of my God, which is new Jerusalem, which cometh down out of heaven from my God: and I will write upon him my new name." I love that promise! Twice God stated that if a Christian will take the little bit he has and will do right by

God with that little bit, God will look at what he has as a mark of honor. When a Christian puts his stamp of excellence on the little bit he has, God will take His pen and sign His name to it. God wants the Christian to work with the little bit he has so that it is worthy of God's signature.

During Youth Conference, I was bombarded by teenagers asking me to sign their Bibles. As a rule, I usually do not sign Bibles during that week. However, a group met me the Sunday morning after Youth Conference and asked, "Would you sign our Bibles?"

"I really don't think I should," I replied.

One of the fellows said, "We traveled 30 hours to hear you preach. That ought to be worth a signature." I signed their Bibles.

During our Sunday school Fall and Spring Programs, I sometimes sign baseballs and footballs or other promotional items. The point of this illustration is that people find someone who they think is famous or well-known, and they want his mark—his signature—on something that is theirs. God said, "I would like to sign your work. I would like you to so work that you take the little bit you have and make it worthy of bearing My signature." That concept arrested me when I read those words. I wonder if the sermons I preach on Sunday mornings, Sunday nights, and Wednesday nights week after week are such that God would like to sign His name to them and say, "Those are my works." I wonder if God looks at the life that I live and would like to sign His name on me, saying, "His life belongs to Me and is worthy of bearing My name." I wonder if the work each of us does is worthy of the name of God. Jesus is saying, "Do the best with what you have. Use what you have as though you were royalty. Put your stamp of honor upon it."

The seven churches listed in Revelation chapters 2 and 3 actually existed and are representative of what any one church could be at any given stage of the church's life. None of these churches exist today because of one major fault—they did not balance truth. Each church had something out of balance that eventually destroyed that church.

The church in Philadelphia also had an imbalance. The church did not possess much strength. It was a fragile church and a new church. In quantity, this church did not have much. Jesus said to the pastor of this church, "Even though you don't have much, you must

be careful not to act like you don't have much. If you are not careful, you will fall into the trap of thinking 'Well, we just have a small
handful of people. It doesn't matter if we practice for the service at
all. We just have 40 people coming to church, so it doesn't matter if
the soloist practices the song. We have just a small group of people;
we don't have to pick out the congregational songs ahead of time—
I'll pick them out while I sit on the platform as the service starts.
Those 40 people aren't very important anyway. Someday I'm going to
have 400 people. When I have 400 people, then I am going to be prepared. We will run our church in a first-class manner. It will be clean
and well decorated. Right now since we only have a handful of people, we won't decorate much. Our choir won't practice." Jesus warned
this church that they would die if they thought that the little bit they
had was not worthy of the quality of God's message. When a church
equates quality with size, their ministry has been killed.

First Baptist Church does not do things first class simply because
it is a big church. If a teacher has a Sunday school class with only
three students, he should run that class of three like we run our services at First Baptist. If he does not, maybe that is why he is still running three in his class. Jesus was giving the church in Philadelphia a
great secret of church growth. Jesus said, "I decide which churches
grow. I will build my church."

Who builds a church? Jesus does! The pastor does not build a
church. The deacons do not build a church. Choir members don't
build a church. Staff men don't build a church. Sunday school teachers and ministry leaders do not build a church. Jesus builds a church!
Jesus decides how much He wants to build a church by how a church
handles what they are given.

People sometimes say, "Brother Schaap, you do things like
Brother Hyles did." Yes, I do. However, when I was a bus captain, I
also operated my bus route the same way. I also conducted my college classes the same way. When I taught a lesson in the singles'
department, it was a well prepared, well thought-through, well
prayed-over lesson. I realized that whether I had 10 or 20 or 40 or 50
or 5,000, that the number should never decide what kind of quality
I gave to a job.

Brother Hyles gave an illustration about when he was a college
boy at East Texas Baptist College. At age 21, Brother Hyles became

the pastor of a church outside the city limits. He was so excited when he went to Bible class on Monday morning. All the preacher boys were in that class. Brother Hyles sat on the front row. The professor walked into class and said, "Fellows, what did the Lord use you to do this weekend?"

Brother Hyles jumped up and said, "Professor, God called me to pastor a little church...."

The professor interrupted and said, "Sit down, Mr. Hyles!"

Brother Hyles was shocked. He couldn't figure out what he had said wrong. Other men stood up and testified about their weekend. When they all finished, Brother Hyles raised his hand and asked, "Professor, what did I do wrong?"

"Mr. Hyles," the professor answered, "you said that God called you to a *little* church. For your information, there are no *little* churches."

Brother Hyles stood and asked, "May I try again? God called me to a *big* church out in the country."

A bus captain says, "I've just got a little bus route. I only had 13 on my bus," so he doesn't prepare much for his sermon on the bus. Oh, those 13 aren't important?

I was out east preaching for a Hyles-Anderson graduate. On Tuesday afternoon following the morning services, we went to lunch. While we were en route to the restaurant, the pastor said, "Brother Schaap, I want you to pray for me."

I said, "Why is that?"

"This is a good work that God has given me here," he said. "But you know, one day the big church is going to come. One day the will of God is going to come and find me, and I feel that God is letting me cut my teeth here and grow and develop at this church. Would you keep your eyes open, and when the day comes that you have the confidence in me, would you put my name out for a larger church?"

I didn't say anything to him. We stopped at a stop sign. I said, "Stop here for a minute." I pointed to a house on the street and said, "Who lives in that house over there?"

The pastor said, "I don't know."

I said, "Oh, it doesn't matter anyway. They are just plastic people. They are just pretend people letting a pretend pastor preach to them, waiting for the big leagues some day." We drove on a little further and came to another stop sign. I pointed to a house across the street and asked, "Who lives in that house over there?"

He said, "I don't know. I've knocked on their door, though."

I said, "I'm sure you have. I'm sure you've talked to those plastic people. They're just pretend people who don't have any feelings or emotions or heartaches or hurts or sins. Their souls don't need to be saved; they're just pretend people. You're just practicing on them anyway."

We didn't go out to eat that day. The pastor turned the car around and dropped me off at my hotel. He didn't even say goodbye to me. Several months later, I received a letter from that pastor. Enclosed was a picture of the pastor holding a tombstone. In his letter he wrote, "Brother Schaap, I just wanted you to see a picture of my tombstone I bought. I'm staying in this city. I'm going to be buried here with real people who have real heartaches."

I receive a letter from him nearly every week. In my last letter from him he wrote, "Brother Schaap, I cannot tell you the joy I feel about pastoring. Are you as happy about pastoring as I am? Do you feel the same way I do when you walk into the pulpit and preach the eternal Word of God to God's people? We're running 280 now and pushing for 300. We're going for 400 during our Fall Program."

That's what I like to hear. Here is a man who at first looked at his quantity and decided what his quality would be; he was already injecting that cancerous cell of death. How big does your bus route have to get before you want to give it first-class treatment? How big does your Sunday school class have to be before you finally pray over those students? How many people do you have to have in your department before you finally get serious about loving them, providing for them, and making sure your department is decorated and attractive for them? If you are a custodian in your church, how many people have to attend your church before you take your custodial duties seriously and make sure the church sparkles before the first member walks in?

The biggest sin of the church in Philadelphia was that they had let their quantity decide their quality. If we apply that same principle to child-rearing, I guess a man who has five children should be more involved in his child rearing than I should be because he has five kids, and I only have two. I guess my two children aren't that important. What idiocy! Each person is an eternal soul.

I suppose our deaf department is not as important as our Bible clubs because there may be only 100 deaf members and probably 200 in the Bible clubs. At what point do we get serious that a soul is a never-dying, eternal being created in the image of God, and each person is important by himself? Are the truck drivers in our truck stop ministry only important if over 30 attend, but they're not important if only 19 attend? Are the 75 to 100 sailors important during the Fall Program, but the motley crew who comes on a summer Sunday night is not important at all? When a Christian starts deciding his quality of work by the quantity he has, he has damned his work to a spiritual perdition. One day he will be nothing but a history book illustration because he did not have the character to have the quality for the small quantity he was given.

Whatever a Christian does, he must do it so well that God Himself would want to put His name on it. A man who feels that his wife is not all she should be, diminishes the quality of his love and the quality of his time and the quality of his affection. Because a husband is not all he should be in his wife's mind, she diminishes her love because his quantity of gifts and talents are not what she thinks they should be. Women who come to me and say, "If my husband were so-and-so, he would have one incredible wife." If her husband is not worthy of the quality of affection she wants to give him, why did she marry him?

One of my deacons said to me, "We went on vacation, and I'm so glad to be back home." I know how he feels. I don't like visiting churches on vacation. I usually try to go to a place where I am anonymous. However, I always regret it because of the typical scenario. You drive into a church's parking lot where your muffler falls off because the lot is full of potholes from the gravel's not being properly graded. The church sign is tilted, and the previous pastor's name is crossed out with the new pastor's name written in on the sign. The word "Baptist" is misspelled on the sign. You get there five minutes before the service is supposed to begin, but the service doesn't start until 20 minutes after the scheduled time. You trip over broken pieces of concrete outside. When you get to the front door, you meet a man who should have won a statue contest. He hands you a bulletin and grunts, "Hello."

Nobody shakes your hand. Nobody asks your name. Nobody asks

where you are from—you feel so warmly greeted! The pianist plays a piano that is horribly out of tune, and she obviously needs a few more lessons. You sit there thinking, "Boy, we're off to a great start."

A song leader gets up to lead the song, and it's obvious that he not only does not know how to lead a song, but he is the only one courageous enough to stand in front of the crowd. He says, "We're going to sing all five stanzas of 'One Day.' " It's obvious that the song leader and the piano player have never practiced together. After you sing a couple of congregational songs, the song leader says, "We'll now hear from the girls' trio."

In the very back row, a teenage girl gets up who is dressed improperly. She walks toward the front, points at another girl who gets up and heads to the piano. The girl announces, "Sheila's not here tonight. Pray for her. She ain't feeling well. We didn't have time to practice, so we're going to do the best we can."

You sit there, and under your breath say, "Oh, God, help us!" The trio becomes a solo, and the only girl who really can sing is the one who is sick at home where you wish you were right about now. Some guy gets up when she finishes singing and says, "And all God's people said...." You want to shout, "You could do a whole lot better!" Instead you join the rest of the congregation mumbling, "Amen."

You wonder if God is even remotely close to that area or if He tiptoed out a long time ago. Then comes a sermon that is long on time and short on content. You endure the sermon and then sing about 15 verses of "Just As I Am" for no reason at all because those people have not walked an aisle since that church was built. The baptistery is full of cobwebs and spiders. Nothing happens. During the dismissal prayer, you bolt out of that church shouting, "Thank God I am free!" We've all been there!

You return to your home church, where the choir marches out right on time, and the organist has already been playing a prelude of some peppy, lively music. The house of God is alive! You walk inside and say, "It's good to be home!"

I am not criticizing any church because it is small. Cleanliness costs nothing. A straight, freshly painted sign costs very little. Spelling a word right is cheaper than spelling it wrong and having to do it over again. A church must never use the excuse that because their church is small or poor, that the church can't be clean. Anyone can have a clean storefront room. The chairs can be set up straight and in neat rows. The service can start on time. The pastor can have a plan and a program. Whether it is the deaf ministry, the Spanish ministry, the blind ministry, the truck stop ministry, or the great services at First Baptist Church on Sunday morning or Sunday night or Wednesday night; regardless of the size, everything should be first class. Quantity should never decide quality.

John 1:39a says, "*He saith unto them, come and see.*" Verse 46 continues, "*And Nathanael said unto him, Can there any good thing come out of Nazareth? Phillip saith unto him, Come and see.*" John 4:28 says, "*The woman then left her waterpot, and went her way into the city, and saith to the men, Come, see....*" That is exactly what evangelism is— come and see! Come and see Jesus!

If a poll were taken on why people visit a church, the main reason is because someone who believes in that church said to the visitor, "Come and see what we have." Can you say about your marriage, "Come and see a marriage that is worthy of the signature of God upon it"? Can you say to an unsaved, dying world, "Come and see a family that gets along, a family that is worthy of God's signature on it"? If the pastor and his wife were invited over for dinner, many wives would have to do major reconstruction to their house. Christian lady, is your home worthy of having God's signature on it because it is done rightly? Sunday school teacher, can you bring God to your Sunday school class and have Him write His name upon it? Christian, could you say to your unsaved neighbor, "Hey, you ought to come see how we teach the junior-age kids," or "Come and see my adult Sunday school class," or " Come and see my bus route," or "Come and see our pastor," or "Come and see our church service!" Come and see!

Families have come to First Baptist Church as visitors because of the invitation of one of our members. I know of one visiting family in particular who lived very far away. When these folks came to visit, they said, "Wow, we've never seen anything like this!" Before long, that family put their house up for sale to move to our area.

When people come to see a church, they ought to see that something is different. Those greeters who stand outside our church doors before the services say, "Welcome to First Baptist Church. I'm glad you're here." I want those greeters to say that every time with enthusiasm. If the greeters aren't glad the visitors are at church, why should the visitors come? Jesus said, "Come and see."

When I was a bus captain and picked up our bus on Sunday, at times our bus was such a mess from garbage. The teenagers who used the bus the day before for soul winning forgot that there were people coming after them and would see what they had left behind. Every place a Christian leaves should be a better place for his having been there. That holds true for the restrooms, the buses, the Sunday school classrooms, and the church auditorium. When a Christian leaves a place, he should make sure he picks up every piece of trash he sees. He should be able to say, "This place is a better place for my having been here." If every Christian adopted this practice, most of the custodians wouldn't be needed except to disinfect the bathrooms. No, the average Christian walks into the church restroom and says, "What a mess!" and then leaves a bigger mess. Church members ought to be able to say, "Come and see our restrooms. They're the cleanest restrooms in the whole country."

I visited Disney World one time and left saying, "God, why don't Your people see that Your work is bigger than Mickey Mouse is?" A place like Disney World being cleaner than a Baptist church irritates the fire out of me. There is no trash on the floor of their restrooms. Clean is cheap! Clean is character! Clean has nothing to do with money. Clean has to do with the desire to say to an unsaved world, "Come see how we do things here."

In some churches, the Sunday bulletin has streaks through it because the copier wasn't working correctly. The brochure may even contain misspelled words. I don't appreciate a member of the First Baptist Church staff having a letter sent out with misspelled words. If someone works for me, I want everything he sends out to be proofread carefully. A staff member of the First Baptist Church represents the pastor and the church; but, ten thousand times more importantly, he represents the LORD JESUS CHRIST!

After I became the pastor, our church printed a very nice color brochure promoting some of our ministries. We reprinted 30,000 of those brochures because of one typographical error. I looked at the brochure with the error, and I said "Reprint it."

One of the staff men said, "Nobody will catch that mistake."

I said, "That is not our standard of excellence—whether or not anyone will catch it. Our standard of excellence is whether it is right or wrong."

The brochures with the errors were trashed and reprinted. Quantity wasn't the issue—we printed 30,000 of those brochures. However, I don't care if we print three or 30 million of them—First Baptist Church is going to do it right. If something isn't worth doing right, why waste time doing it in the first place?

Jesus said, "Come and see the place where I lay My head." Was it a big palace? No. It must have been a quaint, non-extravagant little place. Jesus didn't have a big palace, but what He had must have been so impressive that the men decided to follow Jesus. If someone came to your home tonight, church member, and saw how you and your wife get along or how you and your children get along, would they be impressed?

Some have taken what God has given them and demeaned it because it is not very big. A Christian is a child of the living God. The President of the United States is not as big as Jesus Christ. I'm a child of the King. If Jesus Christ is my King, then I am royalty. Therefore, how I dress, how I shine my shoes, how I knot my tie, how I choose my clothes, how I brush my teeth, how I comb my hair, how I walk, how I talk, and how I live all represent who I am.

I am angered when I see how careful the world is to take care of worldly things. In II Peter chapter 3, Peter said that this entire world will be burned up with fire. Disney World will be burned up.

Brother Tom Vogel, the academic vice-president of our college, and I were talking about the Museum of Independent Baptist History that we want to build out at the college. We were talking about some ideas, and Brother Vogel asked, "What kind of museum do you see?"

I said, "Have you ever been to the Hall of Presidents at Disney World? I'd like to see a model of Brother Hyles sitting at his desk in his office. A visitor could sit down by him, push a button, and ask him any kind of question. The answer would come out in Brother Hyles' voice from one of his sermons or Bible studies. I also want to walk into another room and have a model of Dr. Lee Roberson preaching."

Brother Vogel said, "You've got pretty big dreams for that museum!"

Why should the world have all the gizmos and all the good stuff?

Is not our Baptist heritage more important? John Kennedy, Abraham Lincoln, and the other Presidents are not the only important people in this world. If our Baptist heritage is important, I want to preserve it and do it right. I'm tired of the world's telling fundamentalists how we ought to do it. I want to show the world how to do it.

At the Masters' Golf Tournament, the vendors' candy is wrapped in the same color of paper as the grass so that if someone inadvertently drops a candy wrapper, it can't be seen on television. It aggravates me that someone is so meticulous that he makes provisions for slobs!

When I visited the Air Force Academy, I was impressed with how cadets greeted each other in passing and how cadets asked for permission to pass a senior officer. What an operation! There was no paper on the ground. There was no bubble gum on the concrete. I went inside the bathroom, and it was spotlessly clean. I was so convicted that the Air Force Academy would care more for their properties than the people of the First Baptist Church care for theirs.

I told Brother Randy Ericson, our maintenance engineer, "You're going to hate my guts one of these days. I've been patient with the refurbishing of our old buildings. I understand that if a building is old and unused, I don't expect it to be clean and nice. But Brother Randy, as we refurbish these old buildings, I expect them to be spotless and neat and clean. I want to be able to walk inside a building and say, 'This is the First Baptist Church way of doing it.' "

Every Sunday school class should be clean and neat. Every bus used on Sundays should be clean and neat. A mother should be able to get on a Sunday school bus and say, "My house is not as clean as your bus." There are no little bus routes! If a bus captain thinks that way about his bus route, it was a giant mistake giving him a bus route.

1. There is a big difference between pretty good and excellent. To me, there is one huge difference between pretty good and excellent—mediocrity. Mediocrity is not pleasing to the Lord Jesus Christ. I don't believe in mediocre special music.

One day I asked Mrs. Colsten, "You like to use Brother Harold Snure and his daughter April for special music, don't you?"

She said, "Yes, because they always practice whether or not they are singing."

I like people who are going to practice and practice whether or not they are asked to sing. I am not interested in a person's singing; I'm interested in his preparation. Brother Hyles said, "Greatness is in the preparation, not in the delivery."

I was talking to a pastor recently and asked him how his church was doing. "I don't know," he said. "I don't know if they will let me remain as pastor much longer."

I asked, "What's wrong?"

He said, "I was telling the people, 'Folks, summertime is coming. Let's be sure we dress properly at church. Make sure you ladies wear hosiery....' "

A man in the back interrupted me and hollered out, 'Hey, where do you find that in the Bible?'

'I didn't say it was a sin,' I answered. 'I just said it would be appropriate for us to look like we belong in church.' "

If a Christian's guideline of right and wrong and propriety are based wholly on, "Is it a commandment? Is it in the Bible?" that is pretty sorry living. No commandment says, "Thou shalt wipe off the mirror after you splash on it" or "Thou shalt flush the commode." If the only reason why you do things is because you have to do it, then you have a sorry Christianity. I want my First Baptist Church members to look like First Baptist Church members. I want everybody outside the walls of First Baptist Church to know that the members are glad to belong to a church that does things the right way.

On Mackinaw Island, no man may visit the Grand Hotel without wearing a jacket and tie. Our nation has a slob mentality. Americans want to dress sloppy. A couple of our church men asked me if they could wear their shorts to our Men's Golf Outing. I said, "No. You go to First Baptist Church."

They said, "It's hot. Why can't we wear our shorts?"

I said, "The same reason why Tiger Woods or Jack Nicklaus does not wear shorts.

"Well, it's not a professional game," they said.

"No," I agreed. The First Baptist Church Men's Golf Outing is more important than a professional golf tournament. It is the children of God getting together. We're a step above the professionals. We are going to look like Christians out there on the golf course."

Some might say, "Where does the Bible say a man can't wear shorts?" That standard is not in the Bible; it's in the First Baptist

Church code of conduct. It's called the First Baptist Church way of doing things. Someone who represents our church should look right.

Occasionally, I will have problems with some men on our church softball teams who don't want to get their hair cut properly. I'm tired of our softball commissioner, Brother Paul Burke, having to go to a team and tell a coach that a certain player cannot play because his hair is too long. Then, after Brother Burke leaves, the coach lets the player play.

That team won't be playing again! Our First Baptist Church softball players will get their cotton-pickin' hair cut, or they won't play in our league! The men will not wear jewelry and play on our teams. If a player is ashamed to be a man, he will get off our ball teams.

A coach said, "Well, I've been trying to get that player to come back to church." Every player knows exactly what First Baptist Church believes about standards! A softball player will look the part or get off the ball field.

I am eternally patient with young converts and folks who are new to church. If a man walks in off the streets with long hair and jewelry, that doesn't bother me. I'll teach him the truth. However, it irritates the fire out of me when a young man has gone all through our school system, graduated from Hammond Baptist High School, attended Hyles-Anderson College, was privileged to sit under Brother Hyles for many years. Yet, he has a punky little attitude that says, "I can wear my hair any way I want to." No, sir, not here!

2. **Excellence is in the details.** The pastor should not have to go into a Sunday school class and take down pictures of Jesus with long hair because a teacher is not thinking about the details. Once a month, I inspect each Sunday school class in our church.

Teacher, why not buy a bucket of paint and paint your classroom? Clean that room and make it look sharp. Care for the details so that when the kids walk in on Sunday they can say, "This looks nice."

Each Christian must take care of the details of what God has given him. Ecclesiastes 9:10 says, *"Whatsoever thy hand findeth to do, do it with thy might."* That word *might* doesn't just mean strength; it means "do it with all the power and imagination and ability and creativity; do it with all that you have in you."

3. **Excellence not extravagance.** There will be no brass railings or stained glass windows in the new auditorium of the First Baptist

Church of Hammond. It will be beautiful, but not extravagant.

My friend, Brother Jack DeCoster, is the world's largest egg farmer. His egg farm is incredible. He runs his egg farm with more cleanliness and more efficiency and more detail than 99.99% of all the Baptist churches I have ever visited. He takes care of chicken manure in a more efficient manner than any bathrooms I've seen. I've visited Brother DeCoster several times, and Brother DeCoster once asked me, "What do you think, Jack?"

I said, "I hate it! I don't even like you any more."

He asked, "Why?"

I said, "Because you embarrass my profession at how efficient you are with eggs and pigs." No one is allowed to walk inside his pig pens without first taking a shower. All of their uniforms are stacked nicely and neatly.

While I was there one day, Brother DeCoster took an employee to task. Boy, was he upset! He grabbed the guy and said, "Why is that uniform out of place?"

The man said, "I'm sorry."

Brother DeCoster said, "I don't want sorry. I don't want an excuse. We don't make mistakes here."

Ushers, what does your jacket closet look like? Kitchen worker, every little nook and cranny in our kitchen should be cleaned. Those who use the church kitchen should leave it cleaner than they found it.

Every place First Baptist Church members go, I want people to be able to say, "First Baptist Church has been here."

4. Being first class is not an act. Someone said to me, "Brother Schaap, you like to have classy things. Is that kind of an act?"

"Don't you ever tell me that what I do for Jesus Christ is an act," I said. "If my Saviour does not deserve my best, then I ought to get out of this business and go do something that does deserve my best."

Mediocrity is not very impressive to Jesus Christ. I don't want to maintain or be mediocre. There are 463,000 residents in Lake County, Indiana. We are sitting smack dab in the backyard of many millions of people in the Chicago area. We have a small mission in Jilin City, China, in the most populous nation in the world. It would take over 100,000 churches like First Baptist Church to make a difference in China. However, we have a great opportunity here in the Chicago area. I want things done first class because that is what Jesus deserves. I want Jesus to think that everything I do, everything I touch, every sermon I preach, and every lesson I teach is worthy for Him to say, "Hang on a minute. Let Me sign My name on that. I want to be associated with that." In every area of a Christian's life, he should so live so that God Himself would say, "Can I sign My name on that? I like the way you do that." Whether it is our athletic program or our cheerleading program or how the mission men cut the grass for the widows—it should all be done as if God Himself were going to inspect the work.

The landscapers for the Master's Tournament should come to watch the mission men cut grass because the mission men do a better job. Recently, a major storm came through our area, downing trees and power lines everywhere. The whole subdivision looked like a war zone. Brother Harrell, who takes care of the landscaping at my house, comes to work on Saturdays. When I came home on Saturday evening after the storm, my house and yard looked like he had taken a vacuum to the whole property. It was neat as a pin. I was so proud to pull into my driveway that I wanted to tell everyone, "Tim Harrell does my lawn." He's a Bible teacher during the school year and cuts grass in the summer. If he teaches Bible like he cuts grass, I would want to sit in his class.

I want to be able to say, "Come and see," to people outside First Baptist Church. I want to say, "Come and see our bus routes. Come and see our duets and our choir. Come and see how we do things at First Baptist Church." The quality of our work testifies of what Christians believe. We believe in a Saviour Who is worthy of our best.

CHAPTER ELEVEN

Contentment Vs. Compromise

"I know thy works, that thou art neither cold nor hot: I would thou wert cold or hot." (Revelation 3:15)

WHEN A CHURCH gets out of balance in certain areas, it eventually crashes. These churches in Revelation did not go out of business because the Moslems took over or because the Crusades succeeded or failed. The churches did not die off because of Nazism or Communism; they died because they let themselves die. A church does not have to die. A church can keep doing what it was called to do from the beginning and keep growing. Of course, a church has its ebbs and flows, peaks and valleys, and good times and setbacks; but the church does not have to die.

The last of the seven churches described in Revelation 2 and 3 was the church at Laodicea. Most theologians who are misguided in their eschatology believe Laodicea is the last church age, and that we are now living in the Laodicean age. No. The church in Laodicea is an example of another phase of the seven phases that any church may go through at any time, or a church may go through any number of the phases simultaneously. Because the First Baptist Church of Hammond has so many ministries, it could be possible for the deaf ministry to be going through one phase while the blind ministry is in another phase, and all the other ministries could be experiencing yet another phase. God is simply telling these pastors in Revelation that the big thing to notice is that there are strengths and weaknesses in a church; and if a church becomes unbalanced, it will crash and no longer exist.

Revelation 3:14-17 says, "*And unto the angel of the church of the Laodiceans write; These things saith the Amen, the faithful and true witness, the beginning of the creation of God; I know thy works, that thou art neither cold nor hot: I would thou wert cold or hot. So then because thou art lukewarm, and neither cold nor hot, I will spue thee out of my mouth. Because thou sayest, I am rich, and increased with goods, and have need of nothing; and knowest not that thou art wretched, and miserable, and poor, and blind, and naked.*" When I read this portion of Scripture, it appears that God is criticizing these Christians for doing well. The folks in Laodicea had increased in goods; yet, nowhere in the Bible does it say it is a sin to be rich. These people appeared to be very content; however, God sees it as a contentment that brought compromise.

The Bible has much to say about being content. In Philippians 4:11 the Apostle Paul says, "*...I have learned, in whatsoever state I am, therewith to be content.*" I Timothy 6:6 says, "*But godliness with contentment is great gain.*" I Timothy 6:8 says, "*And having food and raiment let us be therewith content.*" Hebrews 13:5 says, "*Let your conversation be without covetousness; and be content with such things as ye have: for he hath said, I will never leave thee, nor forsake thee.*" III John 10 says, "*Wherefore, if I come, I will remember his deeds which he doeth, prating against us with malicious words: and not content therewith....*" Contentment is good. However, contentment out of balance leads to complacency. If I do have good things, the tendency is to be too content. When I am too content, I tend to get complacent.

Contentment out of balance leads to compromise. Compromise is to take the extreme middle position on any issue, which is the least defensive position and the least offensive position.

I like being content. I love going home. *Home* is my favorite English word. I love going home and being greeted by my wife with a hug and kiss and a warm smile and that twinkle in her eye that says she is glad I am there. I like coming home and having my son say, "Hey Pa, how you doing?" I like to spend time with him at home. I like what I have. I like the car I drive and the clothes I wear. I like the wife I have and the children I have. I am a content man. I feel like being content is one of the great secrets to the victorious and happy Christian life.

Brother Hyles taught that contentment comes from either getting everything you want or wanting everything you have. That is a marvelous philosophy. I am doing the job that I want to do. I would rather preach at the First Baptist Church of Hammond than anywhere in the world. I am content with the Bible I have. I am content with my Saviour. I'm content with the house God has given me. I'm content with my financial status. I'm content with both my problems and my pleasures.

Jesus was warning this church in Laodicea that if they were not careful, they could get so content that it would lead to complacency which would lead to compromise. As a result, they would find themselves guarding their contentment at the expense of conviction. In a church like First Baptist Church, a man can enter our system, learn our preaching and philosophy, and become a faithful, valuable worker at his secular job. Before he knows it, he's making decent money at his job. This often happens to our college young men. A young college man may start off at $8 an hour. He then works his way up in his job while he is in college; and by the time he graduates, it is not uncommon for him to be making $35,000 yearly. His position and salary are almost too much because when he accepts a position at a church, he will not be making that kind of salary.

This young man can become very content with his life. He is making good money, driving a nice pick-up truck, and wearing nice clothes. Sometimes he becomes so content that he doesn't want to take a stand at work. He doesn't want to risk anything or lose his job. Contentment can force a Christian into the extreme middle where everything is good—good God, good people, and good Devil.

Several lessons can be learned from the church in Laodicea.

1. **God does not measure the value of a church in the content and quality of its buildings or possessions; rather, God measures the value of a church in the fervor of its spirit and its works.**

Jesus said to the church in Laodicea, "You have everything that should bring contentment, and you are a very content church. You have riches. You have increase of goods."

God never comes inside a church and says, "Boy, you must be some church. Look how pretty these buildings are." God does not look at the new auditorium First Baptist Church is building and say, "Wow, with that new auditorium you are building, you must be some church. I'm impressed." No! God looks at the fervor of the spirit of a church and at the energy of the work of a church to decide whether or not it is good.

How much fervor the church members bring to the church auditorium is more important than how ornately the church auditorium is adorned. How excited the church gets when souls get saved is more impressive to God than how many bodies are sitting in the church pews. God looks at the zeal and energy a Christian brings to his bus route and Sunday school class to measure the strength of a church. God looks at the fervor and passion a soul winner has when he knocks on doors or passes out tracts trying to get the Gospel to someone. God looks at the energy a Christian spends in his prayer closet begging God for His Spirit and the growth of the church. God doesn't look at the chandeliers or the spotlights or the padded pews or the big public address system.

In the Old Testament, God says that He doesn't find any pleasure in the strength of a horse or the power of a man's legs. Rather, God looks at the zeal of a man's spirit and the fervent passion he brings to God's ministry. The song says, "Ere you left your room this morning, did you think to pray?" God doesn't want, "Just a Little Talk with Jesus"; God wants "Sweet Hour of Prayer." God wants the fervor and the energy in the prayer closet. That's how God measures a church.

When I was a full-time teacher at Hyles-Anderson College, I taught a class called Homiletics (the preparation and delivery of sermons). One of the requirements for the class was preaching in a bar. A few of the students put it off until night before the semester ended. They really didn't want to go. I told these men, "You've got one week left. You cannot pass this class unless you complete all the requirements which include bar preaching." I decided to take them bar preaching.

We drove up to Halsted Street in Chicago to a bar. (Later, we discovered it was a black gay bar.) After we parked, I said, "Fellows, you go inside, and I'll stand out here and make sure you are safe."

One student said, "Brother Schaap, it is jam-packed full of people."

"Wonderful," I said.

Another student asked, "What do we do?"

"Walk inside, go way back in the back where the pool tables are," I instructed, "grab a cue stick, and say, 'Fellows, this game is over. I'm going to talk to you about Jesus.' "

My students said, "You don't mean that, do you?" (I didn't tell the fellows that when I go bar preaching, I always say, "Excuse me," while standing with my back against the door and my hand on the doorknob—ready for a quick getaway.)

The preachers went inside, and I waited outside the bar. A female police officer walked up to me and said, "Hey, what are you doing here?"

"Waiting for my buddies," I answered.

She asked, "Are they crackers like you?"

"Yes, ma'am, they're white boys like me," I answered.

"What are they doing in there?"

I said, "They are preaching."

"Whew!" she exclaimed. "You've got lots of courage—more than I have. I'm getting out of here!" (I didn't tell the men what the police officer said until we got in the car and left!)

When the preacher boys came out about 15 minutes later, I asked, "How did it go?"

One said, "Man, were we scared! There was a pool table in the back surrounded by a group of guys drinking liquor. Brother Schaap, I grabbed a cue stick and jumped up on the pool table. One of the men grabbed a cue stick and was ready to hit me when another fellow stopped him and said, 'Hey, just a minute. What do you want, boy?'

I told him, 'I'm a Baptist preacher.'

The man said, 'You're in a gay bar.'

I said, 'Well, God loves you, too,' and I started preaching."

I imagine God was pretty excited watching that preacher boy from Heaven. I also bet God was glad that He was in Heaven and not down there in that bar!

One day in Homiletics class I said, "Fellows, we don't have enough zeal. I'm tired of your getting up here with a sweet little talk. I want you to get some fire! I want you to get excited about your preaching!" The whole class continued to be sort of boring and was going nowhere. Finally I said, "That's it. From now on, I'm going to tell you where to preach."

I began assigning places for these preacher boys to preach. I assigned a couple of them to preach at a school. These men walked onto the campus of a Catholic middle school which had several hundred students. They walked inside, and the nuns were polite to them. They walked into the school office and said, "We're here visiting the school. We are in Christian education ourselves. We would like to take a tour of your school and visit one of your classrooms."

The priest agreed to let them go anywhere they wanted on the campus. He shouldn't have said that. Our preacher boys walked into a classroom where the teacher was at the front of the room teaching. They sat down, and the teacher asked, "Who are you gentlemen?"

They said, "We are young ministerial students studying for the ministry."

She asked, "Would you like to speak a word to my students?"

One of the college students said, "I would be glad to." He preached the Gospel for 30 minutes. There were 35 children in that class and one nun. When he finished preaching, he gave an invitation; 36 hands went up saying they had trusted Christ as Saviour! The preacher boy didn't think the class understood what he meant, so he said, "I mean if you are not trusting Mary, you are not trusting your baptism, you are not trusting your Catholic school or church, and you are trusting Jesus alone, I want you to stand." All 35 students *and* the nun stood. All 36 said the sinner's prayer and were saved! God looks at that zeal and that passion to get out the Gospel.

God looks at those missionaries who went to the Congo on a survey trip and won 1,650 souls. He doesn't say, "What kind of buildings did you have?" God didn't look at the Apostle Paul and say, "What kind of buildings did you have in Lystra when you were stoned?" Paul did not have a building, but God was impressed with the fervor of the spirit of that old, bug-eyed Jew, not the quality or content of Paul's goods.

God is not looking at the padded pews or the nice carpet of a church. He's looking at the "amen" level of the high school kids and the deacons and the Sunday school teachers and the men of the church. He's looking at the "amen" level of the staff members and the assistant pastors. God wants to know the passion brought into the pulpit by the pastor. God wants to know the passion brought into the service by the Christians. God wants to know the passion a Christian brings to his bus route and his Sunday school class. God wants to know the passion a choir member brings to the choir. God wants to know the passion a church member brings to his ministry. God is not looking at the quality or content of the buildings of a church. God is looking at the zeal of a church.

People have asked me, "Is your church going charismatic?" I'm tired of some critics saying "charismatic" every time someone in the church has the fire of God. Do you think Paul was charismatic when he got so excited preaching in Athens and Lystra that they dragged him out of the cities and beat him and stoned him? I'm tired of a bunch of deadhead Baptists criticizing other excited Baptists by calling them charismatics because the critics are too lazy to get anything done.

God asks the Christian, "How is your bus route doing?"

Some reply, "Well, we're content. God, did you see our bus? It has air conditioning." Neither God nor I are impressed with your air-conditioned bus; however, we are concerned with your filling that bus with riders. I don't want the First Baptist Church to ever lose its shout and its enthusiasm.

God was saying to the church at Laodicea, "I am not against your having good things, but I don't like your contentment to the point of complacency and compromise."

2. **Things hinder my knowledge and devotion to God.** The Apostle Paul said in Philippians chapter 3 that things hinder my knowing about God and hinder my fervor for God. Before Paul was saved, he became a Pharisee because he believed that things and position were very important. Being a Pharisee was very important in those days, much like becoming a member of the Masonic Lodge or a member of the Lion's Club or like Fred Flintstone was a member of the Water Buffalo Lodge. Paul thought he was somebody. He was a Jew of the tribe of Benjamin. He was a Pharisee and trained at the feet of Gamaliel. After Paul was saved, he realized that all his heritage and

training meant nothing. Those laurels were so important to Paul; yet, Paul came to the point where he realized that God valued them to the same degree as dung. (Dung is what you shovel when you own a farm.) Paul pointed at a pile of dung and said, "You know that degree I got at that famous school? That's the value of it right there." Some people work so hard to be accepted in the academic world; and yet, Paul said such acceptance has the same value as dung.

Too many people have elevated the possessions and positions of this world too highly. One may say, "Do you know what kind of a car I own?"

God said, "I value any car the same as a manure spreader." God is not impressed with our things. Things are a hindrance to knowing God because the pursuit of things takes energy to get them. Any energy spent on getting things—even good things—is energy that cannot be used to get out the Gospel. I think of all the energy and hundreds of hours spent in the necessary rituals of life like cleaning buildings. I wish we could just say to our custodians, "You all spend a hundred hours knocking on doors and passing out tracts instead." But we have to fulfill the necessary rituals of life. We have to cut our grass. We have to wash our dishes. So much energy has to be spent on just living and breathing; why waste more energy pursuing things until you are so tired you just flop in bed? Then come Sunday morning you say, "I'm so tired. I can't run my bus route."

God was saying to Christians, "It's not that you are pursuing bad things, but the pursuit taps you of energy that could have been spent getting out the Gospel."

Paul wasn't criticizing someone's having a nice car or a nice house or a nice wardrobe. Paul was saying that the pursuing of those things taps energy. Remember when Jesus was touched by that woman and He stopped and asked, "Who touched me? I perceive that virtue has departed from me." The Greek word for *virtue* is the word "energy." Jesus was saying, "I feel like somebody plugged into Me and drained me."

Counseling people drains me. I feel like folks pull all the energy out of me. Though I want to help people, I don't want to waste any energy because it is too precious to me. I only have so many spiritual BTU's to give.

God is not criticizing Christians for having nice shoes on their feet. God is not against a Christian driving a nice car. Paul and Jesus were not saying, "Things are bad." Paul and Jesus were saying, "Be careful how many things you pursue because it takes energy to go after those things. It takes time and money and life. You are losing a lot of virtue because that energy could have been spent knocking on a door and telling someone how to get saved." When I stand before the Judgment Seat of Christ and look my Saviour in the eyes, realizing He gave it all for me, I will say, "I wish I had given Him more."

I'm happy for my members when they get a new car or a new house; however, pursuing things hinders a Christian's fervor for God. A church like First Baptist Church has to watch it. As a couple goes from their first-year apartment to a small cottage to a nicer house, they must be careful not to get into the habit of saying, "Nicer, nicer, nicer." Getting nicer things is not the object of life. That couple needs to find a place where they want to put down their roots and stay there.

3. **The pursuit of things robs me of investing more in the work of Christ.** Pretend for a moment that as Christians we really believe there is a Hell, and we want to get people out of Hell as much as Jesus does; that is the only thing that really matters in life. Then stack up all the money we spend on things. When we think of our loved ones going to Hell and look at all of the money we have, I wonder sometimes why we Christians don't just take all of their money and say, "I've got a nice enough house. I don't need any more clothes. I don't need anything, God. I just want to give everything I can to get lost souls out of Hell."

Christians, if we really believe in our hearts what the Bible says about Hell, are the pursuits in life and the things we want really as important compared to taking that money and getting a missionary to the foreign field and getting out the Gospel?

A pastor, who is in a big building program, recently said from his pulpit, "I've got good news, and I've got bad news. The good news is, we have all the money we need for the building project." The congregation got excited. The pastor continued, "The bad news is the money is in your pockets."

I believe with all my heart that the Great Commission is not to a group or to the so-called "universal" church. I believe the Great Commission is to local churches. I believe the command to go into all the world and preach the Gospel to every creature is personally given to the First Baptist Church of Hammond. I also believe that God never commands me to do something that is impossible to do. If I believe God has given me the Great Commission to get the Gospel to the entire world and we are not getting the Gospel to the entire world, then the problem is with me; God would not command me to do something I cannot do. If God has commanded me to do it, then I believe First Baptist Church can do it and should be doing it. I have to believe that what First Baptist Church has is all that God needs. Every illustration in the Bible tells me that God never failed in a miracle because the human instrument did not have what God needed. If a miracle failed, it was because the man would not give what he had. God is limited because a Christian will not tithe. God is not limited because a Christian will not give God one million dollars or any amount of money for that matter.

A child wrote me a few days ago and said, "Dear Brother Schaap, pray for me. If I get one million dollars, I'll give it all to you!" Buddy, I am praying! That child is not going to get one million dollars. I just hope that child mows a lawn and pays his tithes and then gives a generous offering to God.

Sometime in my lifetime, I would like to get to the point where I can give it all to God. I want to see what God could do if I gave it all. D. L. Moody was challenged by the statement, "The world has yet to see what God could do with a man totally yielded to Him." When I heard that statement, I said, "God, sometime in my lifetime, I would like to qualify for that."

What if there was a band of people whose goal was to get to the point where they could give it all to God? So many Christians are in bondage to credit-card debt and mortgage payments that they seemingly cannot do any more for the Lord. If Christians could get out of debt, they could get to the point in their life that they could say, "You know, I was making $600 payments to the mortgage company and $400 to my credit card. Now that I'm not in debt, I can give that amount to the Lord's work."

What would happen if a church like the First Baptist Church of Hammond got "turned on" to giving it all? I'd like to see what could be done by the power of Heaven multiplying its force, coupled together with our sacrificial and obedient giving. I believe the Gospel could get to the world! For eternity, I would like to see the millions of souls that were saved because of people who gave it all.

Let me be practical. When you go to the store, you don't have to get everything you want. When you are deciding whether to purchase an item, think to yourself, "If I don't get that item, I'll probably have the same quality of life. What if I took the money I was going to spend on that item and put it into missions or into the church building fund?" What if each of us so lived that every time we saw something we would like to have we just didn't buy it, but took that money and invested it in the Lord's work.

I wonder about that boy who gave his sack lunch of five loaves and two fishes. If he had eaten his lunch, the next day no one would ever have known about it. However, because the boy gave what he had, his story is still being told. What if each Christian so lived that every time he went to make a purchase, he said, "I was going to get five of those, but I think I'll just get two and take the rest of the money and give it to the Lord's work'" There would be no difference in our style of living, but God could multiply that money a thousand-fold.

4. Contentment should be found in my walk with God, not the things God gives me. Revelation 3:20, *"Behold, I stand at the door, and knock: if any man hear my voice, and open the door, I will come in to him, and will sup with him, and he with me."* God wants to sit down and fellowship with a Christian and have the Christian find his contentment in God's presence and in walking with Him. God is saying, "If you really want to get serious about serving Me, the key word for things is the presence of Christ."

If you have ever walked with God for a couple of hours at one time, you know the satisfaction that fellowship gives your soul. When I spend time in my prayer closet and feast on the Word of God, I find myself saying, "God, can I spend a little longer with You? This is so much fun and so pleasurable to me, I feel almost guilty doing it." Christians who have never felt that way, haven't yet spent enough time with God. Rushing around the house with your Bible in one hand and getting dressed with the other hand is not walking with God.

When I ask my son to pray for a meal, he sometimes adds "Lord, thank You that we can spend some quality time as a family." The way

I feel when my son prays that is how I want the Lord to feel when I say, "Lord, I want to spend some quality time with You."

Years ago, a friend invited me to go to Eduardo's Natural Pizza restaurant with him. I asked, "What is natural pizza?"

"It is spinach pizza and broccoli pizza," my friend said.

"I never want to try that," I declared. "It sounds gross! *Pizza* doesn't mean healthy; it means 'greasy, high cholesterol, heart attack!' "

My friend said, "You haven't tried it."

I finally agreed to go the restaurant with him, but I said, "Okay, I will try it, but I will not like it." After arriving at Eduardo's, my friend ordered a pizza with half spinach and half broccoli. I fully intended on going to White Castle after looking at the pizza.

The pizza arrived, and it looked pretty good. I reluctantly took a bite of the pizza. Immediately, my taste buds came alive and said, "Hey, you up there in the brain! This is good stuff!" The little guys on my tongue were saying, "Bring on some more; this is good!" After my fourth piece, I felt like a bloated elephant, and I was excited about Eduardo's Natural Pizza!

One day, I went to another friend of mine and said, "Let me take you to Eduardo's Natural Pizza." As I expected, his response was the same as my original reaction—"Natural Pizza! I want pepperoni. I want sausage." I convinced him to go with me. As he took his first bite, I watched his face as the same signal I had experienced went from his taste buds to his brain.

I have since taken several of my friends to eat natural pizza, and they always say the same thing: "I had no idea how good natural pizza was." That is exactly how I feel about trying to get Christians to walk with God. I say, "You want to walk with God?"

The response is, "Walk with God? I want rock 'n' roll. I want television. I want funny comedians. I want sexual fornication. I want the garbage can of America."

Driving by Eduardo's Natural Pizza is not the same as eating it. Carrying the Bible until you have big biceps is not walking with God. When a Christian walks with God, gets in His Word, and feasts upon the manna of Heaven, he will never be satisfied with the garbage can of this world!

Jesus was saying that contentment should not be in the things a

Christian possesses, but in the Person he loves. I'm possessed of the Saviour, and He is a whole lot of fun. I share everything with Him. There is no secret that I have ever kept from God. He knows every sin and every wicked thought. I tell God everything. The song says,

> And He walks with me, and He talks with me
> And He tells me I am His own,
> And the joy we share as we tarry there,
> None other has ever known.

God can give a joy that nobody else has ever known. Most Christians want the high cholesterol sin—the sausage and pepperoni of the world that clogs the spiritual arteries and gives him a spiritual heart attack and stops him from functioning.

5. Compromise is not measured in my distance from the world but in my closeness to Christ. The world is getting worse and worse. The Supreme Court of 50 years ago would never have sanctioned homosexual intimacies. As the world gets worse and worse, the Christian feels that if he keeps the same distance from the world, then he is doing fine. He feels like he is separated from the world. He does not think of himself as a compromiser because he is never closer to the world than he ever was. He says, "I'm not like the world. You would never catch me looking like the world, acting like the world, talking like the world, or thinking like the world. I'm a separated Christian."

The truth of the matter is, as the world moves further away from right, if the Christian remains the same distance from the world and moves with the world, the Christian will eventually **be** as worldly as the world **was** in the past. He has moved further from God by moving with the world. That Christian does not even recognize how worldly he has become.

In the last ten to fifteen years, many churches have begun an incredible experiment. They do not yet know what will be the outcome; and by the time they discern the outcome, it will be too late to change. Churches have brought drums and electric guitars, theater lights and drama, and Hollywood actors and rock 'n' roll singers—men with their long hair and earrings, and females wearing mini-skirts. With their wiggles connoting their sexual behavior, they sing rock 'n' roll songs with Jesus words. These churches are attracting huge crowds. The fastest growing churches in America today are the compromising churches. Many of those churches now run 15,000 to 20,000 weekly in attendance. These churches do not understand where this experiment is taking them.

The members say, "We're not singing the world's songs," but they are putting the world's music with Jesus words. They have changed the tradition of getting up on Sunday morning and getting dressed up and going to church, wearing their blue jeans and tank tops for church. Even if these changes are not wrong, these churches have no idea where these changes are going to lead them down the road. I believe that the compromising of standards is going to lead to a corruption of Christianity in a magnitude this world has never seen. This trend could very easily be what Paul preached about in II Thessalonians when he said about the coming of Jesus Christ, that Christ will not come until there first comes a falling away. That "falling away" is the Greek word *apostosia*. This word is used only three times in the New Testament, and every time it refers to a doctrinal, theological departure from the faith. Each time the word is used for people's walking away from and leaving the truth of the Bible.

With thousands of churches experimenting with using the world's techniques, Christians are no longer keeping their distance from the world. Instead, they are gaining on the world. Christians are actually catching up to and embracing the world. The number-one Christian contemporary music group is now the number-five secular group in the world. Christians are getting close to the place that Elton John was in 1970's. In the same year, Elton John was voted the number-one female singer and the number-two male singer.

Compromise is not measured by distance from the world. In Revelation 3, Jesus said, "*These things saith the Amen.*" The word *Amen* is capitalized and is referring to Jesus Christ's personal name. The word *Amen* comes from a Greek word which means "so be it," or "I agree with that."

If I say, "The Bible is the Word of God," Christians would say, "Amen" which means "I agree with you." *Amen* literally means, "I stand with you there." If Jesus is "The Amen," that means Jesus is saying, "I am the One Who defines where we stand." Jesus said, "A

Christian better not decide where he stands. A Christian better let Me decide where he stands. I am The Amen. I decide where Christians ought to stand."

Instead of walking toward the world, a Christian had better turn and walk closer to Christ. I better make sure I am standing beside the One Who decides where I stand. Christians compromise by looking at the world and deciding separation by the world. The world does not decide how separated I am supposed to be. The world is nothing to me. I am not trying to be different from the world; I am trying to please my Saviour. It is the pleasure of Christ, not the world's sarcasm, that decides if I am doing right. The world's bragging on me or persecuting me does not matter. The world is not a factor in my stand. A Christian will begin to compromise if his stand is decided by, "Well, I'm different from the world." The world does not tell me how separated I am supposed to be; Jesus Christ tells me how separated to be. The measure of compromise is not separation from the world but devotion to the Saviour.

Compromise is the external manifestation of a lukewarm heart. When Jesus said, "I wish you were cold or hot," some say that *cold* means "liberal" and *hot* means "fundamental." Jesus would not say, "I would rather you be a liberal than lukewarm." Jesus was saying, "I want you to be as refreshing as cold water or as hot as boiling water." He wants the Christian to be inspirational and delightful and charming or a stir-it-up, kick-it-in-the-kneecap, and bless God! let's-get something-going-here kind of a Christian. After all, who wants to drink lukewarm water? The hot and the cold are not used to illustrate good and bad. God **never** gives a Christian permission to sin. God is simply saying that Christians should be cool and refreshing and helpful, or be a mover and a shaker who makes things happen. A Christian who can't be a leader can at least be refreshing. A Christian who can't preach a sermon and kick over the microphones can at least say "Amen" when the pastor does. Jesus doesn't want a Christian to be lukewarm and stand in the middle and say, "I wonder if the pastor should have kicked over those microphones? What do the visitors think?" That type of attitude is the attitude of a compromiser.

The Bible says that good news is like a refreshing messenger. Good news is like a good cup of cold water on a hot day. God wants us to be refreshing and supportive. If a Christian can't be the bus captain who visits for ten hours and brings in a bus load, at least he can be the teacher who looks at the bus captain and says, "Man, I'm glad you did that! Bring them on in! I'll teach them the Word of God." Jesus wants Christians to be refreshing and supportive or boiling hot in zeal and enthusiasm. Jesus does not want Christians to be compromisers in the middle.

First Baptist Church has gotten over the hump of Brother Hyles' death. Though we will remember him and honor his memory, and we will always cherish the wonderful years we had with him, our church has gone ahead because Brother Hyles would want us to. It is pleasing to Brother Hyles. More importantly, it is pleasing to his Saviour that First Baptist Church has gone on.

Some wonderful things have happened. First Baptist Church has grown about 1,800 in the last two years. We've started almost 20 new adult Sunday school classes. We're excited about growing.

The point is that every time growth is present, so is the temptation to compromise one's moral testimony. Let me warn those who want to get hot or cold. Great temptation does not come to lukewarm people. The safest place for a Christian is the extreme middle where he doesn't offend anybody, he doesn't build anything, and he doesn't get in the way and make waves. When a Christian is in the hot zone, it is going to be hot in more ways than one. If a bus captain decides to double his bus route, the biggest temptations and attacks are ahead of him. The Devil is painting a huge target on his back, and he had better walk very circumspectly because the biggest temptations come to those who want to grow. When a Christian sticks his head above the crowd, the Devil will be right there to try to snap it off.

I knew when coming into the arena of building the First Baptist Church that I would face temptations and pressures like I have never before faced. I have told the Lord many times, "Lord, I know that I have a bigger target on my back than I have ever had before. I know that those who want to tear me down will zone in on me. I know that all Hell will try to crumble me. If I crumble, then just think what will happen to the ministry of the First Baptist Church." I have warned the members of First Baptist Church that as we decide to get cold or hot, we had better hang on tight because Hell and Satan are not happy. I am not scared of Satan, but I have respect for his power. I don't taunt the Devil. I simply say, "God, if I can humbly be used of You, I submit myself to do so. I would rather die trying to be used of God as to live in the extreme middle zone of never really trying to be hot or cold. I want the First Baptist Church to go for it! I want us to humble ourselves, go forward on our knees, and say, "By the grace of Almighty God, let's see what He has in mind for us."

CHAPTER TWELVE

The Role of Gender in Church Growth

"I will therefore that men pray every where, lifting up holy hands, without wrath and doubting. In like manner also, that women adorn themselves in modest apparel, with shamefacedness and sobriety, not with broided hair, or gold, or pearls, or costly array." (I Timothy 2:8, 9)

CHURCHES GROW NUMERICALLY for a variety of reasons. For instance, a church may grow because of effective marketing tactics. They may have good advertising. They may have good literature or a radio or television program. Consumers know that not everything which is marketed well is necessarily worthy of its marketing. Some churches grow just because they are excellent at promoting what they have.

Some churches grow because of good preaching. First Baptist Church certainly grew under the excellent preaching of Brother Hyles, and we are still keeping the preaching hot. A church may grow because of a strong music program. Some churches grow because they have an outstanding outreach ministry or soul-winning program where the members are getting out and spreading the Word.

Numeric growth does not necessarily imply spiritual growth.
I believe some churches make that statement who are hiding behind
their laziness. However, that statement is true. For example, at a
recent gathering of 80,000 teenagers for a religious meeting, a very
prominent preacher spoke. The Gospel was never mentioned one
time. How sad! Probably tens of thousands of unsaved young people
attended that meeting. What a harvest of souls that could have been.
I am not pointing a finger; I am merely saying that just because a religious group has a large crowd does not necessarily mean that spiritual growth is taking place.

Some of the fastest-growing churches are nothing more than
rock concerts, social clubs, fitness centers, or well-choreographed
entertainment. When First Baptist Church first began plans for
building a new auditorium, I took a few of our church men to visit
several other mega-churches where thousands of people attend
weekly.

These churches had phenomenal weight rooms and fitness centers. One church had a fitness room, costing nearly $10 million, that
was larger than half the size of the present First Baptist Church auditorium. This fitness room was very impressive; however, I would like
to clear out all of the exercise equipment, bring in bus kids, and have
a huge revival! I am not against a fitness center, but I do not believe
that is the calling of the local church. Not only that, it's not in the
Bible.

Many of the churches we visited had a huge rock 'n' roll set up
in the middle of the platform with drums and a rock sound system.
When our group of men talked to these people about our new auditorium, the leaders told us what kind of sound system we would
need. I told them, "We don't have rock concerts in our church."

Several years ago, one of the most well-known charismatic
preachers in the world was exposed. He appeared to be performing
phenomenal miracles on his television program. He would walk out
into the crowd and say, "I'm thinking of a lady from Newbury,
Connecticut, who is wearing a blue dress and is sitting in the middle
section over here." The preacher would then walk over to a lady in
a blue dress and point at her, and say, "Ma'am, God's Spirit just
spoke to me. Are you from Newbury, Connecticut?"

"Yes, I am," she would say.

"God told me that you have cataracts in your eyes," he would then say.

"I do," she would answer. "How did you know that?"

"God is speaking to me right now," he declared. The preacher continued talking to the lady and told her the names of her husband and children and revealed other details about her life. She was shocked because this preacher had never before seen her. The preacher would then supposedly heal the lady of her cataracts. The woman was so stunned by all of the revelations that she appeared to be healed.

Later, investigators discovered that the preacher had trained a group of intelligent young men who were to act as public relations experts and greet people when they entered the auditorium. These men would get the names of the visitors and find out a few details about them such as where they were from and why they were at the meeting to be healed. Then these greeters would escort these visitors to a place reserved especially for them. After seating the visitors, the men would go back, write down the information they had learned, and relay the information to an unseen P.A. booth. The preacher would be fed this information through a surgically implanted listening device in his ear. His healing ministry was a big farce. This preacher was drawing huge crowds. My point is, just because someone can draw a big crowd doesn't necessarily mean he is producing any spiritual growth.

Strong, lasting, scriptural growth is our goal at First Baptist Church of Hammond. First Baptist Church is trying to get every number we can. I am not trying to build a big church; I am trying to reach as many people as I can. I believe First Baptist Church has the answer with a good, solid, balanced program. If a person comes to the First Baptist Church, he will hear the Gospel, and he can get saved. He will learn how to build a family, how to establish a home, how to rear children, how to get his kids in a good Christian school, and on and on. We'll take a bus kid from the bus routes of Chicago all the way to earning a Master's degree at Hyles-Anderson College and then help him to get to the mission field. We will even help him raise the money. First Baptist Church is a wonderful factory for helping people find the will of God for their lives.

First Baptist Church is a big church and has proven again and again that we can get a crowd. I want to keep getting a crowd. However, when we get that crowd, I want to do something with them. I want to build a foundation with a younger generation—those in their twenties and thirties. I told a young man in my office, "You're in your middle twenties. If I can't get you to understand what I'm all about, I might as well close my Bible and go home. If I fail with you, I wonder if I have any hope."

Many of us in our thirties and forties "caught it" from Brother Hyles. I'm not worried if Brother Terry Duff, the first vice chairman of our deacon board, "caught it." I'm not worried if Colonel Richard MacCormack, the chairman of the board of deacons, "caught it" from Brother Hyles. I'm not worried if those who sat under Brother Hyles' ministry for years caught it. Most of us who have been in First Baptist Church for many years have caught what we were taught over the last many decades. Those about whom I am worried are in their teen years, in their college years and twenties and in their early thirties who have not yet established themselves rock solid as to where this ministry is going. I have a fear that those who "caught it" have not solidly planted their feet deeply in what could be the next surge of church growth across the country.

The leadership of Hyles-Anderson College decided to cancel the evening college program. One reason why is that the dean of evening college came to me and shared his fear that the evening college preacher boys were not getting all they could get if they attending day college. Some of the faculty members like Dr. Wendell Evans, Dr. Ray Young, and some other teachers who taught exclusively in the day college, were not influencing the evening college students. However, the main reason why the evening college program was canceled was the discovery that many of the married college men were living very comfortable lifestyles.

I talked to three married men who were making $70,000 or more yearly and were attending college on Monday, Tuesday, and Thursday nights. They had Friday nights off and had a couple of hours of ministry work on Saturdays. These men had very comfortable lifestyles. I asked these men, "When do you learn how to live by faith? When are you going to have to find out what it is like to get your prayers answered? How are you going to go to the mission field and live on about $20,000 a year and rent some property or clear off some land and build a building? How are you going to go to Guyana, take a machete, and clear out the jungle to build a building, and start a boat ministry? How are you going to go to the Philippines and have 1,600 in church on one day and have 1,200 of them saved, if you don't know that God answers your prayers? You don't need God. You make $70,000 and have an easy schedule with eight hours of sleep at night. You don't need God at all."

I decided that I am not going to have our college turn out a bunch of "wannabe Baptist look-a-likes." I want some on-fire, hairy-legged men who know how to stand up, cry aloud, spare not, and preach. I want our Hyles-Anderson College preacher boys to be able to stand up and declare, "God answers prayers because I know personally that He answers prayers." I don't want our preacher boys reading some prayer book from Prayer class and living on someone else's borrowed faith; I want them to have their own personal faith.

A couple of those college fellows said to me, "Brother Schaap. If you cancel evening college, my family can't survive."

Bless God! I'm tired of that kind of namby-pamby, wishy-washy, yellow-bellied, yellow-spined, wannabe-a-Christian-but-ain't-got-the-guts-to-live-it kind of Christianity. First Baptist Church and Hyles-Anderson College are never going to stand for that kind of laid-back, lazy, good-God, good-Devil, good-grief, go-home mentality. We want a hard, firm edge. We want a Christianity that cuts deeply and makes a difference.

Many years ago one of our graduates hired Anita Bryant, the Florida Orange Juice celebrity promoter, to be in a citywide service. This pastor had 10,000 people show up in the Civic Auditorium on his first day of starting a brand-new Baptist church. On week number two, he had zero show up for church.

Bringing in a big name person will draw a large crowd. Many churches are bringing in big names from the rock 'n' roll industry and from the so-called Christian contemporary music industry. I am sure if I brought in some big-name southern Gospel rock-a-billy music group, First Baptist Church could draw a big crowd. However, it wouldn't be called church, and there would be no solid foundational growth.

Sustained, solid growth is a by-product of proper gender roles in a church. I Timothy 2:3-7 says, *"For this is good and acceptable in* *the sight of God our Saviour, Who will have all men to be saved, and to come unto the knowledge of the truth. For there is one God, and one mediator between God and men, the man Christ Jesus; Who gave himself a ransom for all, to be testified in due time. Whereunto I am ordained a preacher, and an apostle,…a teacher of the Gentiles.…"*

The book of I Timothy is called a pastoral epistle because it was written to a pastor on how to build and maintain a local church. At this point in his ministry, Timothy was probably pastoring the largest church at that time—the church in Ephesus. Timothy was a young man, about 40 years old. Paul was saying to Timothy, through the inspiration of the Holy Ghost, that the biggest objective on God's agenda is getting people saved. Getting people saved is the reason why Jesus came and is the heartbeat of God. *"…God our Saviour; Who will have all men to be saved.…"* Paul said that was the reason that God ordained Paul to be a preacher and a teacher of the Gentiles. The whole reason that God called Paul to be a preacher and Timothy to be a pastor was to get lost people saved and saved people out soul winning and getting more lost people saved. That makes sense.

In verse 8 the phrase, *"I will therefore that men pray every where,"* didn't make sense to me. Why are we jumping to men praying when the main objective is to get people saved? Then in verse 9 Paul continues, *"In like manner also, that women adorn themselves in modest apparel.…"* When I was a younger preacher, I would study this Scripture and say, "God, I know it all makes sense somewhere, but it doesn't make sense to me."

Paul tells Timothy that the purpose of a church and being a pastor is getting people saved. Then he says that men should be praying, and women should be dressing right. This passage just didn't seem to make sense.

God is teaching us a great truth about how to build a solid, growing church that sustains its growth generation after generation after generation. The gender role must be right in a local church; otherwise, the growth of a church is sporadic, temporary, and unstable. Meteoric growth is a lot of fun. However, I want to grow and build, grow and build, and grow and build.

What is happening in so many churches today and even in some of our Hyles-Anderson College graduates' churches is that they

make the unscriptural mistakes of minimizing preaching and bringing in drama. What a tragic mistake! The Bible does not say that
God manifests His Word through drama. The Bible says in Titus 1:3,
"*But God hath in due times manifested his word through preaching....*"
Preaching is not something that was done in the 1940's and in the
1950's, and now has been outgrown. To the contrary, preaching was
ordained of God in the Old Testament. God ordained men, such as
Isaiah, Jeremiah, and Ezekiel to name a few, to stand up and literally make fools of themselves! God told Isaiah to cut off his clothes to
show God's people that they were going to be stripped and naked.
Some of those preachers did some embarrassing things! God chose
preaching as a tool, not simply as a modem cultural event. God wants
a man to stand, take the Bible, read a few verses, holler and scream,
and tell His people what is going on in their lives.

I like it when people come by my office and say, "You've been in
our house. You've been a fly on the wall. You know exactly what is
going on." No! God has ordained preachers to say what the Bible
says.

I don't mind a good skit in Youth Conference. However, we are
never going to have drama or skits replace the preaching in Youth
Conference. Skits are to grab the minds of the unspiritual young kids
and to prepare them to hear the preaching of the Gospel. I like a
good skit. We have crazy skits in Vacation Bible School, and we
laugh a lot. The truth of the matter is, we are going to try to teach
and preach some truth to them.

I think churches are making a mistake in their choice of music.
So-called fundamental churches, and even some of our Hyles-
Anderson College graduates, are bringing in very worldly music with
barroom and rock-concert rhythms. The Bible does not teach that
any particular rhythm is a sin, but of what is the listener reminded
when he listens to that music? Where did the style of music come
from? Where was the rhythm inspired? When a Christian hears,
"Amazing grace, how sweet the sound," he doesn't say, "Oh yeah,
that reminds me of a rock concert I recently attended." Some
churches use the rock-a-billy, hillbilly, "beaty" kind of music, and the
listener might say, "That reminds me of Nashville."

First Baptist Church is not trying to have Nashville here! We are
trying to have church here. Other songs may cause the listener to

think, "That reminds me of some of those rock 'n' roll groups or rap groups." First Baptist Church is not trying to have a rock concert here! We're trying to have a Rock of Ages concert here! These churches are bringing in music that is exactly like the world's music.

I recently received a letter from a Southern Baptist pastor. He said, "I listen to your preaching on the Internet. I like your preaching. I've been searching all across America for that kind of preaching. My denomination doesn't have anything like that. They are teaching in the seminaries and our pastors' schools to copy the unchurched world's techniques to reach the unchurched people. To me, that seems shallow and inefficient and unscriptural. What do you think?"

I agree with this pastor. I think using the world's techniques is shallow, inefficient, and unscriptural. I want to say to this pastor, "Brother, why don't you come on over to the independent Baptist side? We'd love to have you." I'm not interested in finding out what Madison Avenue or Hollywood or the world has to teach me about church building. God wrote a Book to tell me how to build a church.

What does the role of gender have to do with church building? God said that if a church doesn't get the men and women in the right roles and in the right order, it will not have a good, solid foundation on which to build and then to sustain growth. I can build a church without men and women understanding their roles, but to sustain growth with a good, solid foundation, generation after generation, men and women must learn what their roles are in the church.

I Timothy 2: 8 says, *"I will therefore...."* The word *therefore* means "based on what you just read." We saw in I Timothy 2:3 that because God is a Saviour, He wants to get all people saved, and He calls preachers to build churches to get people saved. Timothy now is saying, "Based on this premise, I want the men to do something." Verse 8 continues, *"I will therefore that men pray every where, lifting up holy hands, without wrath and doubting."*

Man has a specific role in the local church. I believe God is teaching the following three principles regarding the man's role in the church.

1. *Men should lead the public services.* The word *pray* in verse 8 doesn't simply mean we are to pray before we eat or before an offering. The word *pray* has the idea of leadership. It is taking the role of public praying. The word *pray* does not always simply mean "praying to God." It is actually a courtroom term, and the word *pray* is often used in legal terms regarding a lawyer petitioning a judge or a court and has to do with procedure and leadership. God wants the men of the church to establish the procedures of the church and to enforce them. God wants the men to lead in executing the procedures of the church.

That doesn't mean a woman cannot sing a song in a public service. She is not leading the congregation when she sings. She is just inspiring and encouraging. That is why at First Baptist Church, a man reads the Scriptures. We have a man for a pastor and men sit on the platform. It is a statement that men lead the First Baptist Church.

2. Men should teach the men. God does not want women teaching the men in the church. In First Baptist Church from junior age and older, the boys and the men are taught by men.

3. Men should petition the leadership when problems arise. One meaning of the word *pray* is "petitioning the leadership." Another role of men in the church is, if there is a problem in the church, the men should initiate solving the problem. It amazes me how many times a couple will come to my office, and the husband will not open his mouth one time. Husband, if you told your wife to do all the talking, I don't mind the wife being the husband's mouthpiece. But it bothers me when I look at the husband and say, "What are your feelings about this?" and he looks at his wife and says, "Do I have any feelings about this?" It bothers me when I go to a restaurant and the woman orders for both of them. If you want your wife to order for herself, that is your business. My wife does not order for me. My wife doesn't choose my clothing for me. My wife doesn't put on my socks or pick out my shoes.

One of the safeguards of the local church is if a wife has a problem, the wife should go to her husband and say, "I'm concerned about something, and I want to put it in your hands." One of the worst things a woman can do is pick up the phone, call her friend, and say, "I've got a problem, and I want to tell you about it."

I don't believe it is wrong for a woman to come to the pastor to discuss a problem because she is petitioning the man that is the leader of the church. The problem that God is addressing is that men should handle the problems of the church. That is the purpose of the deacon board. The deacon board of the First Baptist Church is comprised of men. In Acts 6 when a problem arose in the church of Jerusalem, God had the men solve the problem. That is God's method. He uses men to lead and solve the problems.

I Timothy 2:8 also says, "...*lifting up holy hands, without wrath and doubting.*" In Bible days, it was very common for a man who was a warrior or for a man who was protecting his own property to carry a weapon. It was also a common practice to carry a shield. Typically, the man would carry his weapon in his right hand and his shield in his left hand. When this man came upon another man, he had several ways of greeting that man. First, he might lay down or sheath his sword, hold up his right hand, and greet the man. They did not shake hands. From a long distance, a man might hold out his hand, and that action was saying, "I have no weapon in my hand, and I did not come here to hurt you." However, the man would still be holding his shield which told the other man, "I'm not here to hurt you, but I don't trust you either."

Sometimes, a man might keep his weapon in his hand, put down his shield, and hold up his left hand which said, "I don't trust you so much that I am going to put down my weapon, but I am willing to expose myself. I will put down my shield and not defend myself unless I have to do so." If a man had total trust, faith, and verity, he would sheath his sword, lay down the shield, put up both hands which indicated, "I'm coming to you defenseless and with no malice."

I spend up to seven hours a week helping churches across the country that have the kinds of problems I am addressing right here. Sometimes smaller churches have power plays by men. A man has a weapon in his hand. He gets power by getting on the deacon board or some other position, and he wants to wield authority and have power. Paul is teaching that the men of the church need to understand that the local church is not a place for a man to defend his position or exercise his power. Strong men need to be chosen who are secure enough in their masculinity and manhood and totally onboard with the pastor that they are not sitting with their weapon in hand saying, "He better not do that," or sitting in the crowd with their shield up saying, "He had better get off of that topic." When men in the congregation say, "The pastor irritates me with some of the things he preaches," they have their shields up.

God is teaching that if a church wants to be a sustained, growing mega-church, it must have many men who leave their weapons and their shields outside, walk in, and say, "I am exposed and vulnerable to you spiritually, Pastor. I am willing for you to go right into my heart with the weapon of the Sword of the Word of God." Men who are not willing to conform to the preaching of the Bible from the pulpit will cause a major problem with the growth of the church.

Growth is not just how many kids the bus captains can bring on their buses. Growth is determined by the number of men who walk into the church and say, "I'm laying down my weapon. I'm not here to prove any point. I'm here to let the pastor go straight into my heart with the double-edged Sword of the Word of God."

Many men hide behind their shields when they enter the church. Taking that stance is a great crippler of future growth because those men are not allowing the Spirit of the Living God to use the Word of God, which is quick and powerful and sharper than any two-edged sword, to pierce their hearts. Fundamentalism needs a revival of hairy-legged men who are strong leaders of business and strong men of employment who are regularly at the altar of their churches; men who say, "I may have a position of power or authority, but, God, that is not why I am in this church. I am in this church service to have my pastor stick me right in the gizzard!" Men should regularly bend their knees at an old-fashioned altar and say, "God, I needed that message."

It bothers me when men want to sit in the pews and let their children and their wives walk the aisles. It bothers me greatly when I see women at the altar and their husbands scurrying outside. Sustained growth isn't caused because a church has hot-shot staff members who know how to have a big day during a program. No! Sustained growth is caused by hairy-legged men who have enough courtesy toward God to listen to the man of God and make things right at the altar.

The altar of every old-fashioned Baptist church should be filled with men. Women and children should have to say, "I wish I could get to the altar, but Dad is in the way." Whatever reasons a man gives for not listening to the man of God and responding to the message shows he has his shield up. If a man is spitting venom during a sermon, he has his weapon in his hand. A man takes leadership by raising both hands and saying, "I have no shield to protect me. I have no weapon. Let me have it, Pastor!"

Any preacher who yells and screams and has a halfway decently organized sermon outline can touch the heart of a woman. Unfortunately, women tend to be by nature more spiritually minded. Eve was more interested in being like God than was Adam. The serpent said to Eve, *"For God doth know that in the day that ye eat thereof...ye shall be as gods, knowing good and evil."* The woman said, "That's what I want," and took it. I don't think she took of the fruit because she wanted to usurp the authority of God. The Bible says that Adam was not deceived. Adam knew that the serpent's statement was a lie out of Hell, but Adam let his wife take the lead. Why didn't Adam step out, take Eve's hand, kneel with her, and make sure their hearts were humble before God?

Too many men visit the restaurants and the sports stadiums more than they visit the altar of their church. This applies not only to older men, but to all men. That generation who caught Brother Hyles at the end of his ministry, when he was settling his ministry, preparing for the inevitable, and getting it good and solid to hand over to the next man, didn't see Brother Hyles when he was in that vibrant growth stage of his 40's and 50's and early 60's. The church was strong, but these younger men never caught that white-hot, fervent, passionate hunger for the God Who Brother Hyles loved. They loved Brother Hyles, but they did not catch His God. The young generation of men, ages 25 to 35 years of age need to be at the altar just as much as the older men. The gender role of the male is leading, stepping out, and responding to the preaching. Strong women will follow a strong man, but strong men will not follow women. Many churches have many men in them, but they are not strong men, so the women lead them.

If the men are to step out and take the lead, then what is the role of the woman in the church? Look at I Timothy 2:9, *"In like manner...."* Just as the men have a leadership role that determines the sustained growth of a church, likewise the women also have a vital role that helps secure the sustained growth of the church. Verse 9 continues, *"In like manner also, that women adorn themselves in modest apparel, with shamefacedness and sobriety; not with broided hair, or gold, or pearls, or costly array, But (which becometh women professing godliness) with good works."*

If the goal of the church is getting people saved, the men should be stepping out and leading in the soul winning. Who should be building the bus routes? The men should! Men should be building the Sunday school classes and leading in the starting of more classes and sending more people to the mission field and raising more money. The men should be saying, "How can I help, Pastor? How can I do my part to get more people out on the mission field?"

The women manifest the character of the church. Women validate the leadership of the men by their manner of dress and manifestation of spirit. Paul is not saying that women should not fix their hair or wear jewelry. He is simply stating that the character of a church is manifested in strong men responding to the preaching of God's Word and women validating that leadership. God was saying that the women put their stamp of approval on the role of the man by the spirit of followship and the dress of femininity. When a woman carries feminine grace and charm and stands in support of the role of the male leadership, she is making a powerful statement that says, "I validate the role of male leadership."

How do the people in the world know that First Baptist Church is the right kind of church? The world looks at what First Baptist Church ladies wear when they go to the supermarket. The world knows what First Baptist Church women look like. A church member cannot go anywhere in this Calumet region without people saying, "I know what church you attend." The church ladies validate the message of the pastor.

When our teen girls or ladies wear clothing that is not in line with the pastor's preaching, they are wearing a big neon sign that says, "I don't agree with what my pastor preaches." High school and college girls who want to strip half-naked and go mixed swimming with the boys are invalidating the message of this church. They are undermining the authority and the message of this pulpit, as well as the male leadership of this church. The church will not grow on harlotry, on a Southern-Baptist style of worldly evangelism, nor on rock concert music. If the First Baptist Church does go down, it will go down with the cry, "Thus saith the Lord!" still thundering from the pulpit! If that type of preaching kills the crowd, then so be it! We are not going to get a crowd at the expense of our standards. The pulpit will not be sacrificed because of the modern generation. The Bible says that ladies validate what the pastor preaches when they walk out of the church doors and dress according to the preaching.

Husbands may not disagree with what I say, but they put up their shield because they have to go home with a wife who disagrees with the preaching. The husband has to listen to his wife's nagging statements such as, "I'm tired of that preacher preaching on how I dress. That's all he talks about!"

Women show the validation of the pulpit ministry and the leadership of the men not only by the way they dress, but also by the spirit they manifest. The role of a woman is to have a spirit of followship. Verse 11 says, *"Let the woman learn in silence with all subjection."* The word *subjection* is a military term which means the same thing as when a sergeant says to a soldier, "fall in," and the soldier lines up in military order and follows the direction of his leader. The soldier organizes himself to follow the commands of the leader. That is exactly what subjection means—a soldier follows the command of the leader.

Some say, "You're trying to put women under foot." No. Everywhere the Gospel is preached, women are magnified. God is saying that women are so powerful in their testimony that they don't even have to open their mouths. All a woman has to do is let people see how she dresses and how she treats the male leadership. That woman will make a statement more profound than even the men who lead because nothing is more validating or powerful than a woman at whom people look and say, "She's one of those First Baptist women. You can sure tell who they are."

> **"God is saying that women are so powerful in their testimony that they don't even have to open their mouths."**

Feminine, godly, humble women inspire men of character to accept the challenge of leadership. If a woman, who trots to my office and talks about her miserable husband, would dress nicely, put on a little perfume, act a little feminine around her husband, and stop bossing him would instead encourage him, and use her charm and

grace and the tools of the trade, she could get that man to do nearly anything she wanted him to do. If Eve could get Adam to deliber-
ately, willingly, knowingly damn mankind to Hell, a woman can get
her "big boy" to do anything she wants him to do. Many a woman
has left her feminine charm that inspires her man to do righteousness
to wagging her tongue like a vicious weapon and has slashed her husband's spirit until he lacks the confidence to do anything. That man
knows that if he even feebly raises his head, he will be cut down with,
"Who do you think you are?"

The human reason I stand in the First Baptist Church pulpit is
because I know I have my wife's confidence. With my wife's confidence, all Hell better watch out. Every real man feels this way. I personally know of only one man who is doing anything substantial in
God's work whose wife is not on his side. I know some men, who are
in the ministry, whose wives are not on their sides, but these men are
not reaching their potential. When a husband comes home from visiting his bus route, his wife should say, "I'm so proud of you. That
church is so fortunate to have a man like you." Her husband would
be pumped up with ten tons of nitroglycerin and ready to charge Hell
with a squirt gun.

However, that husband who comes home and his wife says, "You
promised you would be home, but you put in 30 more minutes on
that bus route! You love those stupid bus kids more than you love
me!" is not excited about getting up Sunday morning and running his
bus route.

A man's role is to respond to the preaching and step forth and
show by example in leadership that he is behind the policies. A man
is supposed to step out and say, "Follow me, Sweetheart. We're going
some place."

When I was dating my wife, sometimes she would be worried
about the future, as all women are. I would tell her, "Baby, stay with
me. I'm going some place."

Then I would go back to my room and plead with God, "Lord,
where am I going?" Men are supposed to lead in all areas including
child rearing and marriage. I sat in the office the other day with a
man who couldn't think of any activities to do with his wife for a
date. I quickly listed 25 things he could do, and the man said, "Wow!
I never thought of those."

I said to him, "That's your problem. You don't think." A woman's role is to validate the leadership and the preaching by how she dresses and by how she follows and submits.

In sustaining church growth, both men and women have the role of passing on their faith to the next generation. I Timothy 2:13-15 says, *"For Adam was first formed, then Eve. And Adam was not deceived, but the woman being deceived was in the transgression. Notwithstanding she shall be saved* [not saved to go to Heaven, but she will salvage the mess she got mankind into] *in childbearing, if they continue in faith and charity and holiness with sobriety."*

God is saying, "Eve, you made a horrendous mess! You brought damnation to mankind when you sinned and gave the forbidden fruit to your husband. Your purpose was to keep Adam from messing up his life. Eve, if you want to redeem yourself and save the mess you created, you better team up with your husband. The two of you can salvage the mess you got into by passing on the faith to the next generation."

Parents, are your children serving God? I don't necessarily mean full-time Christian service. Are your children serving on the bus route with you? Does Dad go off to the bus route and do the soul winning? Does Mom go to Phoster Club and the children stay home? Dad, get your family together and say, "We, as a team, are going to serve God."

Joshua made a tremendous statement when he said, *"...as for me and my house, we will serve the LORD."* Parent, don't you drop your child off for Teenage Soul Winning and then go have a cup of coffee. Why don't you drive for teenage soul winning? We need to have a revival of families, as teams, serving God.

Brother Bob Hooker, who is in charge of our sailor ministry, was asked how he got his six daughters loving God, turning out right, and serving the Lord. Brother Hooker said, "I got my whole family involved in my ministry. My girls saw sailors getting saved in our house, and they had a part in that."

Dad, please don't leave your family behind. Husband, please don't leave your wife behind. As a team, parents must train the next generation.

Let me make three final observations.

1. **Godly men are often forced to keep peace through their**

marriage covenant at the expense of their spiritual contribution to the local church. A woman can force her husband to walk away from his covenant promise to God, his spiritual call to the ministry, and his love for his church. The husband may want to get involved in a ministry, but he took a covenant oath with his wife that he would stand by her and protect her and love her. The result is that the wife and the husband are not involved in anything. She has nagged him and nagged him. She may even say, "We should leave this church and go to a smaller church where we could be more involved." Honey, anyone who can't get involved in the First Baptist Church of Hammond won't get involved anywhere! First Baptist Church has over 100 ministries. If a member can't find a ministry in this church, the problem is a warped spiritual appetite. The problem is not that the wife cannot get involved; the problem is a heart and attitude problem. The husband needs to lead the wife and say, "Honey, we're going to get involved. I'm for you, and I love you. Let's do something together in this church."

The only people I know who talk about leaving First Baptist Church are the people who do nothing in our church. I have not yet had a bus captain come to me and say, "I'm leaving this church." I have had one man who was involved in a ministry leave our church because his wife made the decisions at home. The truth of the matter is, many men will never reach their potential because the woman won't let him, and the husband knows he has to live with her.

Many a man comes to my office and says, "Brother Schaap, could I just bleed in a man's office? I want to tell you man-to-man that I want to do something for God, but every time I try to raise my head up, my wife just slams it down." That man needs to hit an altar and tell God, "I commit the whole mess to your hands. I want to lead, but You are going to have to help her follow." The man cannot go home and be a big bear or insult her or get mad at her. The man needs to look at his wife and say, "One of these days, I want God to turn your heart so we can serve God together. That's my goal."

2. **Godly men often hide behind the needs of their wives rather than exercising creative leadership.** Why doesn't a man spend a little money on his wife? Why not take her out to eat? A wife may not want her husband to serve God because the husband hasn't bought her a new dress since Noah stumbled off the ark.

A couple came to me for counsel, and I asked the husband, "When was the last time you bought your wife a dress?"

He said, "I don't know."

He looked at his wife and she said, "The one I have on is the last one you bought me. You paid a dime for it at the Salvation Army because you finally broke down and gave me some change ten years ago!"

Is it any wonder that couple is in my office with marriage problems? A man won't spend any money on his wife, and he wonders why she doesn't want him to serve God. In her mind, serving God is an excuse to spend less time with her and less money on her.

3. **Godly men can often get involved at the expense of their family.** A man should never step away from his family and say, "I'm too busy serving God to spend time with you." That is a lie and a contradiction to the Bible. A Christian can serve God and have a happy home. A couple can win souls, help build the church, and have a happy marriage. A family does not have to choose between serving God and having a happy family. You can have both, and the happiest families in our church prove that is true.

CHAPTER THIRTEEN

A Greater Sin Than Sodomy

"And turning the cities of Sodom and Gomorrha into ashes condemned them with an overthrow, making them an ensample unto those that after should live ungodly; And delivered just Lot, vexed with the filthy conversation of the wicked." (II Peter 2:6, 7)

I AM NOT A one-issue preacher. I am not a one-issue political person. Really, I am not a one-issue anything. If I had to make one issue in my life, it would be, "God loves you, and wants to save you from Hell." Aside from that one issue, I do not make an issue about many things. However, I am going to make an issue about something very important.

Several issues regarding homosexuality have been in the news lately. First is the issue of the United States Supreme Court passing a landmark decision that no state can pass a law prohibiting sodomite sex. Many newspapers are publishing that this Supreme Court decision may be one of the planks of future Republican and Democratic platforms. President Bush has come out strongly saying that marriage is between a man and a woman. Thank God for a President who is not afraid to look in the eyes of the Supreme Court justices and say, "You're wrong!" Every one of the 2004 Democratic presidential hopefuls gave their assent to some type of a civil union between two men or two women.

Secondly, widespread news coverage has been given to the homosexual Episcopalian bishop who was elected. I like what one of my church members, Dave Sisson, said to me. "Why the outcry about the bishop's being homosexual? You have to be a priest before you can be a bishop. So I guess it's okay to be a homosexual priest but not a homosexual bishop." The Episcopalian church is due for a major split. I'm glad to see that there are a few with some backbone in the Episcopalian movement.

A third issue concerns a major religion having a terrible problem with its leaders and pedophilia.

Recently, on a talk show, the host was interviewing a woman who was a priest in her religion. She said, "I am now going to tell you everything the Bible says about sodomy. Here it is." She remained silent for a moment, and then said, "That is it. Nothing. The Bible says nothing about homosexuality."

The talk show host said, "Since you don't know what the Bible says, I will read it to you." After he read one or two passages from the Bible, he asked the woman, "What qualifies you to be a priest in any religion since you don't know the Bible?" It's a sad day in our country when a talk show host, who makes his money entertaining people, knows more Bible than does a priest or a bishop or a preacher.

Volumes of information regarding sodomy has been published in newspapers and broadcasted on radio and television. Many people are taking the dangerous, extreme, middle-of-the-road position. I hate the middle position. Know what you believe and stand with it! Because a lot of bad information has been published concerning this issue, I want to address the matter and show how it relates to church growth.

The Sodomite community has taken the beautiful word *gay* which means "happy and cheerful," and has perverted it to describe the sodomite lifestyle. I like the Bible term *sodomite* better. The word *sodomy* comes from the word "Sodom" and means "burning or scorched." Genesis 13:10 and 11 says, "*And Lot lifted up his eyes, and beheld all the plain of Jordan, that it was well watered everywhere, before the LORD destroyed Sodom and Gomorrah, even as the garden of the LORD like the land of Egypt, as thou comest unto Zoar. Then Lot chose him all the plain of Jordan; and Lot journeyed east: and they separated themselves the one from the other."*

Genesis 13 records the story of a good man named Lot. The Bible calls Lot a *just* man meaning a "justified man." I believe Lot was a saved man and is in Heaven tonight. However, Lot made a tragic blunder. Lot had to separate from Abraham for several reasons. Abraham told Lot to choose which way he wanted to go with his family and servants to settle, and Abraham said he would go in the opposite direction. Lot looked toward the plains of Sodom, a land the Bible says looked like the garden of God.

Let me point out that just because judgment does not fall immediately on a particular sin, which may appear to some people to be very appropriate and enjoyable and natural, does not mean that human experience supersedes the Word of God. Before God destroyed the land of Sodom, it looked just like the Garden of Eden. Christians must not make the mistake of judging between right and wrong based on what a situation looks like before judgment day. Committing fornication and living together for a while may look good to young people. Living together seems like a good idea in the pea-sized brain of mankind, but the Bible says that God will judge whoremongers and adulterers. Fornication may look good when a boy is 16 years old and his hormones are flushing through his system at 100 miles per hour, but it will not look good to him on the other side of judgment when he realizes what a tragic blunder he made. Teenagers must not let a pretty little girl or a handsome boy and the external attractiveness of the package determine what is right and wrong.

Recent newspaper editions showed two sodomite men, who look like well-dressed business executives, living together in their penthouse in New York City. They have lots of money, drive a Mercedes, and have all the fine things; they just happen to be "gay." Which ever way the world wraps that package of sin must not determine the rightness or wrongness of the sin. Sodom may have looked like the Garden of Eden, but that was before God destroyed it. Genesis 18:20 and 21 says, *"And the LORD said, Because of the cry of Sodom and Gomorrah is great, and because their sin is very grievous; I will go down now, and see whether they have done altogether according to the cry of it, which is come unto me; and if not, I will know."*

The word *grievous* means "severe." Sodom was known for a particularly severe sin. Whatever sin it was, God said it was a grievous or a severe sin, and the city was known for that particular sin. God said He would go down from Heaven and see if that report was true; and if it was true, God was going to deal with it.

In Genesis 19, God sent two angels to Sodom to see if what God had heard about Sodom was true and to report back to God with their findings. The angels went to the house of Lot, the born-again Christian of the city. Genesis 19:4-5 continues, *"But before they lay down, the men of the city, even the men of Sodom, compassed the house round, both old and young, all the people from every quarter; And they called unto Lot, and said unto him, Where are the men which came in to thee this night? bring them out unto us, that we may know them."*

This crowd was not the welcome wagon of Sodom coming to greet these men who were visiting Lot. The word *know* in this verse is exactly the same Hebrew word used in Genesis 4:1 when God said that Adam *knew* his wife, and she conceived a child. This verse is not talking about the men saying, "Hello, my name is Jones; Nice to meet you." No! This verse is talking about an intimate, physical relationship. That word *know* is used again and again in the Bible to describe a husband and wife knowing each other and having babies.

These sodomite men in the city of Sodom came to Lot's house, pounded on the door, and said, "Two men came to see you. Bring them out. We want to have intimate, physical, immoral acts with these men." I wonder what the sin of Sodom was!

The story continues in Genesis 19:6-8. *"And Lot went out at the door unto them, and shut the door after him, And said, I pray you, brethren, do not so wickedly. Behold now, I have two daughters which have not known man; Let me, I pray you, bring them out unto you, and do ye to them as is good in your eyes: only unto these men do nothing; for therefore came they under the shadow of my roof."*

I do not know ancient Hebrew customs, but this account is the biggest affront to my moral, righteous attitude that I have ever encountered in my life. Lot was willing to bring out his single, unmarried daughters to these Sodomite men. He was saying, "You may rape my daughters, but just don't touch these men."

No wonder God said that there was a grievous sin in Sodom. No wonder God said that there was a sin in the city of Sodom that was so perverted, so distorted, so dishonorable, so absolutely nauseating, that it would change a man like Lot so much that he would actually freely offer his two virgin daughters to be raped by a group of perverts in the city.

Genesis 19:9 says, *"And they said, Stand back. And they said again, This one fellow came in to sojourn, and he will needs be a judge: now will we deal worse with thee, than with them. And they pressed sore upon the man, even Lot, and came near to break the door."* These inhabitants of Sodom actually began the process of violating Lot. These sodomites told Lot, "You think you are better than we are. You are judging us as though we don't know what is right and wrong. We want those male visitors in your house. Bring them out." The sodomites didn't want the daughters of Lot, and they even proceeded in an attempt to violate Lot.

In verses 10 and 11, the angels step in. *"But the men put forth their hands, and pulled Lot into the house to them, and shut to the door. And they smote the men that were at the door of the house with blindness, both small and great...."* These sodomites were stricken with blindness. At this point, anyone would think these men would say, "God is angry at us" and go home. However, they didn't. Rather, verse 11 continues, *"...so that they wearied themselves to find the door."* Their inability to see did not stop these men as they continued to search. They wanted what they came to get, and nothing—not even blindness—was going to stop them from getting it.

When I reread this story about sodomy, I can't believe that some Christians watch television sitcoms with a central theme based on sodomite living. Actors portray homosexual characters. These same Christians say, "I don't agree with their lifestyle, but it is good acting; and it's funny." Those shows are garbage out of Hell! I would rather a man feed his family from the local garbage dump than let his family watch that kind of trash on the television.

God takes action in Genesis 19:24, 25: *"Then the LORD rained upon Sodom and upon Gomorrah brimstone and fire from the LORD out of heaven; And he overthrew those cities, and all the plain, and all the inhabitants of the cities, and that which grew upon the ground."* God's opinion of sodomy lies at the bottom of the Dead Sea. Sodom and

Gomorrah and the other cities of the plain are now at the bottom of the Dead Sea. Archeologists cannot even get to those cities for excavation. God said, "I'm going to bury those cities. I'm going to cover them with salt. Mankind will never get to the cities. I will permanently bury those cities so that everyone will know my opinion of the sin of Sodom." God sent the same ingredients that are in Hell upon Sodom.

Deuteronomy 23:17 and 18 says, *"There shall be no whore of the daughters of Israel, nor a sodomite of the sons of Israel. Thou shalt not bring the hire of a whore, or the price of a dog, into the house of the LORD thy God for any vow: for even both these are abomination unto the LORD thy God."* In this passage of the Bible, the word *dog* is not referring to an animal. Rather, a dog in Bible times was a man who dressed up like a woman and sold himself as a prostitute. God was simply saying that He did not want any transvestites, cross-dressers, or prostitutes. God does not want boys dressing like women. God doesn't want women dressing like men. The verse says that those who did so were an abomination to Him. God doesn't want anyone looking look like a whore or a sodomite. God doesn't want a Christian dressing like them or acting like them. The word *abomination* means that God is nauseated and about to throw up.

Deuteronomy 29:23 says, *"And that the whole land thereof is brimstone, and salt, and burning, that it is not sown, nor beareth, nor any grass growth therein, Like the overthrow of Sodom, and Gomorrah, Admah, and Zeboim, which the LORD overthrew in his anger, and in his wrath...."* The sin of Sodom made God angry and wrathful. *Wrath* is heated-up anger. The sin of Sodom made God so angry that He poured out Hell on earth on the sodomites.

I Kings 14 speaks about a king who was a weak leader and made terrible decisions. His name was Rehoboam; he was the son of Solomon. Rehoboam split the kingdom because of foolish decisions, and then he let the kingdom fall apart. Verses 21-24 say, *"And Rehoboam the son of Solomon reigned in Judah. Rehoboam was forty and one years old when he began to reign, and he reigned seventeen years in Jerusalem, the city which the LORD did choose out of all the tribes of Israel, to put his name there. And his mother's name was Naamah an Ammonitess. And Judah did evil in the sight of the LORD, and they provoked him to jealousy with their sins which they had committed, above all that their fathers had done. For they also built them high places, and images, and groves, on every high hill, and under every green tree. And there were also sodomites in the land: and they did according to all the abominations of the nations which the LORD cast out before the children of Israel."*

Do you know why God sent the Israelites into Canaan and told them to kill everyone—man, woman, boy, girl, and animals? That was an act of mercy from God. Those nations like the Canaanites, the Ammonites, the Hittites, and the Hivites were populated mostly with sodomites. Those nations practiced child pornography and pedophilia, victimizing little children for sexual gratification. They even practiced bestiality. They actually bred animals dedicated for the express purpose of sodomites using them in religious worship services in the most grotesque ways.

Not a week goes by that I do not hear about someone messing up his life sexually because of the Internet. If a Christian does not have the character to control his Internet usage, he needs to get rid of it. I was counseling a man who said, "Pastor, you don't even want to know what is on the Internet. It's everything including animals." That sin is exactly why God had the Canaanites cast out of the country of Israel. That is exactly why God told His people to destroy those people as an act of mercy. He did not want the children of Israel to grow up in that abominable lifestyle and continue that horrible sin. God believed in capital punishment for sodomites.

A friend of mine in Canada wrote me a letter asking me to pray for his country. He said, "If I get up and preach against sodomy as a sin, I could go to jail." At this time, some states in America are considering punishing preachers who preach against sodomy as being guilty of a hate crime. The stars will fall before anyone tells me what to preach in my pulpit! Please don't misunderstand me. I pray for our country's officials every day of the year. I pray for the Supreme Court justices. Christians are to be salt in the community. We are to be righteous, proper, decent, God-fearing, and Christ-honoring citizens, who are wise as serpents and harmless as doves. But we are not supposed to be the kind of people who just sit by when someone says, "I think those gays are nice people."

No! The Christian should step up and say, "They may be nice people, but the sin of sodomy is condemned by Almighty God!" It is incumbent upon all Christians to act as salt in their communities. Sodomy is a hellish, abominable damnation to this nation, to our citizens, and to God's people.

I Kings 15:11 says, "*And Asa did that which was right in the eyes of the LORD, as did David his father.*" What was the first right thing King Asa did? Verse 12 says, "*And he took away the sodomites out of the land, and removed all the idols that his fathers had made.*" Asa even had to put away his own mother because she was a pro-sodomite.

Christian, if you have family members who are sodomites or lesbians, don't be unkind to them; however, **NEVER** let your children spend time alone with them.

Someone once told me, "Brother Schaap, my dad is a homosexual and has a live-in partner. He wants my son to spend a week with him." Then he asked, "What do you think, Brother Schaap?"

What do I think! I don't think a parent should ever let his little boy be alone with any single, unmarried man on any kind of basis overnight—never. I don't care if the man is an uncle or a friend or any other relative. Anyone who spent one week with me in my office and heard the stories I hear would never let his little child stay overnight alone with anyone. I have counseled far too many incest cases since I became the pastor of the First Baptist Church.

God's people need to be wise as serpents. Christians should not harm or insult or curse or sneer at even one sodomite. A Christian should let the love of Jesus radiate from his smile, and he should be kind, decent, and appropriate and try to win them to Christ as he would anyone else; however, Christians should stand up when an individual says, "The Bible doesn't say anything about sodomy." The Bible has a lot to say about sodomy!

Single men should not be constantly hanging around little boys and little girls. Single men and women should be involved with single friends and get involved in some of the adult soul-winning ministries. Doing so is a protection for their testimony. We have come to a day and age in our society where it is not appropriate for those kinds of things to take place.

Romans 1:24-27 says, "*Wherefore God also gave them up to uncleanness through of the lusts of their own hearts, to dishonour their own bodies between themselves; Who changed the truth of God into a lie, and worshipped and served the creature more than the Creator, who is* blessed forever. Amen. For this cause God gave them up unto vile affections: for even their women did change the natural use into that which is against nature: And likewise also the men, leaving the natural use of the woman, burned in their lust one toward another; men with men working that which is unseemly, and receiving in themselves that recompense of their error which was meet."

The word *recompense* means "payment." The word *meet* means "appropriate." God said, "I sent a disease which is an appropriate payment. If you want to act like a sodomite, you will get a disease that is uniquely suited for sodomites." It grieves my heart when I see a little child who has AIDS. That child is the innocent victim of the free will of man. For instance, if I take a gun and shoot someone, that person did not necessarily get judged by God; rather, he is a victim of my free will.

When I was robbed recently, God wasn't judging me. I didn't walk away and say, "God, what did I do? You judged me." No. I was a victim of the free will of man. If somebody wants to act like a sodomite, the Bible says there is an appropriate punishment for those actions; it is called AIDS. Some believe that the way the AIDS disease came into existence was from sodomites.

I Corinthians 6:9-11 says, "*Know ye not that the unrighteous shall not inherit the kingdom of God? Be not deceived: neither fornicators, nor idolators, nor adulterers, nor effeminate, nor abusers of themselves with mankind, Nor thieves, nor covetous, nor drunkards, nor revilers, nor extortioners, shall inherit the kingdom of God. And such were some of you: but ye are washed, but ye are sanctified, but ye are justified in the name of the Lord Jesus, and by the Spirit of our God.*" The church in Corinth had members who had been sodomites, lesbians, adulterers, and whoremongers, but they all got saved and were no longer involved in those sins. Don't ever tell me that a sodomite cannot change. This verse says, "*And such were some of you.*" The verb "were" is past tense. They had become clean and decent and righteous.

Romans 1:32 says, "*Who knowing the judgment of God, that they which commit such things are worthy of death, not only do the same, but have pleasure in them that do them.*" I do not know of any group of people who are more arrogant and more angry toward God than sodomites and lesbians. Sodomy is a filthy disease. It is a sin against Almighty God.

II Peter 2:6 says, "*And turning the cities of Sodom and Gomorrha into ashes condemned them with an overthrow, making them an ensample unto those that after should live ungodly.*" God set an example in the book of Genesis when He destroyed Sodom and Gomorrah. God said, "I thought it would be a clarion call throughout the Scriptures that if anyone wanted to know My feelings about homosexuality, they could look at the example of Sodom and Gomorrah. Let it forever be a statement: Just because I don't judge it immediately every time, doesn't mean I will not do it again."

Let me make several observations.

1. **God hates the sin of sodomy.** Christians should be cordial to sodomites, but they should not fellowship with them nor condone their sin nor watch those ungodly shows featuring homosexual lifestyles on television. The radio and television are full of sodomites. Homosexuality is a filthy, vile, unnatural, unrighteous, ungodly, unscriptural, Antichrist sin.

2. **Sodomy is unnatural and unscriptural.** If an individual can say he was born a homosexual, by using that same logic, I suppose a mission man could say he was born an alcoholic and the drug user was born as a cocaine addict. Mankind was born in sin. How a person is born does not make it right. What God says about an issue is what makes it right or wrong. Some people are born with a proclivity for certain appetites that are more dangerous for them than others. For instance, some children are born cocaine addicts because they were born to a mother who was a cocaine addict.

A person who was abused as a child or who feels that he was born a homosexual still has no justification for his sin of homosexuality. God still hates it! How a person is born the first time is meaningless. Nobody was born righteous. Every person is born a sinner and must be born again. I have never counseled a pedophile who had not himself been abused by a pedophile as a child or teen.

3. **The sin of Sodom was punished by a firestorm of Hell on earth.** Only a few times are mentioned in the Bible where God literally did bring Hell on earth. During the Tribulation, God says that He will take the lid off Hell, open the doors of Hell, and release the creatures of Hell. A literal Hell will exist on earth during that time. For those who want to know what God thinks about sodomy, one of the rare times when God sent Hell on earth was for the sin of sodomy.

Nothing will cause a firestorm of hellfire and damnation like America will experience if this sin does not get corrected in this nation.

   4.   A certain lifestyle gave permission for the sin of sodomy. Ezekiel 16:48-50 says, "*As I live, saith the Lord GOD, Sodom thy sister hath not done, she nor her daughters, as thou hast done, thou and thy daughters. Behold, this was the iniquity of thy sister Sodom, pride, fulness of bread, and abundance of idleness was in her and in her daughters, neither did she strengthen the hand of the poor and needy. And they were haughty, and committed abomination before me: Therefore I took them away as I saw good.*" *Iniquity* is that judge inside the Christian which gives him permission to sin. Iniquity is that reasoning power inside a Christian's spirit that tells him it is permissible to look at pornography; it is acceptable to be involved in Internet sex; it's fine to have an affair; or it's okay to divorce your spouse. It is that justifier inside of a person that says, "You have permission to do wrong."

   The *sin* is the commission—the act or the thought that one thinks or does. The iniquity gives an individual permission to commit the sin. If the sin of sodomy is that intimate, immoral, ungodly, unnatural, unscriptural act of the sexual relationship between men and men and women and women, then the Bible tells what led to the sin of sodomy. God describes the lifestyle of the people that gave them permission to commit the sin of sodomy.

   • *First, the people in Sodom were guilty of pride.* It is that attitude that a person knows more than anyone else does. It is the attitude of a college student who drops out of college because he is God's gift to the human race. It is the attitude that a teenager or young adult knows more than his dad, more than his pastor, and more than the godly deacons of the church. It is the attitude of some young adults that the standards and convictions of a Bible-believing, independent, fundamental, Baptist church are acceptable for older folks, but not good enough for them.

   That is pride and arrogance! That cocky attitude is exactly what started Sodom on the path into sodomy. I will not let the young adults, ages 18 to 25, in First Baptist Church take this church with its convictions and standards and tromp on them as they drink their wine coolers, commit fornication, frequent gentlemen's clubs, and watch their Internet sex. No! I'm going to cry out, "Thus saith the

Lord!" until I am voted out of the First Baptist Church. I will not let my pulpit roll over to a bunch of hard-minded, tough-attitude, cocky, bratty, arrogant young adults who think they know more than the Bible! It's time some young adults came to an old-fashioned altar and said, "God, I need to humble myself." Pride was the iniquity that produced the sin of sodomy.

 • **Secondly, the people of Sodom had the unlimited satisfaction of their appetites.** The Bible says, *"fulness of bread."* In other words, the inhabitants could have anything they wanted. For the most part, this present generation has the attitude of, "Want it? Charge it." Some college students are making $18 to $25 an hour and cannot afford to pay their college bill because they have to pay for their "toys," their pickup trucks, and their computers.

Among the younger generation in America, a mentality exists which dictates a fat-cat society of having everything they want right away. Nothing is wrong with newly married couples living in an apartment the first several years of their marriage. They don't have to have a four-bedroom, three-bathroom house when they are first married and have no kids. I have had people tell me, "I'm 25 years old, and my house has only three bedrooms and two baths, and I only have two cars."

I'm tired of young boys driving their $40,000 pickup trucks and thinking that it is hard to be a college student. Aren't those boys going to be great missionaries toughing it out in the Congo! Americans have every bell, whistle, gizmo, and gadget imaginable. It is not uncommon for me to talk with folks who have three or four computers and that same number of television sets. We Christians don't need all the bells and whistles! We need the Word of God!

 • **Thirdly, the people of Sodom were guilty of idleness.** The people had too much free time. Some men think 40 hours a week in full-time Christian service is a lot of time. That number is less than half of what real men of God work. Most of my staff men have 40 hours in by noon on Wednesday! Anyone who wants to do something for good and for God and for America has to ditch that 40-hour work week and put in about 60 or 70 hours in a week. It is time the younger generation learned how to work, to save their money, to sacrifice for the Lord, and not to live in the nicest condominiums and not to have the nicest material things. It is time Christians did without. The truth of the matter is, our country is so far gone that it can probably only be salvaged by a great depression. To that end, I would be willing to pray if that would shock some Christians out of their filthy, abominable fornications. A hard depression where a man can't find a job, where he would beg to shovel dirt, where he would go hungry day after day, and where he would have to sell his fancy sports car and his fancy clothes, may be the only jolt back to reality for many Americans.

Matthew 11:22-24 says, *"But I say unto you, It shall be more toler-able for Tyre and Sidon at the day of judgment, than for you. And thou, Capernaum, which art exalted unto heaven, shalt be brought down to hell: for if the mighty works, which have been done in thee, had been done in Sodom, it would have remained until this day. But I say unto you, That it shall be more tolerable for the land of Sodom in the day of judgment, than for thee."* This passage is quite an indictment. Jesus was saying to His disciples, "Fellows, you know how bad Sodom was. God sent fire and brimstone and sunk Sodom beneath the depths of the Dead Sea. That plain is now an ocean of salt. Do you know Whom you have among you?"

They responded, "You are the Christ, the Son of the living God."

Jesus said, "That's right. Do you know what a terrible sin it would be to reject Me as Saviour after seeing all the works that I have done, and all the works that you men are doing, all the souls that are being saved, all the lives that are being changed, and all the converts that are being baptized? If Sodom had seen what the people in Jerusalem have seen, had heard Me talk, and had seen My works, Sodom would have repented a long time ago."

First Baptist Church of Hammond members have seen God do great works at the First Baptist Church. We have seen thousands of souls saved and thousands of converts baptized. We see the buses running every week. We have seen our new ministry, the inner-city chapel ministry, have 495 in attendance on one day. We have seen our nursing home ministry have attendances ranging from 200-450. We have seen the works of the deaf ministry with over 400 recently on a big day, and the truck driver ministry with over 30 on a big day. It is difficult to understand how anyone can live in the midst of a place that is really doing the work of God and sit back with a ho-hum attitude, criticize the work, and not get involved. Those same people almost never make a trip to the altar, almost never bring a convert to church, almost never work on a bus route, and almost never bring a child to a Sunday school class, or any other visitor to church. These people sit in the midst of the works of Almighty God and are careless about it. They may say, "Oh, brother, what time is the preacher going to finish anyway?"

Jesus said, "It will be hotter for those people on the day of judgment to be facing God Almighty than it will be for Sodom.

Sodom never saw the great works of First Baptist Church. Sodom never saw the over 200 buses lined up on a big day with over 10,000 riders coming to Sunday school. Sodom never saw 48,000 converts make a public profession on one single day in 2002 on Great Commission Day. Sodom never heard the preaching of Brother Hyles for over 41 years.

As far as church growth is concerned, the most horrible sin is for people to be in the presence of the moving of God and the Holy Spirit of God and take it with a light, cavalier attitude that says, "So what? Big deal. It's not for me." That same attitude also says, "That's for Mom and Dad's generation. I don't have to fall in line. I don't have to run a bus route. I don't have to tithe or give offerings. I don't have to contribute to the bus kids. I don't have to try to help keep the doors open. I can run around in my sports car and live high on the hog, party and drink wine coolers, go to the beach, strip off my clothes, and then fornicate afterward. Hey, I'm a born-again Christian. I can wear my shorts and my bikinis and still be godly."

People, why don't you jump on board? If the works that are done at the First Baptist Church had been done in Sodom, the people in Sodom would have repented a long time ago.

When good godly people are in the presence of the moving of God and do not jump on board, they bring the curse of Sodom to a ministry. Why do big churches die? Because over the decades, people will sit in those big churches. The first group of people will get fired-up and jump behind the pastor, who is growing and building, and they grow and build, grow and build, and then they plateau. When they plateau, people who are sitting in the presence of the moving of God, watching people get saved at the old-fashioned altar, listening to the songs of Heaven with tears in their eyes and a tug in their heart, listening to the preaching of God's Word by God's man begin to have the attitude of, "As soon as we get out of here, we're going to have a good time and party, and go fornicate. We're going to turn on the television and get over this religious nonsense." That's why big churches die!

It is time some young adults jump on board. Some young couples who sit back in the shadows of the church need to move to the front. They need to see the passion of the choir members when they sing. They need to see the intensity and the passion of the preacher when he preaches. Those who need to jump on board are those who fight for the back seats in the church and run as far from the preacher as they can. They never sit near the front, do not get involved in the service, do not teach a Sunday school class or work on a bus route, and probably never win a soul to Christ.

To those who sit in the middle of God's moving year after year and never let their heart be stirred and never shed a tear, God says, "If Sodom had seen what the First Baptist Church sees, they would have been at an altar a long time ago. Sodom would not be buried on the bottom of the Dead Sea."

I would hate to stand before Jesus Christ as a child of God the same way Lot is going to do one day. God says, "Lot, you spent time with Abraham, My friend. You saw Me call him out of Ur of the Chaldees, and you saw him walk by faith. You chose to walk away from Abraham and to go to the well-watered plains of Sodom. You lost your wife, your daughters, and your sons-in-law."

Church member, don't sit with a ho-hum attitude in the midst of God's doing of great things. Don't just sit and watch. You will not want to face Christ at the Judgment Seat of Christ if you do.

It's time closet Christians and silent witnesses come to an old-fashioned altar and said, "God, this church is my church. The Bible is my Book. Brother Schaap is my pastor. I am going to do everything I can in my power to make sure I am a part of what is happening here. I'm tired of sitting on the bleachers criticizing the quarterback. I'm going to jump into the game and play with him."

CHAPTER FOURTEEN

Taming the Destroyer

"Lest Satan should get an advantage of us: for we are not ignorant of his devices." (II Corinthians 2:11)

Growing churches attract the attention of the Destroyer. Satan seeks out vulnerable Christians and preys upon them. Growing churches often have a high casualty rate of very hurting Christians who have become corrupted and disabled by the Evil One. The fact that Christians are tempted and targeted by Satan should not be strange. Likewise, the disappointment that some of those who are tempted and targeted become victims by means of their own lust is not a peculiar truth.

It is a fact that many Christians are vulnerable, not necessarily because they are bad Christians, but because they are a threat to the kingdom of darkness. A Christian is vulnerable because Satan knows if he can get a Christian to stumble, his stumbling might cause many, many others to be distracted and to become casualties in the ministry. The Bible says that Christians are not ignorant of his devices. We know that Satan preys upon vulnerable Christians. The great tragedy, however, beyond the sin is the sad truth that so very many of those Christian casualties never get back in the battle.

It is unfortunate, but not unrealistic, to expect casualties in battle. When we went to war with Iraq, we knew there would be American casualties. It would have been foolish to assume that somehow nobody would even have an accident. While traveling the streets of America, there will be accidents; so to invade a foreign country and topple their government will doubtless bring casualties. The key is to keep those casualties minimal.

We must recover the casualty, strengthen the casualty, and get that hurting person strong enough so that he can reenter and enjoy a productive life. How tragic it is when a person does not recover when it is possible to do so. How tragic it is to be a casualty who never gets back on his feet to reenter and to enjoy a productive Christian life. One of the great tools that Satan uses is not just to tempt a Christian to stray away from the truth and to become a casualty, but also to keep that casualty from ever getting back on topside again. I am not saying back to where he once was but at least back in the flow of life.

The very fact that a person is living means God is not done with him. The fact that he is alive means God is not finished with him. God has a task for him; He has opportunities for each person to perform. No, perhaps not to the same degree or with the same title or position the casualty once held, but that really is not important. The important matter is to recover the casualty.

Not only does Satan tempt Christians out of the battle, he also takes them further away in their very human efforts to regain their spiritual strength. First Baptist Church of Hammond has, in some ways, become the Mayo Clinic of fundamental churches. Many people come here from across the country and literally from around the globe. These people come quietly and covertly through our doors. They sit quietly in the services desiring anonymity, desiring a place where they can be nurtured and restored. How important it is to have a church like First Baptist Church of Hammond in this country. Would to God that every church would become a spiritual medical facility to help facilitate that restoration. How privileged First Baptist Church is to be a place where hurting people are welcomed. First Baptist members, sitting all around you are hurting people. You do not have a truly accurate idea of this unless you have been one of those hurting people, or you are the pastor who counsels hurting people. Then you would know how many people, within the small perimeter around you, are very hurting people.

Scores of people, who are part of the First Baptist family, may appear very strong. They are here trying to get help spiritually, as are those medically ill who go to Mayo Clinic for help. Do not be deceived by the outward appearance of very strong people who might be in this church. They need a place where they can come and not be quizzed or investigated or become an object of a spotlight. Always be aware that First Baptist Church has been, for many years, a spiritual resort where people can come and find strength and encouragement. My prayer is that First Baptist Church can always be that to the people.

Therefore, it is incumbent upon Christians, as those who have a mandate from God's Word, that we respond scripturally in love and mercy to those who are our hurting patients. Let us respond to those who are part of that army of casualties who have been wounded in the battle—whether in the battle of a broken marriage, or in the battle of child rearing and parenting, or maybe in the battle of just living as a Christian in a very dark and decadent society. To whatever battle these Christians have fallen victim, it is incumbent upon the church to make sure we heal them properly. The unscriptural handling of broken people can result in the contamination of the spiritual hospital. Many a hospital, because of the poor procedures in handling hurting people, has become quarantined and sometimes even forfeits the right to further help hurting people.

I do not ever want the First Baptist Church to become quarantined or to become decommissioned due to a failure to understand this message. This message is aimed principally at those who are the hurting people; but the ones who will profit from it most are those who are the "doctors and nurses," so to speak, who are helping these hurting people.

The children's rhyme says, "Jack and Jill went up the hill to fetch a pail of water. Jack fell down and broke his crown, and Jill came tumbling after." The whole focus of this rhyme is that Jack never recovered his crown. He never put that crown back on his head. He fell, and the fall took him away from a position and brought him into an arena that the little child's rhyme never reveals what happened to him. The implication is that when Jack fell down and broke that crown, he lost his opportunity to serve, and he never recovered.

Let me explain why some hurting people never get back up on that broken leg. It is because the broken leg never healed properly. I am not referring to a physically broken leg; I am talking about the spiritual broken leg. You went to the "doctor," we counseled together, and you came here to the "hospital." My preaching and our Sunday school classes and our programs here began to work on you, but somehow, long after you should have been healthy and even back jogging again spiritually (not running a race, not entering the marathon let alone winning it, but back jogging again), you are still laid up in the hospital bed labeled with the status of "unrecoverable."

I have carefully and practically examined this subject as to why week after week I counsel the same people who rarely, if ever, get back up to walk again. They never recover! Why? In my counseling, I have found 11 characteristics of people who do not get back up when they have fallen down.

1. The casualty makes himself the center of his world. When you fall and tumble, suddenly the world revolves around your problem. All that matters to a patient brought into an emergency room is his problem. The doctors and nurses run to his aid with all kinds of expensive equipment. They stop the hemorrhage from a severed artery and set the broken bones. The doctors and nurses fix the emergency problems, stabilizing the vital signs and getting the heart pumping regularly. They may have to give his fluttering heart a jolt of electricity to get it beating a regularly. For a while, every loved one and friend is huddled outside; their total focus is on that hurting person. That patient becomes the center of everyone's world; however, that is not the normal way of living. At some point, those doctors will transfer that patient to another room. Perhaps he will be placed in a cardiac care unit or an intensive care unit. For a while nobody else can visit the patient, or visitors may be limited to a spouse or the immediate family members. For a while, the center of the world is that patient in that hospital room.

Normally, as that patient heals and recovers, less and less attention is paid to him; and the patient stops paying so much attention to himself. He may start asking questions like, "How are things back at work? How is the family doing? How was the church service?" He starts asking about the world beyond his room. When a patient is habitually wrapped up in only his world, which is his hospital room, his hurts, his heartaches, his sorrows, and his problems, he is called an intensive care patient or an emergency room person.

Sometimes the patient is so focused on himself, he has to be literally strapped down so doctors can perform surgery on him. Perhaps the patient is so focused on his pain, he thrashes around and may even hurt people trying to help him. All that matters to the patient is subduing the pain and getting over the immediate consequences of an accident or a traumatic incident. A person has to recover to the point that when the doctor walks in, the patient says, "Hey, Doc, how are **you** doing?"

However, suppose every time the doctor walks in, the patient complains, "Oh, Doc, I still have this pain, and this still hurts," or "The nurse is not taking care of me." As long as it is always me, me, me, the patient will not recover. As long as he is focused on himself and his pain and his heartache and his problem and his trauma and how people are treating him and as long as he is the center of his world, he will not recover. His recovery is impossible.

At some point, the doctor says, "Look, we have done all we can for you. I can refer you to pain management or to a rest home or to some specialist, but we have done all we can. As long as you are focused on your problems, we cannot help you any further."

In the same way, there is only so much that a spiritual hospital can do. When a person comes to church with a trauma, for a while the church understands that. For a while that hurting person's whole world is, "I cannot believe this is happening to me," or "I cannot believe my son broke my heart," or "I cannot believe my daughter is pregnant out of wedlock," or "I cannot believe my husband is never going to be normal again and the provider for our home," or "I cannot believe my wife has committed adultery and broken my heart," or "I cannot believe my child is crippled and will never walk again," or "I cannot believe my child is mentally disabled," or "I cannot believe they are never going to see," or "I cannot believe they are never going to hear." I cannot believe, I cannot believe, I cannot believe.... It is acceptable for a certain period of time for the hurting one to let that trauma hit him and impact him, but at some point the healing process begins with his saying, "How is everybody else doing?"

Many times I have gone to a graveside service of a little child where I heard Brother Hyles say, "Mom and Dad listen to me now. I am going to talk to you because you have living kids. That child in that casket can no longer be parented, but you have other kids, and you had better get your mind off the child you lost and get it on your other kids. You had better get your mind off the fact that you have lost a child."

I thought to myself, "That seems harsh." No, his was good advice. Brother Hyles knew that those parents could not go home and say to their children, "You do not know how hard it is. I loved that child." Their other child wants to say, "I am still a living child. Do you care about me?"

Look at the world beyond you. Life is going on while you are trying to figure out how to go through life. Most of us miss life because we are trying to figure out how to live while we are missing the privilege of living. When the doctor walks in a patient's room, the healing process begins when the doctor says, "How are you doing today?" and the patient responds, "How are you doing, Doc? How are my kids doing out there? How are the nurses doing? How is your family?" The doctor knows that when that patient starts talking that way, the healing process just turned, and that patient is getting out of the hospital really soon.

Brother Johnny Colsten is in charge of our hospital visitation. When he walks in a hospital room, many times the person is groaning and says, "Brother Colsten, I am so glad you are here. I do not think I am going to make it. I have had a bad day."

There is nothing wrong with making that kind of a statement. The patient is in the hospital because he is hurting, and the focus is on the patient; still, the healing process begins when Brother Colsten walks in the room and the patient says, "Hey, Brother Johnny, how was church Sunday?" Brother Colsten knows that patient is getting better. He is getting his mind off himself because the body is beginning to heal to the point where the patient is not focused on his own problems.

2. **The casualty has a very shallow repentance.** Repentance includes a sorrow of heart; it is an emotional disappointment that you have done wrong against a holy God. Repentance comes when you understand that you are guilty in the presence of a holy God.

Repentance can be for salvation to bring a sinner to faith. It can be the repentance of a Christian who realizes he has sinned and has disappointed himself, as well as his mom and dad or husband or wife or his family or his church. Most importantly, he has disappointed a holy God.

In I Corinthians 5, a man was committing incest with his stepmother. Paul wrote to the church in Corinth and said, "You have a woman and a stepson living together and sleeping together, and you are all puffed up about their sin. Fornication is wrong. You should tell them it is wrong. Pastor, you should preach against their sin of fornication. In fact, I am disappointed, pastor, that you have not thundered out from the pulpit that fornication is a sin." By the way, fornication is still a sin. The couple who lives together before marriage is committing a sin against a holy God.

It grieves my heart, but how much infinitely more it must grieve the heart of a holy God, when an individual commits adultery against his family or violates his marriage vows. Many times when I say to a husband or wife who has been unfaithful, "Do you understand that you violated your commitment to your spouse?" the unfaithful one will retort, "Well, you do not know what my spouse has done to me." True; but, you are the offending party."

The Apostle Paul continued his exhortation to the pastor by saying, "That boy is living in sin; and Pastor, you had better tell that boy he is living in sin. If you do not tell him he is living in sin, I am going to come to your church, and I am going to tell him face to face that he is living in sin! I am going to go so far as to say that I am going to have Satan get ahold of that boy for the destruction of the flesh; not to kill him, but to put him through the wringer and make him understand what a grievous and egregious error he is committing."

It disappoints me when I see people in my congregation who want to run to my office, but they never run to the altar. Repentance begins when you are humble enough to leave that cotton-pickin' pew, walk down and kneel at the altar, and bow your head and say, "God, I have sinned against Thee." Repentance does not begin by trotting off to the pastor's office and asking me to forgive your sins. You did not sin against me. You sinned against the laws of the Bible. I did not write the Ten Commandments; God did! It is important for you to understand that this shallow kind of flippant attitude that says, "I'm sorry, I broke my parents' hearts" is one of the great reasons why some individuals will never get back up. He never went down low enough to fall on his face and cry for mercy.

The Bible tells us of the haughty attitude David had when he had taken Bathsheba and the flippant way he handled his sin. David knew he had sinned, but he devised a plan. He said, "I will bring Uriah home from the battle, and he will sleep with his wife. Since she is expecting a baby, no one will know it is my baby. Everyone will assume the baby belongs to Uriah and his wife Bathsheba."

David did bring Uriah home; however, Uriah, being a more ethical man than his boss at that time, did not sleep with his wife. David realized he was in a pickle. With his still flippant attitude, he was saying, "Uriah, you are expendable; as the king, I am not!" David sent Uriah to the front line of the battle where he was killed. The haughtiness of sin! That kind of arrogance says, "**I** am the center of the universe. **I** am the great King David. **I** am the one who reigns supremely. **I** sit on the throne. If **I** go down, the whole nation goes down."

Let me tell you something, David. God can bring you down and shove your nose right down in the sewer! When the prophet Nathan stuck his finger in David's face and said, *"Thou art the man,"* David had no place to hide. There was no one else to blame. The result of that confrontation was David's acknowledgment of his sin, his broken spirit, and the penning of Psalm 51.

Psalm 51 should be a psalm to which every Christian runs and reads again and again and again. *"Against thee, thee only have I sinned...Create in me a clean heart...Deliver me...."* Psalm 51 is the repenting cry of David. David said, "I have sinned against Thee, God! I am wrong! You are right. I am sorry, and I apologize."

Some of you teenagers trying to get back up, have broken your parents' hearts. Every single day for one month, go to your mom and dad the first thing in the morning and say, "I hurt you deeply, and I am sorry."

If your mom and dad say after five or ten days, "You do not have to say it again," then the next day say, "I have sinned against you; I hurt you, and I am sorry." If you have sinned against your spouse and you have been unfaithful to your vows, the most important thing you can do is go to your spouse and say, "I love you. I hurt you. I am sorry."

I am appalled at the incredible unwillingness of many an offender to do that. Many times when I recommend apologizing, the
offender will bristle like a dog that is caged in a corner and trapped
as if I am poking a stick at him and trying to taunt him. It is amazing
how the offender will become riled and say, "I am not going to do
that." But, my friend, you are the one who sinned! There needs to be
more than a shallow show of disgust at getting caught. You begin to
show God your sorrow by lying on your face saying, "God, against
Thee and Thee only have I sinned. I am sorry I brought reproach and
shame to You."

Our Baptist churches need to learn a little bit of old-fashioned
Holy Ghost repentance. There need to be some contrite and broken
spirits. The sacrifices of God are not bullocks with blood flowing from
the altar; the sacrifices of God are a broken and contrite heart.

What is a broken and contrite heart? It is a heart that hurts, realizing it has shattered the confidence of God and has brought shame
to Calvary. You spat in the face of the Saviour. You sinned against
Christ. It is time that God's people understand this concept.
Repentance is not just for the unsaved people. God's people need to
repent. The Bible says in II Chronicles 7:14, *"If my people, which are
called by my name, will humble themselves...."* God is looking for His
people to have that broken and contrite heart. That verse is not
addressing unsaved people; it is written to born-again people.
Shallow repentance will never get you back topside from the sin you
have committed.

**3. The casualty is quick to point the finger of blame at
someone else.** Blaming someone else for your sin is always the fin-
gerprint of the Destroyer. After all, he is called the accuser of the
brethren. When I find somebody who cannot recover from a sin after
it is well past the time he should have gotten back up on his feet,
dried his tears, pulled back his shoulders, picked up his chin, and
said, "I am going back to serve God"; I find the reason is he is blaming someone else. He should hold up his head high, look at his
spouse, and say, "Thank you for forgiving me. Let's go on with life."

And yet, long after that, he is still down in the mullygrubs, still
depressed, still beating himself to death. What I find is a person who
is saying, "If you knew who I had to live with, you would understand
why I can't recover." Please tell me the chapter and verse where the

person with whom you live gives you the right to fornicate! Name the chapter and verse where the parents you have give you the right to get pregnant out of wedlock! Name the chapter and verse where you get to sniff cocaine because you have a hard boss with whom to work! Tell me the chapter and verse where you have the right to get drunk on Friday nights and fornicate with the whores and harlots of this world because you have a rough family life!

Not one excuse you have to act like an animal is in the Bible. Sin is a choice you make. *"But every man is tempted, when he is drawn away of his own lusts, and enticed. Then when lust hath conceived, it bringeth forth sin: and sin, when it is finished, bringeth forth death. Do not err, my beloved brethren."* (James 1:14-16) God is saying, if you want to point the finger at anybody, go look in a mirror and say, "You, buster, are the reason you sinned. You are the one who broke your marriage vows. You are the one who brought an illegitimate child into the world. You are the one who brought shame and reproach to a godly mom and dad. You are the one!"

4. The casualty will not follow the basic simple diet of obedience, patience, and faith. There is no complicated, magical potion. When you come to my office and say, "Brother Schaap, I've got a problem. My child is wayward" or "My marriage is blown apart by sin," I am not going to use some magical potion. I do not have pills you pop that make you godly. The Bible contains the pills—66 books of pills.

Instead, I am going to tell you, "Let's get you on a schedule of reading the Bible and going to church regularly. Let's get rid of the bad music and replace it with some good music. Let's set a schedule of praying and talking to God regularly. Perhaps, let's get you into Reformers Unanimous and get some more Bible pumped into you. Let's be sure you are part of some kind of service group so you are doing something for others."

I repeat, "There are no magic potions." If you want to be a godly Christian, the formula is:

> *Trust and obey,*
> *For there's no other way*
> *To be happy in Jesus,*
> *But to trust and obey.*

Name any fine Christian who you hold up as an example or mentor, one of whom you would say, "That is the person I would like to be like." I will tell you how that person became a godly Christian. He read his Bible, prayed every day, and he grew, grew, and grew. That is the formula! The great Johnny Colsten, who is stable in spite of his stroke. How does he keep on going? Brother Colsten reads his Bible, stays on schedule, goes to church, keeps on with his duties, and loves his wife. He follows the simple diet of patience, faith, and obedience.

Most people want quick fixes. There has never been a quick fix except salvation, and it took God from the beginning of the foundations of the world to bring redemption to you. It took Jesus 4,000 years to get to Calvary. Nothing is fast with God. Everything is patient, painstaking, and slow. Churches are not built overnight. Lives do not recover overnight. Though you might pray the sinner's prayer and get saved at that very moment, the true Christian walk is for a lifetime.

I like what Dr. Wendell Evans said, "You do not measure Christianity in years; you measure it in decades." When you have been a Christian for ten years or out in the ministry for 10 or 20 years, then tell us how you are doing. After the Devil finds your address, TP's your house, breaks out the windows, burns it to the ground, and you escape with your attitude right and your head held up high, then tell me how you did it. Until then, I do not want to hear about how wonderful your Christianity is.

I admire what a man told me recently. He said, "Brother Schaap, I had an emergency and could not reach you because you were on vacation. At first I got angry at you and God. Then, I thanked God I could not get in touch with you because I had to go God." Ten thousand times better than I am at counseling, God is better at healing you in the prayer closet.

> O what peace we often forfeit,
> O what needless pain we bear,
> All because we do not carry
> Everything to God in prayer!

I recently talked to a husband and wife who were having marriage trouble. I asked, "Where are you going for counseling?"

He said, "To a psychiatrist."

"Is he helping?"

"Oh yes," he assured me. "He is helping a lot."

I asked, "How long have you been going to him?"

"Three years, once a month, $125 a session," he answered.

"You are suckers," I said. "Why are you seeing me now?"

No matter how good a counselor I am, I know Somebody Who is called The Counselor. Isaiah 9:6 says, "...*his name shall be called...Counseller....*" If you want the right counsel, you go to God and fall prostrate on your face, stay down there, and do not come up for two or three hours.

I marvel when people come to me and say, "I have an emergency. I have problems."

When I ask, "How long have you prayed about this matter?" they say, "Well, I have prayed about it."

I ask again, "No, how long have you prayed about it. Have you prayed two or three hours a day, every day for several weeks?" I would like to say to those people with these earth-shaking problems, "After you have been on your face for two hours every day, seven days a week, for 30 days, then come see me." If you do that, you will not need me.

By the way, when you lie on your face, you do not have to say anything, just listen. The best praying I do is when I have my mouth shut, and I am listening.

You say, "God talks to you?"

Yes, He does. How many thousands of times verses come back to my mind or thoughts enter my mind. Would you like to know where I get most of my sermon ideas? On my face. I do not read commentaries. I get on my face and start praying for my church folks, and God says, "Here is how I would fix that." I get my pen and paper, and I write furiously. Then I preach the truth I got while I was praying, and the ones who need my message the most will sleep through my sermon or will not even come to the preaching service at all. Then these same people come to my office and say, "I have a problem." I feel like saying, "Doofus! I just gave you the answer a few moments ago, but you were not in the service."

The truth of the matter is, you go to God and spend hours with Him. Do not feel that somehow the basic simple diet is not going to work for you. It will work. I promise you it works. The Bible is guaranteed to work for anyone who uses it. God's Word will work for deacons. It will work for teenagers. It will work for broken homes. It will work for broken hearts and broken marriages. It will work for pastors and Sunday school teachers. It is a one-size-fits-all Bible. It is even better than those adjustable caps. You stick it on, and it fits right away. God's Word fits your problem no matter what your problem is.

5. **The casualty can become convinced other people are out to destroy him.** The only person who will not let you recover is you! If a patient walks around the hospital saying to doctors and other patients, "You are the problem. You are the reason I am sick," the doctors will put that patient in the psycho ward. It is amazing that a teenager will say, "I would make it at Hammond Baptist High School, but the kids won't let me." What kids? I got tired of hearing that statement, so when a teenager blames other Hammond Baptist kids for his failures, I have the following conversation with him:

I ask, "What kids?"

The teenager hedges, "Well, you know, **they** won't let me."

I ask, "Who is 'they?' Give me a name."

The teenager dodges again, "Everybody knows who **they** are."

"Okay, tell me the 'everybody' or tell me the 'them,' " I order. "Tell me somebody."

The teenager still hesitates. "Well, So-and-So." (He will finally name another student.)

"You're telling me So-and-So has it in for you?"

The teenager sidesteps my question again. "Well, he doesn't really have it in for me."

"Who has it in for you? Nobody has it in for you," I offer.

You are listening to a little devil. You are listening to the hissing serpent of Hell's future residents who are telling you the reason you cannot get up is because everyone who knows about your problem is going to get you for it. As the pastor, do I have it in for you? Do the assistant pastors or the choir members have it in for you? Or maybe it is Ray Young, the college co-president, who has it in for you. In fact, if you talk to any of the people you think have it in for you, you will find that none of those people have it in for you.

May I tell you the great truth about all the people who you think have it in for you? Do you know who those people are thinking about? They are thinking about themselves! You sit there and say, "I think So-and-So has it in for me." Do you know what So-and-So is thinking about? He is thinking about his problems, his difficulties, and what the pastor thinks about him. His life is consumed with his problems. Most people are not that good of Christians; they do not think about others that much. I think about my bills. Do you walk down the street thinking, "Oh So-and-So's problems."? No, you are thinking about your spouse, your children, or your car. It is me, me, me, me; and those are the good Christians. We are too busy being selfish to worry about your stupid problems.

When I walk down the alley shaking hands with approximately 700 to 1,000 people every Sunday, those folks are thinking, "What does Brother Schaap think about me?"

They have their kids with them, and they tell them, "Here comes Brother Schaap; get your hand out." After I shake the child's hand, the parents say to the child, "Oh, you did such a good job. Brother Schaap was so proud of you." Those parents are not worried about the kid down the line who spit on me. Each parent is thinking about his kid and how his family was presented to me. How do I know? Because I am thinking about how each person thinks about me.

Do not give us so-called good Christians so much credit that we are actually concerned with you. You give us way too much credit when you say, "They are all thinking about me." Why would others think about you? It is not entertaining or enjoyable, and thinking about you brings no pleasure or benefits.

The other day, I was talking to a nurse in our church, and I asked, "When you nurses get around each other, do you discuss nursing and patients?"

She said, "Oh, no! We talk about our miserable marriages and our kids. We will be assisting in the operating room sometimes, and as the doctor is cutting out a gallbladder and we are passing him tools, we talk about what we watched on television."

I said, "You have got to be kidding!"

She said, "We don't care about that patient. We don't even know who he is."

Wow! That is really encouraging.

Do not get to the point that you think, "I am the center of the world; thus, everyone must be thinking about me."

6. **The casualty becomes preoccupied with fixing the prob-**

lem and thus neglects the business of living. If you have taken a major tumble, but you are able to get up and go to church, and you are physically able to read your Bible, and you are physically and mentally capable of spending time with God talking and listening, then you do not have a significant enough problem to justify the world's shutting down. You have kids to rear. You have a husband or wife who needs loving, laundry that needs washing, meals that need cooking, and a house that needs cleaning.

You are physically functional where you can go to church, listen to the preaching, and attend a Sunday school class. You are physically able to drive or to be driven. You can get out of the car and walk in to the church under your own power or be wheeled in, pushed in, strolled in, or escorted in, and sit and listen to my preaching.

Brother Randy Rodgers, a faithful member of First Baptist Church, is in a wheelchair. Brother Randy and I talk quite a bit together. He came to me with some parenting questions recently. He was concerned about some issues with his children. I said, "Brother Randy, let me just make a statement to you. In spite of your concern, like so many parents who are good parents, while you are going about the business of being concerned about child rearing, you are accidentally rearing good kids."

Remember Brother Hyles' story, "Get up in the morning, bathe, eat breakfast if you can, and go to work. The next morning, get up, bathe, eat breakfast if you can, and go to work."

What he was saying is, get on with living while you are trying to fix a problem. As long as you are focused on fixing that problem, you are not going to fix your problem. If you have a real emergency, we will all know about it. It is called a funeral. Too many of you are trying to quickly fix the problem and not going about the business of living this wonderful thing called life.

You will say, "Life is miserable. Life is not good. I have this huge, big problem!"

Are you breathing air? Can your eyes see? Can you hear? Are you handicapped? Are you in a nursing home? Are you physically disabled? Can you walk? Do you have a job? Can you run, walk, talk, speak, think? Can you pray and read your Bible? If you listed all the things you think are problems in your life, the truth of the matter is, you have let one festering boil on your neck shut down your whole body; and you are sitting in bed whining, "I can't get up. I've fallen, and I can't get up!"

Well, rise and get on with the healing process! Get out of bed and start going on with life! Too many people never get back up because they are so focused on how to get back up and what they are going to do when they get back up. Their attitude is, "Nobody cares much about me. I am the center of my universe" You have kids and a family. You have a job. Go on with the business of living while you are trying to figure out how to fix your problem.

7. The casualty wants to get back into position too quickly. You have taken this tumble. You come crashing down, and in one giant leap you want to go all the way back up to the place from where you fell. That is not going to happen! You are not going to get back into the position that you once had. You walk back up one step at a time. You cannot skip any steps. If you were a bus captain or a Sunday school teacher or a deacon or held some other position and you lost that position for whatever reason, you cannot just get back up there. You may never make it all the way back up to the top. Go the first step.

I have sat by the hours with people and told them, "I cannot pull you up to where you were. Go the first step. You do not really want to come back up to the top because you are not willing to take the first step."

They will moan and say, "No, I do. I was a pastor, and I lost it." Or they will say, "I was a missionary or assistant pastor, and I lost it."

You are not on top now. You are down on the bottom. Step up one step.

I am thinking of one of the most talented pastors who ever stood behind the pulpit. He lost his ministry. I tried everything in the world to help him. I met with him and said, "I will help you, but you have to go that first step. Just like you preached for years, you cannot get back up on top and may never get back up to where you were, but you have to take the first step. Why don't you come back and be a bus driver or a bus worker? Just take one step at a time. You cannot have the prominence you once had if you do not take the first step."

Folks, you cannot jump back to where you were just because you feel bad since you lost something. Take the first step. Don't get back too quickly.

8. **The casualty is more interested in saving face than in glorifying God.** Again and again, I have told people, "You are not the issue! God is!" It is all about Jesus Christ, and your sin does not have the right to dethrone my Saviour. Your problems are not so great that you can say, "God, hang on a minute; it is not about You. It is about me right now." Your saving face is not nearly as important as your glorifying the Saviour.

> Let's talk about Jesus,
> The King of kings is He.
> The Lord of Lords supreme thru all eternity,
> The great I Am the Way, the Truth, the Life, the Door;
> Let's talk about Jesus more and more."

Jesus is really what life is all about.

Your guilt and your shame may bring you to say, "Oh God, what have I done? I am embarrassed to show my face at that church."

Jesus answers, "Just like I hung on a cross for you, and I showed My face to Hell itself." If your Saviour had the guts to hang naked, embarrassed, and in shame for your sake on the cross, you ought to have the guts to walk back into church and say, "I was wrong. I have sinned. I am very sorry, but this is where I belong." Do not let some sin keep you from walking in the church doors.

Christ lives inside of you, and you have brought shame to Him. He is willing to say, "I will never leave you. I will never forsake you. Wherever you go, I am with you." If God is willing to stick out His neck that far for you, you can stop worrying about saving face. Nothing looks more wonderful on your face than humility. For some reason, there is a shekinah glow about that kind of person; the humble of heart have a beauty that is indescribable.

9. **The casualty misses the basic fact that he has sinned against God, not against his self-image.** You did not write the law which you broke. You did not write the Ten Commandments! God did! It is very important to understand that you did not even break the commandment of your spouse. Your spouse did not write the law "Thou shalt not commit adultery"; God did. I did not write that commandment. First Baptist Church did not write the law. You did not sin against First Baptist Church. You sinned against God—the only Person Who can forgive you. I can help you, but I cannot forgive you.

10.   **The casualty is desperate for another human being to forgive him and make things right again for him.** When you are down
on the bottom, you may need a helping hand. First Baptist Church
and I are going to be the first people to run down and rush to you and
say, "We will help you. Come on up." However, I cannot restore you
if you are looking to me as God. When you come to my office and
say, "Brother Schaap, I have messed up my life," I will love you, I will
comfort you, and I will help you. I may point you to some wise people to get regular counseling. The truth of the matter is, the only person who can change you is God. *"For it is God which worketh in you
both to will and do his good pleasure."* (Philippians 2:13) I cannot
change you; only God can. When you are down on the bottom, go
ahead and run to us. We will help you, but we are going to keep saying, "Turn to Jesus. Look to Jesus. Talk to Him."

11.   **The casualty has a hard time forgiving those who seem to
have a hard time dealing with his problem.** When you are down on
the bottom, may I remind you that those of us who did not tumble
with you are not going to fall apart properly to please you. We have
work to do. We have to stay strong so you can lean on us. I may
stretch down to you and say, "Give me your hand; I will help you."

It is amazing how people, who have fallen, are so quick to say, "I
cannot believe you are not handling this properly." If you violate your
marriage contract and you commit adultery or fornicate, do you realize that your spouse may have a hard time dealing with it? It is not
uncommon for your spouse to have a little bit of a hard time with
your sin, and you should not be so upset that they have a hard time.
If you will be patient, I will get your non-offending husband or wife
to treat you right and restore you.

If your mom and dad are having a hard time dealing with the fact
that you are carrying an illegitimate child, just because mom and dad
sulk and pout, get angry, and raise their voices, that is pretty normal
behavior. Mom and dad have a right to be ticked off because you
sinned. Mom and dad have a right to raise their voice and say harsh
words, "I cannot believe you did this to us!"

You cannot look at them and say, "I can't believe you are not
dealing properly with this situation." Did you know that you brought
on some of their anger? Be patient with people who have a hard time
putting up with some of your faults. Your parents will get over it, but

keep in mind that when they were your age, they might not have shamed their loved ones; so they might have a little hard time understanding why you would.

Sometimes a teenager or young adult will come to my office and say, "Okay, so I smoke and drink a little bit, and I fornicate. I have a girlfriend, but hey, it's 2004; my parents will have to deal with it."

I say, "Your mom and dad are not going to 'deal with it.' Your mom and dad are not required to deal with it. You have thrown garbage in their face, so do not get upset if they shake it off and spit it back at you. Be patient with them. With counsel, we will get your parents to behave properly so they can help restore you."

Many Christian casualties never get back in the battle because of these 11 reasons. Satan would like nothing better than to keep those broken people from ever getting topside again. However, God is not finished with them yet. God has a work for each of them to finish. First Baptist Church and I am here to help those casualties get back on topside. We are here to recover and strengthen the casualty and to help him become a productive Christian—one step at a time.

OTHER BOOKS AVAILABLE
BY DR. AND MRS. JACK SCHAAP

Dating with a Purpose
(Common Sense Dating Principles for Couples,
Parents, and Youth Workers)
by Dr. Jack Schaap

The Debt Series by Dr. Jack Schaap

Marriage: God's Original Intent by Dr. Jack Schaap

Preparing for Marriage by Dr. Jack Schaap

Living on the Bright Side by Cindy Schaap

A Wife's Purpose by Cindy Schaap

A Meek and Quiet Spirit
(Lessons for Wives and Mothers
from Women in the New Testament)
by Cindy Schaap

Silk and Purple
(Lessons for Wives and Mothers
from Women in the Old Testament)
by Cindy Schaap

The Fundamental Man
(An Authorized Biography of Dr. Jack Hyles)
by Cindy Schaap

From the Coal Mines to the Gold Mines
(An Authorized Biography of Dr. Russell Anderson)
by Cindy Schaap